ENCYCLOPAEDIA OF WOMEN IN SOUTH ASIA (NEPAL)

ENCYCLOPAEDIA OF WOMEN IN SOUTH ASIA

(In 8 Volumes)

Nepal

(Volume 6)

Editors

Sangh Mittra, Bachchan Kumar

KALPAZ PUBLICATIONS

Delhi-110052

Encyclopaedia of Women in South Asia *(Nepal)*
(International Studies, Women)

Rs. 7000 (Set)

ISBN: 81-7835-187-0 (Set)
ISBN: 81-7835-193-5 (Vol. 6)

Published in 2004 in India by
Kalpaz Publications,
C-30, Satyawati Nagar, Delhi-110052
E-mail : Kalpaz@hotmail.com

Laser Typesetting at : Shree Vaishnavi Creations, Delhi
Printed at : Mehra Offset Press, Delhi

Contents

1. **Historical Background, Geography and People** 1
Location and Area • Weather • Population • Ethnic Composition • Languages • Religion • Historical Background • Constitution and Government • Rana Rule • Epistemological Issues • Division of Labour • Centres of Higher Learning • Substantive Issues • Means Used • Women's Rights Movement • Short Term Intervention Strategy • Long Term Intervention Strategy • Gender Equality and Democracy • Elections • Sex and Marital Status • Right to Identity • Right to Property • Right to Contract.

2. **Education and Employment** 53
The Donors • Parental Attitude • Literacy Programmes.

3. **Social Status** 63
Preference for Sons • Constitution of 1990 • Work Load • Marriage • Poor Health • Educational Opportunities • Violence • Inheritance • Role in Agriculture • Trade Union Act • In Judiciary • Social Condition • Economic Condition • Education Condition • Health Condition • Political Condition • Sexual Exploitation • Empower Dalit Women of Nepal.

4. **Discrimination Against Women** 97
Convention on the Elimination of all kinds of Discrimination Against Women (CEDAW) • Legal Framework in Nepal • Constitutional Framework • Fundamental Rights • Rights of Equality • Positive Discrimination in Favour of Women • Right to Freedom • Right to Property • Right Against Exploitation • Gender Discrimination and Legal Rights • Abortion Laws • Unsafe Abortion • Proposal for Reforms • Property Rights • Economic

Dependency • Lack of Equal Inheritance Right to Women.

5. **Women's Participation in Government** 125
Access to Resources • Access to Credit • Economically Active Work Force • Women in Agriculture • Employment in the Organized Manufacturing • Working Conditions • Women in the Tourism and Related Sectors • Self-employment and the Informal Sector Workers • Women Entrepreneurs • Child Labourers • Problems of Employment • Changing Structure of Employment • Employment Status • Wage Employment and Earnings • Ethnicity and Caste Factor in the Structure of Economic Activities • Women's Entrepreneurial Activities • Market Production • Contribution to the Social Production Process • Wage Employment • Economic Opportunities • Plans and Programs • Development Plans on Women • A Platform for Action • Policies • Centrel Level • District Level • Project Interventions • Social Mobilization • Sectoral Issues.

6. **National Policy** 175
Nepalese Law • Adultery Titles of Law and Terminology • Rules and Customs • The Revenge of the Husband • Sanctions Against the Adulteress • Control by the State's Representatives • Widow Burning in Nepal • Literary and Historical Sources • Widow Burning in the Ain of 1854 • Regulation for Satî According to the (Muluki) Ain27 • The Abolition of Widow Burning • Differences between Nepal and India • Widow Burning and Asceticism • AI warned against Criticizing Shariah • Amnesty International 1999 Annual Report • Position of Women • Inheritance of Property • Forced Labour and Slavery.

7. **Womens in Politics** 217
Women in Parliament • Problems • Rule of Ranas • New Constitution Favoured Women • Reason for Low Political Participation • Meaning of Democracy • Gender Equity • Socio-cultural Fields of Gender Inequality • Household Level • Community/Societal Level • Socio-cultural

Factors • Patriarchy • Hegemony • Trafficking of Women: Human Rights Violations.

8. The Assessment **249**

PCRW Programme • NGO's and Women Development • Empowering the Women of Nepal • Strategy of USAID.

Bibliography 259

Index 261

1

Historical Background, Geography and People

Location and Area

Nepal is situated in South Asia along the southern slopes of the Himalayan mountains. A landlocked country about 885 km (550 mi) long and 201 km (125 mi) wide, it has two neighbours, India and China, the two largest nations in Asia. The total length of international borders is 2,671 km (1,660 mi) of which the border with China is 1,078 km (670 mi) and that with India 1,593 km (990 mi). The total land area is 141,499 sq km (54,633 sq mi).

Kathmandu is the capital with an estimated 1971 population 195,260. Only six towns have more than 10,000 population : Patan (59,100), Birathagar (45,000), Bhagaon (84,250), Nepalganj (15,800), and Birganj (10,800).

Nepal has three main topographical regions : (1) The high mountains of the main Himalayan range covering one-third of the Country (2) The Kathmandu Valley and (3) the Tarai, a narrow belt which extends alone the boundary with India in the south. The complex mountain mass in the north contains some of the world's highest peaks : Mount Everest (8,847 meters 29,028 ft), Mount Lhotse (8,500 meters 27,890 ft), Mount Makalu (8,480 meters 27, 824 ft), Mount Cho Oyu (8,189 meters 26,869 ft). Dhaulagiri (8,172 metes 26,813 ft), and Annapurna (8,077 meters 26,502 ft). To the south, less than 60 km (100 mi) from the icy heights, is the narrow, flat belt of alluvial land, 45 to 182 meters (150 to 600 ft) above sea level, known as the Tarai. In some places the Tarai is less than 80 km (50 mi) in width. On the northern border of the Tarai are the tertiary ranges known as Siwalik Hills and the secondary ranges known Hills and the secondary ranges known as Mahabharat Lekh. The Kathmandu Valley is a circular basin of only 564 sq km (218 sq mi) north of the central Tarai.

The entire country is drained by three river systems : in the east by Kosi and its seven tributaries, in the centre by the Narayani or Gandak and is the west by Karnali or Gogra. Most of the human settlements are found on the banks of these rivers.

Weather

Nepal's climate ranges from the subtropical summers and mild winters in the south to cool summers and severe winters in the northern mountains. In the Tarai and Kathmandu Valley there are three seasons : hot, rainy, and cold. The hot season lasts from May to June, the rainy from July to September and the cold from October to April. In January, the coldest month, temperatures range between a daily average minimum of 2.2°C (36° F) and a maximum of 17.8°C (64°F) while in the hot months they range between 26.7°C (80°F) and 32.2°C (90°F). The average annual rainfall in Kathmandu is around 152 cm (60 in.). Violent thunderstorms are common.

Population

The population of Nepal was estimated at 14,719,000 in 1980, based on the last official census held in 1971 when the population was 11,555,983. Nepal ranks 45th in the world in size of population.

The population is unevenly distributed : the barren highlands are virtually uninhabited while Kathmandu Valley is one of the most densely populated areas of the world. The average density is 77 per sq km (200 per sq mi), placing Nepal 46th among the nations of the world in this respect. The density of population per square km of cultivated area is considerably higher at 579 (1,500 per sq mi) and Nepal is 17th among the nations in this respect.

In the 1971 census there were 5,817,203 males and 5,738,780 females.

Ethnic Composition

By historical origin, linguistic connections, and religious affiliations Nepalese may be divided into two broad ethnic categories : Indo-Neplese and Tibeto-Nepalese. The Indo-Nepalese group, which comprises nearly 80% of the population, includes the

Pahari, the Newar, the Tharu and the Indians of the Tarai. The Pahari make up nearly half the total population. In social organization and physical appearance they resemble the inhabitants of northern India, though many of these features have been modified in the Nepali environment. The Tharu are also Hinduized as a result of the long and intimate contact with the neighbouring Biharese. The Tibeto-Nepalese category, which makes up 20%of the population, includes a number of ethnic islands without any real sense of common identity. These groups are clustered on the northern and eastern parts of the country where they are subsistence farmers and stock raisers at higher altitudes. Though related culturally and racially to the Tibetans they have developed regional distinctions and cultural variations. The more numerous of the Tibeto-Nepalese tribes are the Tamang, Rai, Limbu, Bhote, Sunwar, Magar, and Gurung. These groups have supplied the bulk of the famous Gurkha contingents to British, and later Indian, armies. Common to most of these groups is the acceptance of a patterned social relationship based on the caste system though less elaborately graded and less rigid in its sanctions than the Indian caste system.

Languages

The census of 1952 listed 30 distinct languages spoken in the country, not counting dialects. Of these 20 were spoken by less than 1,000 persons each. Nepali (also called Gurkhli, Khaskura, or Parbatiya) is the official language, and its use in schools and offices is enabling it to displace the minor languages. It is an eastern dialect of Pahari and is distinguished from western and central Pahari. By percentage of speakers the main languages of Nepal are : Nepali (48.7%), Maithili Pradesh dialects (7.5%), Tamang (6%), eastern Tarai dialects (5.6%), Newari (4.7%), Tharuhati (4.4%), Maithili (3.7%), Magar (3.3%), midwestern Tarai dialects (3.1%), Rai (2.9%), and Gurung (2.0%). Khambu, Yakha, Hayu, Limbu and Thami belong to the Munda group of the Austroasiatic family; Gurung, Mahar, Newari, Sunwar and Murmi belong to Tibeto-Burman family: Nepali belongs to the Indo-European group. Tibetan is spoken by the Bhotias in the north, and dialects of Hindu—such as Bhojpuri, Kumaoni and Maithili—along the southern border. Newari and Pahari show strong Sanskrit influence. Only Pahari and Newari have any literature of their own.

English is the principal second language.

Religion

By the constitution of 1962 Nepal was officially proclaimed a Hindu state. Nearly 89% of the population is Hindu, 9 % Buddhist, and 2 % Muslim. Christian missions are admitted but conversion is forbidden.

Both Hinduism and Buddhism were transported from India, though Buddhism gradually became more associated with countries to the north of Nepal. The simultaneous practice of the two religions, as well as multiple forms of tantrism and animism, shaped the valley's art, architecture, and politics. The art portrays the history of the thousands of gods that make up the Hindu pantheon, as well as the benevolent and malevolent images of Buddhism, and the erotic scenes of Hindu and Buddhist tantrism. There are countless Hindu shrines, small and large, adorned with sculpted stone gods and goddesses, smeared with vermilion powder and strewn with flower petals and bits of rice that are part of rigorous daily worship. Here and there stands that most primordial of religious symbols, the Shiva lingam, an erect phallus shape perched on a yoni, a symbolic womb.

Historical Background

Nepal has never been under direct foreign rule in modern times although it was bound by treaty obligations to Great Britain until 1947.

Constitution and Government

The constitution of Nepal was promulgated by the late King Mahendra in 1962, ad it was amended in 1967 and in 1975. Under the constitution Nepal is a constitutional monarchy in which the sovereignty of the country is vested in the king.

Marriage and family system of various caste/ethnic, cultural and religious groups are different. Dominant Hindu "high caste" groups have a predominant system of monogamy for women and polygyny for men, early and child marriage, prize for virginity/chastity and joint or extended family systems. Different caste/ethnic groups and also both men and women have different historical memory of the past. In Nepal either the history of the "victor" caste, that is Bahun-Chhetris and the men, history is his-story but neither the "vanquished indigenous ethnic groups nor women have any written collective memory of the past. Since the expansion of "Gurkha imperialism" in 1768 under the leadership of King Prithvi Narayan Shah, predatory Nepalese state coercively tried to make the country "Asali Hindustan" through various cultural instruments such as Hinduization, Sanskritization, Nepalization and the Bahunbad synchronized with centralization of power and authority.

Rana Rule

During the 104-year old autocratic Rana rule, both women and indigenous ethnic groups were legally discriminated by the Muluki Ain (National Code) of 1854 and since 1963 women continue to be discriminated by the Naya Muluki Ain. In the last two-centuries, women have been suppressed, oppressed, depressed, and exploited not only by the families and communities but also by the state controlled by the so-called "high caste" men. Dalit women (and also men) have been inhumanely treated as "untouchables." Similarly, women belonging to indigenous ethnic groups continue to be further suppressed and oppressed by the predatory state by denying them to exercise their basic human rights, including minority rights, rights of indigenous peoples and right to education in the mother tongue. Unfortunately, "The invocation of the fiction of "a Nepali mahila", according to Sierra Tamang, "submerges the dimensions of class, caste, ethnicity, religion and age fundamental in the constructions of the different realities of different women, within that of single, collective Nepali, female reality engineered/invented by an elite."

Nepalese society was closed to foreigners till 1950. Therefore, during the Rana rule, Nepalese society changed very little. After the political transformation of 1950, Western donors began to provide foreign aid to Nepal as a part of the modernization/Westernization project. Women also began to raise women's right issues since then. Factors like heavy transfusion of green dollars in the Nepalese economy by the donors, the ever-intensifying process of globalization, Westernization and urbanization, Nepalese society and culture is changing in a very rapid pace.

In Nepal, the last decade of the twentieth century was engulfed by the issues of democracy, human rights, environment, development, empowerment, institutional development good governance, free market economy and gender equality. Gender issues, including women's rights, are very significant because women comprise a little over a half of the total 20 million populations of Nepal. All the Nepalese women suffer from domination, exploitation, suppression, oppression, subordination and discrimination by their men counterpart.

Such a male centered/biased/controlled process of socialization results in the homo-social reproduction of existing discriminatory and exploitative relationship between men and women. It is no wonder that in the global and the South Asian regional context gender inequality has shown its most ugly heads in Nepal than anywhere else in the world. Both Gender-Sensitive Development Indexes (GDI) and Gender Empowerment Measure (GEM) provided in the Nepal Human Development Report 1997 reveals that women's situation in the country is very frustrating. Both GDI and GEM value of Nepal are three times lower than that of the GDI for the developed/industrialized countries (NESAC, 1998). Such a perpetuating hopeless system must change for good.

Gender issues of the past and present remain to be mostly the same. Most of the gender issues have been kept in the deep freeze of state, society and market. If the past is present and present is past in terms of gender issues, neither past and present should be the future nor future should be the past and present. If our planners, policy makers, bureaucrats, political leaders and activists, development experts and practitioners, on the one hand, and people at the grassroots, level, on the other hand, do nothing to change the past and the present, the future is sure to be as past and present. Therefore, the point is to change it and to be able to do so, we must understand both epistemological and substantive gender issues and act accordingly.

Epistemological Issues

There are many epistemological issues that are most subtle, somewhat concrete and abstract but difficult to tackle in favor of women under the existing system of patriarchy. The most important epistemological issues are paradigm of development, manufacturing knowledge and theoretical/ conceptual positions. These issues have strategic values. It may be difficult to gain substantially by achieving some of the substantive issues discussed in the next sub-section of this article until we can achieve substantially on this front.

Paradigm of Development: Women's issues surfaced first in the early seventies under a paradigm of Women in Development (WID) in which development programs were targeted to improve the condition of women. In the late seventies WID was renamed as Women and Development (WAD) with emphasis on changing the positions of women in society. The failure of this paradigm resulted in a shift in the paradigm of Gender and Development (GAD) since the eighties to make everyone gender sensitive and gender responsive.

In Nepal, most of the development programs of the government and of the donors are mixed, partly WID, partly WAD and partly GAD. So far, my sense is that both WID, WAD and GAD paradigms simply failed to deliver results, that is, substantial improvement in women's status-economic, social, cultural, legal and psychological.

Abandoning existing jargonized concepts and creating new ones does not serve our interests but the concepts/ paradigms that we use should reflect the reality of what we want to achieve and what we are doing. In this sense I prefer to use a paradigm of Gender and Public/Private Spheres (GAPS) because there is a gap in GAPS, that is, a gap in the redistribution of reconfiguration of division of labor at private and/or public spheres with the principles of equality and emancipation from all kinds of discrimination, suppression, oppression and exploitation.

Division of Labour

The main problem of gender-based division of labor, that is, women being confined in private spheres and men having privileges in public spheres, is primarily because of industrialization and urbanization. Therefore, in urban and industrial areas, men also should do works at private spheres and women also should do work in public spheres. On the contrary, rural men and women do work at private spheres but the distinction is mainly concerned with less or more works. Often women do work for about sixteen hours whereas men often spend time lazily playing cards and drinking alcohol.

The failure of development in underdeveloped countries, such as, Nepal, is manifested by "development of underdevelopment" and "underdevelopment of development" engineered within the modernization or dependency paradigms. Modernization was a paradigm lost in the sixties and dependency paradigm was gained by the underdeveloped countries since then.

Unfortunately, in Nepal modernization paradigm, which was abandoned in Latin America back in the sixties, continues to mesmerize our planners, policy makers, political leaders and development practitioners alike.

In Nepal, like elsewhere, both WID and GAD have been inserted within the paradigm of modernization. Such attempts have helped women neither to free themselves from the captivity of patriarchy nor to reduce and/or eliminate discrimination, suppression, oppression and exploitation by their men counterpart.

Manufacturing knowledge: When we talk about gender issues in Nepal or elsewhere, archaeology, politics and sociology of knowledge should be analyzed properly because knowledge is power and power is knowledge. In patriarchy, power resides with men, who, therefore, manufacture knowledge for consumption by both men and women. Therefore, in the knowledge industry, men are the producers and consumers but women are consumers only because they are systematically excluded from the production process. A few women do produce knowledge but the production is cloning of men's knowledge than creating women's own.

In Nepal, Nepalese men produce knowledge to some extent, but compared to Western knowledge producers, they are systematically marginalized and ruthlessly excluded. Nepalese men consume consumer items of Western knowledge manufactured in their own historical, cultural, political and economic contexts by Western men and later they export it to the under-developed societies. Such consumer items include Western worldview, Western ideas, Western paradigms, Western theories, Western concepts, Western strategies and Western methodologies.

Centres of Higher Learning

In all the five Nepalese universities-Tribhuvan University (TU), Kathmandu University (KU), Mahendra Sanskrit University (MSU), Purwanchal University (PU) and Pokhara University (PU) or for that matter, almost all faculty members who teach at various departments in most of the universities in the world are men, those authorities who make academic and other decisions are mostly men, and those who design curriculum and write text books and reference materials are men. Women learn the men's worldview and these are reflected in their teaching, research sand writing. Also, Nepalese men and women graduates who join in political parties, bureaucracy, development industry and elsewhere recycle men's knowledge.

Theoretical/Conceptual positions: Nepalese social scientists, be it men or women, have not made efforts yet to generate their own theories and concepts. What they have done so far is either a partial use of Western theories and concepts devoid of contextualization in the Nepalese society and culture or mimicked pre-given theories and concepts available within the ideological domain that they love. In the case of Nepalese feminism, feminists should either choose from a wide range of Western feminist theories, including liberal, cultural, Freudian, Marxist, existentialist, socialist and radical theories by contextualizing them in the Nepalese society and culture or locate their own positions within a wide range of Hindu fictious models such as Sati-Sabitri-bad (symbol of "chastity"), Kali-Durgabad (symbol of "power"), Saraswati-bad (symbol of "education") and Draupadibad (symbol of "polyandry").

Substantive Issues

Some substantive issues were raised in the past and are being raised at the present by various women's organizations. Some of these organizations are about fifty years old and some of them are of very recent origin.

Women's organizations and movement began since 1947 with the establishment of women's organizations, namely Mahila Samiti ("Women's Committee") led by Mrs. Dibya Koirala in 1947, Adarsha Mahila Samiti ("Ideal Women's Committee") led by Mrs. Rewanta Kumari Acharya in 1947, Nepal Mahila Sangh ("Nepal Women's Association") led by

Mrs. Mangala Devi, and Akhil Nepal Mahila Sangathan ("ALL Nepal Women's Organization") led by Mrs. Punya Prabha Devi Dhungana in 1950, Akhil Nepal Mahila Sangh ("All Nepal Women's Organization") by Mrs. Kamachaya Devi in 1951, and Mahila Swyam Sewa ("Women's Voluntary Services") led by a royal family member in 1952.

Thus the first generation of women activists came from different political families but belonging to "high caste," namely, Bahuns. All these organizations were aligned with one or the other political parties, including the Nepali Congress and the Nepal Communist Party, as sister organizations. These various organizations raised the issues of or for political representation of women in high offices.

During the autocratic, partyless Panchayat regime, women were treated as a class by itself and the Nepal Mahila Sangathan ("Nepal Women's.92 Gender and Democracy in Nepal Organization") was the only recognized women's organization by the government. The organization worked on issues related to literacy, law and income generation programs. The UN Declaration on women's right in 1975 forced the Panchayat rulers to do something for the Nepalese women. As a result, HMG-N established the women's Services Coordination Council (WSCC) under the Social Services Coordination Council (SSNCC) in 1977.

The partyless Panchayat political system fell apart in 1990 due to an unprecedented peoples' movement. After the re-establishment of multi-party politically system in 1990, women's right activists raised issues such as equal property rights and reservation of seats in different political positions, jobs and education.

The left leaning women's organizations have been fighting against prostitution, girl trafficking, sexually explicit advertisements and child marriage and also for gender equality, social security and so on. Leftist women activists are believed to be more militant than non-leftist women activists. What is positive about the democracy after 1990 is a proliferation of national and international organizations and network organizations working on women's issues, which are about fifty.

The main thematic substantive issues raised very

forcefully by all women's right organizations and equal right activists appear to have been incorporated in these two themes. After discussing the issues of discrimination and exploitation, I will provide a shopping list of very specific substantive issues raised and means used by various women right activists. Discrimination: Discrimination has been the only rule of game in Nepal. Even nearly after a decade of re-establishment of multi-party democracy in Nepal, gender discrimination against women and girl child is ubiquitous.

It is everywhere from the Constitution and other laws to the families and households. Although the Constitution of the Kingdom of Nepal, 1990 states that there shall be no gender discrimination, the Acts, including the Muluki Ain (National Code), discriminates women from men in several fields, including property rights, divorce, abortion, adoption and tenancy rights. Women are discriminated in governance-state (executive, legislature and judiciary), market and civil society organizations-by exclusion.

Religion, tradition, cultures norms and values that govern the communities and families are also gender discriminatory. Among the religions, Hindu religion and the teachings of "sacred" Hindu scriptures are at the worst in terms of gender discrimination. In spite of women's projection as the goddesses "Durga" and "Kali' as symbols of power and goddess "Saraswati" as a symbol of education, Hindu religion treats women very inhumanely and derogatorily as non-human objects.

Social caste hierarchy, concept of purity and pollution, high prize for chastity and male-based life rituals from birth to death perpetuate Hindu women's status at both natal and husband's home to that of a second class status. Buddhist religion preaches for equality, including equality between men and women but there are some cases of gender discrimination but such discriminations are not as ruthless and severe as in the Hindu religion.

In Islam religion also, there are many gender discriminatory rules and practices. In terms of caste and ethnicity, Bahun-Chhetris practice severe forms of gender discrimination. Among the indigenous ethnic groups, the status of women (cheli/maiti) is very high. Women family members often make household decisions and they have high social mobility. Gender discrimination is minimal among those indigenous ethnic groups who still follow their tradition but those have come under the influence of Sanskritization, Hinduization, Nepalization and Bahunbad, they are practicing more and more discriminatory and conservative social values borrowed from the Hindus.

Social norms and values are biased in favor of boys/ men/sons. In most of the communities, except some very traditional indigenous ethnic groups, sons are regarded as high value cash crop and daughters are regarded as junks. Therefore, sons get preferential treatment from birth to death, especially in foods, clothing, toys/games, schooling/education, parental property, health care, last rites of dead parent, personal respect, social status and freedom from doing household chores. Daughters, on the contrary, are deprived from all those privileges. They are thought to be other's property and liabilities.

Exploitation: Commodification of women and girl child by the state, society, market and media keep the door gender discrimination and exploitation wide open. Nepalese women are exploited in many fronts-household/ family, community and the state. In the cities, many women are sexually exploited as commercial sex workers. Media exploit women as sex objects. Prior to 1950s, women were exploited sexually by the Rana rulers and other high class peoples, on the one hand and through the custom of polygyny by common men, on the other. After 1950s, women are exploited as sex objects, including trafficking of women, commercial sex workers and sex symbols in media advertisements. Women work at home without due appreciation of their contribution in household/ national economy; get less wages/salaries in all kinds of jobs.

Exploitation of women is primarily class based. Poor women are more exploited sexually, economically, politically socially and culturally than rich women. Women belonging to Dalits or "low caste" groups are the ones who are exploited most by "high caste" groups who get their services by paying nominal wages or rewards.

Poor and illiterate women are often heavily exploited by their own family, kith and kin and many innocent women are sold in brothels of India. Some women who are engaged in commercial sex are exploited economically by their brokers and sexually exploited by some law enforcement officers once they are booked. Also, women who work in farms and construction areas are economically exploited by the employer/contractors.

Raging Substantive Issues: The raging national issues, for and against, raised by women's right activists include the following:

For:

- right to inherit parental properties or to equal property rights;
- reproductive rights, including abortion or right on one's own body;
- reproductive health, including family planning and safe motherhood;
- reservation of seats or positive discrimination in education, politics, police, army and public offices;
- equal wages;
- girl child education/out of school programs/Chelibetee class/adult literacy class;
- Production Credit for Rural Women (PCRW)/micro-credit programs and other user's groups, including forest user's groups;
- political representation-national to local (public offices/sphere);
- human rights instruments related to women;
- citizenship rights; and
- women's empowerment.

Against:

- Commercial sex, including traditional custom of Deuki and Badi, and trafficking of women;
- violence against women:
- domestic violence;
- sexual slavery;
- prostitution;
- international trafficking of women;
- incest;
- reproductive rights violations;

- rape;
- sexual harassment;
- sex discrimination;
- medical abuse;
- abuse of women with physical or mental disabilities;
- culture-bound practices harmful to women;
- ritual abuse within religious cults;
- marital rape;
- pornography and abuse of women in media;
- abuse of women internal refugee or relocation camps;
- custodial abuse;
- female foeticide; and
- dowry-related violence and murder.
- child and/or early marriage;
- labor: bonded and girl child labor; and
- female impoverishment.

Local level issues:

- reduction of workload of women and girl child;
- employment for adult men and women;
- income generating skill training;
- children's education;
- food, clothing and shelter;
- health care; and
- access to market.

Means Used

All the above listed peaceful means or the "weapons of the weak," used by women's right activists to achieve some of the above mentioned women's rights are as follows:

- Seminars, workshops, conferences, talk programs on women's rights, including right to inherit parental property, violence against women, reproductive rights, five year plan;
- Publications of advocacy leaflets and reports;
- Interactive programs with the planners, policy makers, political leaders and academicians;
- Delegations to the government, including the Prime Minister and the concerned public officials either to protest against specific government actions detrimental to women and girl child or to press the government to

implement certain plans and programs for them;

- Press statements to protest against government actions detrimental to women and girl child;
- Street demonstrations, mass rallies, and mass meetings either to show solidarity or to protest against specific government actions;
- Sit-in or relay fasting and Gheraos;
- Networking with international sister organizations. Shailaja Acaharya, the then Deputy Prime Minister, advised women activists to flex the muscles, crash the gates of Parliament to Gherao and break some windows, and create loud noise. She implicitly suggested to abandon current soft types of advocacy and lobbying listed above.

These all means to press issues concerning gender equality and equity definitely have some significance but the main gender war to be waged at is at the family level. The family, according to Hartmann, is a locus of "internal struggle over matters related to production or redistribution (housework and paychecks, respectively). It can also provide a basis for struggle by its members against larger institution such as corporations or the state. Will cooking continue to be done at home or be taken over largely by fast-food chains? Will childcare continue to be the responsibility of parents or will it be provided by the state outside the home? Such question signal tensions over the location of production. Tax protest, revolving as it does around the issue of who will make decisions for the family about the redistribution of its resources, can be viewed as an example of struggle between families and the state over redistribution" .

Women's Rights Movement

We can see some features of women's movement in the past. These are:

- The movement started with and continues to be nurtured by women belonging to certain caste, religious and regional groups. Urban Hindu "high caste" groups, that is, Bahuns and Chetris, and the Newars, among the ethnic groups continue to take the leadership in the movement. Women belonging to indigenous ethnic groups, Dalits and Muslims were and are out of the loop. From regional perspective hill women have taken the leadership roles in the movement. Women with good economic background have occupied key positions in the movement.

- Women's movement started spontaneously but in due course of its development it is often either induced by the donors, including INGOs or by the international human rights and women's rights instruments, some ratified and some yet to be ratified by Nepal. ! Most the women's movement is centered in the Kathmandu Valley. There are isolated cases of issues based women's movement coming up from the grassroots level. Campaign against alcohol by Ama Samuha is one such example.
- As most of the women's organizations are affiliated with one or the other national political parties, some women's issues are raised by such organization as directed by their political party in order to use women voters' as their vote bank rather than with a genuine concern for bringing a change.
- Women's movement has confined their advocacy to women's social, legal and political issues but not on economic and epistemological issues. The reasons for such overlook appears to be heavy engagement of gender experts on consulting works provided by international donors and time consuming engagement in advocacy and lobbying activities.
- In the process of Westernization and modernization of Nepalese society, various types of women's movements have contributed to some extent in creating some public, including political, space.

"Over the period from 1917 to 1950 and from 1960 to 1990", according to Lama (1998:328), "women's mobilization was primarily used as a support to a larger political struggle, that is, the fight for democracy....The mobilization of women for women, however, became more frequent after the establishment of the multiparty, democratic regime in 1990." Lama, thus, sees the Nepalese women's movement as "a series of mobilizations of women as women."

Tamang, on the contrary, feels that "the lack of a singular feminist movement in Nepal (a fact often bemoaned) may point to the need for re-conceptualization. What have been hitherto seen as scattered attempts to take up certain issues, may point to emerging forms of different feminism." Each Nepalese woman should think that her individual problems are national problems and the only way to get rid of those problems is to abandon living like, what C. Wright Mills calls, "biography" and live as "history."

Among the donors, the SNV and the GTZ, in sharp contrast to the United States and the World Bank, help to strengthen civil organizations. Many donors have huge amount of aid money in the name of WID, WAD and GAD, women's empowerment, gender equity and equality, equal rights, women's rights and so on. Often these aid money, like any other aid money, do not reach out to the intended beneficiaries.

Most of the money is either siphoned back to the donors' own countries through their technical consultants and staff or evaporated by the Katmandu's elite. Men have neither formed nor there is any need of forming organizations demanding for men's rights because whatever the state, market and civil society have been doing in the past and present are explicit or implicit maintenance of men's rights. On the contrary, women have very lately realized that they should form various organizations to press demands for equal rights for women and men.

Nepalese planners, policy makers, development practitioners and political leaders often treat women as a homogenous group. The Production Credit For Rural Women (PCRW) program introduced in the early eighties through the Women's Development Section, now Women's Development Department, and recently established Ministry of Women and Social Welfare appear to be exceptions. In reality, although the Ministry of Women and Social Welfare is exclusively for women, the remaining Ministries, including education, local development, agriculture, forestry, environment, water resources, land reform, and law, as if, need not to be women-centered at least for some time.

The Constitution of the Kingdom of Nepal, 1990 has recognized Nepal as a multi-caste/ethnic, multi-lingual and multi-cultural society. Though the Constitution declares Nepal as a Hindu kingdom, it is indeed a multi-religious and multi-regional country as well. Therefore, women also should be grouped in four racial categories: Caucasians, Mongoloid, Dravidian and Proto-Australoid. From linguistic perspective, women should be divided into four groups, Indo-Aryan, Tibeto-Burman, Dravid and Munda language speaking groups. In terms of religion, women should be divided into Animist, Bon, Kirat, Buddhist, Lamaist, Hindu, Islam, Christians, Sikh and so on. Women's rights movement has mostly been top down since the Fourties. Women activists coming from either well off or politically advanced families have taken center stage in women's movement and so far there is nothing wrong about it. It is natural because it is always comfortable for women (or men) of such background to participate in social/political activities and to take leadership of the movement. They are the ones who can do something to bring change at the policy making level.

Centralization of power and authorities in Kathmandu provides opportunities to those women who live in Kathmandu to involve in such activities Some women activists who come from rural areas also tend to settle in Kathmandu and launch their activities. Such top-down approach becomes effective in changing laws, plans, policies and programs. Even if the laws, policies, plans and programs should change, women at the grassroots level do not get an opportunity to know, feel and experience about such changes. There is indeed a widening gap between center and periphery, between theory and practice. So far, nothing actually works.

Another side of top-down approach is the gender sensitivity of the donors' own organizations that advocate for gender equality and equity. We know that almost all donors, including INGOs, some NGOs and few government organizations work and advocate for women's rights, women's empowerment, gender equity/equality under the banner of WID, WAD and GAD. One may wonder to what extent the organizations/institutions that advocate and work for gender issues are themselves gender-sensitive. Do they preach or teach?

Recently an INGO has initiated to draft a gender strategy of its own organization. The goal they have set for is "to become a gender-sensitive organization so that men and women have equal opportunities in the society." They have formulated several gender sensitive provisions at the institutional and program levels. At the institutional level they have identified the issues of systems and procedures, hiring practice, equal participation, code of conduct (attitude and behavior), sharing and networking, staff training, and support for the women staff working in remote areas.

The system and procedure include equal number of men and women staff at all levels, including interview panels, focal persons in each program office to look after gender issues. In hiring practices it has become customary to state, "women candidates are encouraged to apply" but they felt that it is not enough. They have accepted that advertisement of recruitment should state categorically about the "policies regarding maternity leave, paternity leave, breast feeding, flexible working pattern after pregnancy up to six months etc." They have also suggested to incorporate gender in job descriptions as well. With regards to support for women staff working in remote areas, the draft gender strategy states that those women staff who work in remote areas of Nepal "may feel the extra burden of working in such areas especially where cultures could be different.

Under such circumstances, instead of discouraging women form working in such areas, we will try to provide support as much as possible to women staff." Similarly at the program level, the gender strategy paper states that gender perspective should be incorporated at each program and monitored during the whole year. The strategy paper states that the organizations should "influence GOs and NGOs in the program areas to be gender-sensitive."

In the past women's movement was welfare oriented. They, therefore, pursued reform approach. After the people's movement of 1990, women's movement has become increasingly movement oriented. The men rulers obviously prefer reform approach. They give less to women and political leaders misuse them as their vote banks. Movement approach has raised some sensation and waves but such waves have not been sustained for long. Often women's right activists are criticized by the men as being induced by the donors. After the initiation of people's war by the Maoists in February of 1996, some Nepalese women have joined in revolutionary wars.

Gender issues, including women's rights, cannot be and should not be the issues exclusive to only one political party, that is. of the Nepali Congress alone, or of the Nepal Communist Party (Unified Marxist Leninist) alone or of the Rastriya Prajatantra Party alone or of the Nepal Communist Party-Maoist alone or of women alone. The issues transcend both political ideologies and women. Unfortunately, in Nepal, political parties have divided women on the bases of their political ideologies and most of the Nepalese men, including planners, policy makers and development practitioners, often believe that such issues are exclusive concern of women, particularity "Sukila saree lagayaka mehaiaharuko metra" ("Women who were sarees neat and tidy").

Short Term Intervention Strategy

- the women's right movement should give due attention to the following short term intervention strategy:
- Shift from Gender and Development (GAD) to Gender and Private/ Public Spheres (GAPS).
- Implement women and girl child first/centered development.
- Expand and intensify current advocacy and lobbying activities by involving activists belonging to various caste/ethnic, religion, language, regional and ideological/ political groups.
- Increase socio-cultural sensitivity within and outside the movement.
- Intensify literacy programs, including functional, out of school program, remedial, non-formal education, mandatory girls' hostel program up to S.L.C.
- Redesign national school curriculum from gender perspective.
- Adopt two pronged approach: policy level & grassroots level on the following five fields-RATOS:
  - I. Research,
  - II. Advocacy,
  - III. Teaching/Training, and
  - IV. Organization building, and
  - V. Social Mobilization.
- Form a single umbrella network/ alliance on women'

rights.

- Intensify grassroots level organization building and campaign for use of various women's user's groups-PCRW, credit and savings groups, forest, Aama Samuha (Mother's Groups), etc. to fight for gender equality.
- Mandatory requirement of gender desegregated data and information on all plans, program, guidelines, progress reports, monitoring and evaluation.
- Develop Gender-Sensitive-Index (GSI) at the institutional level for the Ministries, Departments, Offices, Organizations, Institutions, Donors, (I)NGOs at national, regional and local level.
- Form the Nepalese Women Voters' League (NWVL) at different levels. National constituency, District Development Committee (DDC), Village Development Committee (VDC) and Ward Level to organize public can clarify their position on gender issues and the League should campaign for or against the party or candidate on that basis. The campaign should be something like if any candidates who does not support property right Bill, abortion Bill and elimination of violence against women Bill as proposed by the women's right movement he/she should not get votes of any women voters.
- Draft and pass a Bill about parenting and gender sensitive division of labor at home.
- Intensify demand for positive discrimination or reservation of seats in various political positions, education and scholarship.
- Activate Women's Caucus in the parliament.

Long Term Intervention Strategy

The women's right movement should give due attention to the following long term intervention strategy:

- All the Ministries should work together with Women 's Ministry on gender issues;
- Many indigenous people of Nepal who are not much influenced by the Hindu religion, culture and value still have some tradition that is very close to gender equality. Social values of such societies should be diffused nationwide with pro-active plans, policies and programs of the government and non-governmental organizations.

– Women's should prepare to stage a gender insurgency or a gender revolution to demolish patriarchy. If there can be ethnic insurgencies why cannot we have a gender insurgency? We should remember that in both class-based and ethnic-based insurgencies it is not difficult to use violent means because the enemies are impersonal but in gender insurgency it is practically impossible for women to use violent means against men who are members of the same household. If should be noted here that patriarchy involves power and power does not transfer so easily. Hence, gender insurgency is a necessity.

Women's individual/ personal problems are national problems. It is a fact that until we solve serious problems facing women, national problems cannot be solved. What happen to women are best indicators of the degree of development of Nepal. If women are at the worst, Nepal's development performance is also at the worst and if women get due opportunities then Nepal also gets an opportunity to develop and prosper. Gender issues are embedded in any society and culture. Nepalese society being characterized by socio-cultural pluralism any demand or any practice is rooted differently in different caste/ethnic, religious, linguistic, cultural and regional groups. Socio-cultural dimensions may be a boon for gender equality, if handled properly or an obstacle, if handled wrongly.

Gender Equality and Democracy

Women's development in Nepal has a long history of about a century, but the wavelength of development was different than what is at present. A slow and gradual development of women since 1950-51 has been accelerated after the declaration of women's decade in 1975. A ten years period from 1975-1985 provided an opportunity to take a retrospective look at the role and status of women.

One of the visible achievements of the UN decade for women in Nepal was the establishment of institutions for women in both the government and the NGO sector. But despite some legal reforms intending to improve women's condition, the absence of a truly democratic political environment made it difficult for the people to raise a voice. Democracy in Nepal has enabled the creation of a strong civil society, with a free press, a variety of academic institutions and a large number of NGOs. All these players have performed a valuable role in sensitizing politicians and functionaries on issues of human rights, environmental conservation and the need for gender equity and equality.

Hindu Culture and the socialization of girls and women in Nepalese society has had such a great impact on women that they consciously or unconsciously, enforce the patriarchal system and accept male dominance. Therefore, women are exploited not only by men but also by other women and even by themselves.

The characteristics of the patriarchal society in Nepal have resulted in clear patterns and structures subordinating women. These characteristics include restrictions on educational opportunities, misrepresentation in the media, control over women's productivity, family control over women's mobility, control over parental property, discriminatory religious practices, discriminatory legal system and economic restrictions. Low educational status and various rigidities in the rules and regulations of civil service often limit women's entrance to the bureaucracy. In an effort to change the system, HMG revised the civil service Act (1994) to incorporate provisions by increasing the maximum age for entry for women to 40 years (35 years for men) encouraging lateral entry in second and first class posts to 45 years. In the judiciary, despite recent acts encouraging women's participation women constitute only about 4% of current judicial decision-makers, 5% of total registered legal practitioners and 25% of pleaders and advocates.

The Constitution of the Kingdom of Nepal, 1990 was promulgated as an achievement of the people's movement. However politics is still considered a man's territory. Women's political participation and access to position of power is restricted by them limited access to education and economic resources as well as by their mobility constraints and household responsibilities. In the political sphere women tend to be restricted mainly to grass root level decision making through voting.

Elections

However, they are much less evident in the middle and

virtually absent in the higher levels of decision-making structures. For example in July 1995 only 8% of the 154 executive members in the Lower House were women. In spite of the commit-ment by political parties to allocate 20% of all seats to women candidates, women's candidacy in 1998 parliamentary elections remained at about 5.1 percent. In fact, out of the total of 2212 candidates in 1999 election only 135 were women. Only 12 emerged as parliamentary members, constituting less than six percent of the total number of seats. A progressive step to decrease gender inequity was introduced in 1997 by a royal ordinance that reserved 20% (approximately 36,000) of VDC seats for elected or nominated women representative. But lack of education and awareness of their roles and responsibilities were constraints for effective functioning.

The economic contribution of Nepalese women may be characterized more comprehensively in terms of feminization of low wage low skilled sectors and the concentration of women's work in unpaid or subsistence oriented work. Trends in these sections are upheld by a gender decision of labor, where women perform most life sustaining activities. Women also, have restricted access to credit and capital. There exists a difference in the wage rates of women and men even in urban area. In addition, only 4% of all economically active women work in the formal sector compared to 12% of men. In 1997, 63% of women were employed in unpaid work compared to 24% of men. Nearly 30% of women were engaged in income earning activities compared to 44% of men. Only 7% were employed in "paid job" compared to 32% men. Another challenge to women's economic empowerment relates to credit.

Although 59 percent of Nepalese households are borrowers of credit, there exits a marked gender gap between men and women's access to institutional credit. For example in 1991/92 women access to institutional credit was almost half of that of men (30.4%: 154%). However production credit for rural women (PCRW) program have illustrated that credit can serve as a locus for women's increased mobility, solidarity and overall social mobilization.

But again women's lack of decision making power on how credit is utilized make them dependent again on the men.

A start on the issues of human rights started with the formation of Human Rights Commission Act in 1996 and the establishment of the Commission in 1999. The formation of Women's Right Commission is still in the process. In order to minimize the gender discrimination advocacy on women's right issues, women's right of capacity building, strengthening law enforcement and monitoring of rights should be exercised only by the women's right commission.

Sex and Marital Status

Nepal has its own idiosyncratic legal system that developed in line with Hindu customs over the centuries. The Nepalese legal system is largely an offshoot of The Hindu system. The moulding of Nepalese society and law according to Hindu tradition, began in the fourth century AD during the rule of Licchavi kings. The most notable aspect of Hinduization during the Licchavi period was the introduction of Hindu Varna system, an attempt to allocate places within this system to all Nepalese, regardless of whether or not they were Hindus. However, there was no real systematic attempt to unify and codify Nepalese society until the late fourteenth century during the reign of king Jayasthiti Malla.

Jayasthiti Malla promulgated the "Manab Nyaya Sastra (legal rules for human justice). It was a comprehensive codification of substantive and procedural rules based largely upon Hindu scriptures, Narad and Yagyavalakya Smirities in particular. Rules in Manab Naya Sastra were formulated, based on "gender and caste." Hence, the individual person's social status was the determining factor of law. The social system was envisaged to maintain with a support of stiffer penal system. The penal system was based on the intensity of the crimes, and was determined by the social status of the offenders. Hence, a crime committed by the so-called lower caste person virtually did not attract punishment. The Rules of Human Justice prohibited inter-caste marriage. For instance, if a lower caste man married an upper caste woman, either the penis of the person was cut off as punishment, or the death penalty would have been imposed. The law recognized the customary practices of people. For instance, the husband of woman having illicit sexual relation with another could kill the latter. The law recognized this practice as the right of men.

The modern period of Nepalese law is said to have begun in 1853, when Muluki Ain was promulgated. It is so called because the code introduced the concept of written law as an authoritative source of law. Muluki Ain too was heavily influenced by Hindu dogmas. That is why the Code includes provisions, which envisage reinforcing the Hindu caste and gender disparity systems. For instance, women were not acceptable in the courts as witnesses. In 1964, New Muluki Ain replaced the Muluki Ain, and it was the progressive laws that eliminated caste system, but it was equally regressive as it still continued with "inequality of genders." The Nepalese legal system is largely a reflection of defective value systems related to the structure of the society. The patriarchal domination is deeply imbibed in the social value system, which denies equality of status to women. The denial is "intentionally" designed in order to weaken their position in the society so that the men's absolute control over their personality and sexuality is rendered possible. This value system is defined as the defective value system.

The following three characteristics of defective value system are expressive in the Nepalese legal system:

— disregard of the independent personality of women;
— invisible but absolute control over the sexuality of women and girls; and o commodification of women by men.

Personality is an aggregation of rights, comprising claims, liberty and immunity. Claims indicate simple entitlement over something, like if one works he deserves wages. If the employer denies payment, the employed has a valid claim to have the payment. Power denotes special legal capacity to alter the "legal position of others." For instance, a father may deny to share his property with children (at least in other countries).

The legal capacity of father depriving his children from right to share the property is defined as the "power of father." Liberty is a capacity of making " choice", a man can have wife of his choice, and no other can impose on him. Immunity is an exemption from some liability, like a diplomatic agent is immune from criminal jurisdiction of Nepal. Defects in claims, power, liberty and immunity impairs personality of individual. These values have no gender characters, and modification is acceptable in exercise of such values by women. Ultimately, these values get expression through certain broad types of rights viz. right to identity, right to contract etc.

Right to Identity

Right to identity directly to his/her "self" means every person has a right to have a name and legal safeguard to protect the "reputation." Gender is an identity in itself and as such is protected from infringement upon, or disregard of any kind. But the right to identity itself has no 'gender'. In the eyes of law of personality, every human being, irrespective of sex, is a person, not man and woman.

The right to identity is a strong basis for recognition of the 'nationality' of person. However, in Nepalese law, the situation is different. The Section 3 of the Citizenship Act, 1963, by defining the father as a sole source for Nepalese nationality of the child,12 obviously flouts the right to identity of women. The provision overtly prohibits the mother to transmit her nationality to the children.

Many people take this circumstance as a "weakness" on the part of child imposed by law. However, the view is apparently a mistaken understanding of the fact. In fact, it is a blatant weakness imposed by the law on "women" in order to incapacitate them as the source of nationality of the children. Of course, the provision is an instrument devised to rebut the right to identity of women.

Implicitly, the provision prohibits women to give birth to a child without identification of " man" as his/her father. In turn, the implicit consequence, as a severe dishonor of the right to identity, restrains women from independent exercise of their 'sexuality'. By incorporation of the given gender biased provision in article 8, the Constitution of the Kingdom of Nepal itself has been impregnated by the concept of women's subordination to men's personality, a defective value system practiced over centuries.

Right to Property

The right to property is referred to mean claims, power, liberty and immunity in relation to things and reputation. It enables a person to hold possession of, maintain ownership on, and realize disposal of the goods of property as per their choice.

Except for certain general conditions of limitation, the right to property is absolute and universal. Like the right to identity, it has no element of gender attached to govern the exercise thereof. However, the Nepalese property law prevails over the centuries in contravention of fundamentals of universality, secularity and perfection of women's right to property. The legal system in Nepal has maintained full control of men over women in relation to their property right.

Muluki Ain (State's Code of Laws), promulgated in 1853, was the first confided law in Nepal providing for, among other things, the rules on property. The promulgation of the code in 1853, although Hindu scriptures on conduct of human being heavily influenced it, marked the beginning of modern era of the Nepalese legal system. This is so viewed because the Muluki Ain introduced the comprehensive code of 'legal rules' governing the substantive and procedural realm of law in Nepal.

Until this period, the Hindu scriptures had unquestioningly been treated as the source of 'rights and duty of peoples" in Nepal. The promulgation of the Code was an attempt to introduce a secular legal system, however, in sprit it was deeply influenced by Hindu philosophy on law and society. It is evident from its framework itself, which envisaged reinforcing the caste system and gendering distinctions as the basis of social relations. Hence, in practicality, the code appeared merely a collection of Hindu dogmas and customs. Junga Bahadur Rana, the first Rana Prime Minister and promulgator of the Muluki Ain, also partially abolished the custom of "Sati", the practice of widow burning themselves with the bodies of their husbands while cremated. The practice denotes to absolute denial of "selfness" to women. The custom overtly recognized a proposition that "women's existence is not possible without husband." It was legacy handed down by orthodox "Hinduism."

Rana Prime Minister Chandra Shamsher, politically a ruthless successor of Junga Bahadur, did partially abolished the custom of "Sati" giving way to the recognition of "mortal existence of women" even after death of their husbands. It was the first step to disassociate the "person" of women from that of "men." However, women's position was effectively underestimated in the formal system, like women were not accepted as witnesses in the courts, and similarly they were prohibited to perform disposal of property by independent choice of their own.

These provisions apparently reduced women to "matters of men's property." Having incorporated the dogmas of Hinduism, the Muluki Ain made an attempt to define legal relations of individuals in society in terms of "Kul" (Kin group), Santan (Family lineage), Jat (Caste) and Linga (sex) as the societal bases. His/her caste and gender therefore, determined the status of the individual. Clause of the Section on "Augsabanda" (Partition of shares of property), for instance, allowed the father to discriminate, in matters of property, against his sons born out of wedlock of a woman of inferior caste. Similarly, the Muluki Ain prohibited the son to claim the share in property, if he was born from a "prostitute."

Prostitutes were legally denied the status of a normal human being. The New Muluki Ain, 1964, repealed the former one, and, to some extent, it was proved to be a progressive piece of law. It did away with the "casteism" as a basis of socio-legal relations. It thus created a ground for the movement of ending the oppression and inhuman treated inflicted upon "Dalit" community. Unfortunately, it prolonged the gender discrimination on many matters as usual in the past. The Muluki Ain prohibited daughters from sharing the parent property as "coparceners." This Muluki Ain is still a general law in matters of property in Nepal.

The property of law Nepal defines personality of women in terms of their sex and marital status. The "Aungsabanda" section of new Muluki Ain, in particular, is an intensely gender segregated law. According to clause 16, if a woman is not married till 35 years of age, it qualifies her to share the property with other coparceners. But subsequent marriage would forfeit the share thus obtained.

A woman by virtue of marriage becomes coparcener of the husband's property, and as such is entitled to share the property with the husband. Nevertheless, the right is dependent on certain conditions to be fulfilled: firstly, she has either to reach an age of 35 years or 15 years of marriage; secondly, the marriage should not be broken due to extramarital relation or any thing else; and thirdly, there should not be a divorce. Absolute sexual loyalty is most required condition for entitlement for right to be a coparcener in the husband's property.

The status of a woman is, therefore, clearly subjected to her sex or marital status. The following briefs help to a better understanding of the situation:

Daughters are secluded from "Aungsabandar" (becoming copar-ceners of parental property) for they do not constitute as members of the natal family. It is the "sex" they are endowed with, that deprives them of the membership. However, the sons' position is different. They are recognized as having inherent right to "Aungsa" of the parental property. There are no other grounds of difference but the 'sex' for differential treatment in matters of property between sons and daughters. The identity of a woman as a "person" in the natal family is thus denied simply because of her "feminine gender."

Daughters, unlike sons, have to prevent themselves from getting married if they want to benefit from the property of parental family as coparceners. The legal stipulation is that a woman must reach 35 years of age and remain unmarried to receive the share in the parents' property, is legal instrument, which virtually defines women's personality in terms of their marital status. It implies that a woman is not a 'person' by virtue of her birth as human being, but by her 'condition of matrimonial life'. She is entitled to obtain "Aungsa" by reaching 35 years of age and remaining "Unmarried" implicitly relates her "personality to marital condition, because, then, there is only limited probability of her marriage. That is why there is an explicit provision to return the property obtained in "Aungsa" back to other coparceners in case she gets married subsequently. The acquisition and termination of the right to "Aungsa" has no other basis but the marriage. By marriage a woman is entitled to be coparcener to the property of her husband, but the termination of the marriage takes away the rights too. Here too, the marriage is a sole determining factor of her "personality." The right to succession is also conditioned on marriage. A daughter is prohibited to succeed the deceased parents so long as the sons and sons of the deceased person survive. If no son or sons survive, the married daughters get one share of the property whereas two shares go to the unmarried daughter. Here again, the legal capacity is determined by marital conditions.

A divorced woman can claim alimony from the former husband under condition of her incapacity to earn livelihood of her own. However, the marriage subsequently terminates the right to receive alimony.

A widow is entitled to succeed the share of her husband's "Aungsa", but gets forfeited on consummating sexual relation with any person. Suppression of sexual desires of widows is an attempt to relate property rights to her marital condition. The marriage and sexual relations are prescribed as fundamental elements of women's personality. These elements remain as "condition precedents" for acquisition and exercise of rights over property. The traditional concept of kinship is the fundamental basis of the gender biased property law jurisprudence of Nepal. The Hindu societal value system recognizes only sons having capacity for continuity of ancestral lineage.

Hence, daughters are virtually secluded from having "kinship" relation with the natal family. Fictitiously, daughters are supposed to constitute "kinship" with the ancestors of husband. The "ancestral Kinship" is taken by the property law of Nepal as a "Primary source" of rights relating to identity and property, which, together with right to contract, constitute the 'legal personality' of every individual human being.

Ancestral kinship is, therefore, the most fundamental element qualifying an individual for the membership of the given family. For daughters are considered as having no attachment of "ancestral kinship" with natal family, they are supposed to be disqualified to obtain the membership thereof. The marriage is taken as instrument to create their kinship with husbands' family. Hence, gender based discrimination in the Nepalese society begins at this point-kinship which is a unavoidable qualification for family membership is obtained by son through birth, where as the same is obtained by daughter through marriage. Obviously, a daughter is liability of parents until she gets puberty. At the moment she achieve puberty, she is given away for marriage. This defective value system is pervasive in property and family law of Nepal.

The following examples will abundantly explain the

statement:

- Not the mother but the father is a source of nationality of the children.
- Marriage of girl at the 16 years is valid irrespective of their consent.
- Parents can very much decide who should be her husband.
- Since parents can decide on her marriage, her right to remain unmarried and qualify herself as coparcener to the family property is easily evaded.
- The divorce, extra-marital sex and sexual relation of widow terminate the marital relation and thus the right to obtain "Aungsa" from husband, but such incidents do not bring her back to the station she was at before the marriage. She remains in "Kinshipless" state. In this state she remain with greatly "deformed" personality.

By denying to recognize the rights and interests, a girl child is forced to face several disadvantages and difficult circumstances. A few instances can be cited as follows:

- For not taken as members the family, daughters are simply the liability. Hence, investment on their education and other development opportunities is something like "watering the neighbor's flower plant." Rampant ignorance and illiteracy is therefore the result of defective societal value system. Ignorance subjects women to vulnerability of exploitation of all forms.
- 16 years as a minimum legal age for marriage, is desperately awaited by parents. The marriage being an unavoidable religious and moral obligation of parents, it is a chance never to miss. Hence, child or early marriage is common phenomena. Such marriages lead to early pregnancies, leading to birth of unhealthy child and larger maternity deaths. Hence, right to property is integrally related with reproductive and health conditions of women.
- Uneducated wives are virtually enslaved, and taken as "machines" to procreate children for their husbands.

The property law of Nepal defines the personality of women in terms of their sex and marital status. The "Aungsabanda" section of new Muluki Ain, in particular is an intensely gender segregate law. According to clause 16, if a woman is not married till 35 years of age, it qualifies her to share the property with other coparcener. But subsequent marriage would forfeit the share obtained.

A woman by virtue of marriage becomes a coparcener of the husband's property, and as such is entitled to share the property with the husband. Nevertheless, the right is dependent on certain conditions to be fulfilled: firstly, she has either to reach an age of 35 years or 15 years of marriage; secondly, the marriage should not be broken due to extramarital relation; and thirdly, there should no be a divorce.

Absolute sexual loyalty is the mostly required condition for entitlement for the right to be coparcener in the husband's property. The status of a woman is, therefore, clearly subjected to her sex or marital status.

The following analysis helps to better understanding of the situation:

– Daughters are secluded from "Aungsabanda" (becoming coparceners of parental property) for they do not constitute member of the natal family. It is the "sex" they are endowed with deprives them of the membership. However, sons' position is different. They are recognized as having inherent right of "Aungsa" to the parental property. There are no other grounds of difference but the "sex" for differential treatment. The identity of a woman as a "person' in the natal family is thus denied simply because of her "feminine gender."

– Daughters, unlike sons, have to prevent themselves from getting married if they want to be benefited from property of parental family as coparceners. The legal stipulation that a woman must reach 35 years of age and remain unmarried to receive the share in the parents' property, is a legal instrument, which virtually defines women personality in terms of her marital status. It implies that a woman is not a "person" by virtue of her birth as a human being, but by her" condition of matrimonial life." She is entitled to obtain "Aungsa" by reaching 35 years of age and remaining unmarried implicitly relates her "personality" to marital condition, because thus there is only a limited probability of marriage. That is why there is an explicit provision to return the property obtained in "Aungsa" back to other coparceners in case she gets married subsequently. The acquisition and termination of the right of "Aungsa" has no other basis but the marriage.

- By marriage a woman is entitled to be a coparcener to the property of husband, but the termination of the marriage takes away the rights too. Here too, the marriage is a sole determining factor of her "personality."
- The right to succession is also conditioned on marriage. A daughter is prohibited to succeed the deceased parents so long as the sons and sons' sons survive, the married daughters get one share of the property whereas two shares go to unmarried daughter. Here again, the legal capacity is determined by marital conditions.
- A divorced woman can claim alimony from the former husband under condition of her incapacity to earn livelihood of her own. However, the marriage subsequently terminates the right to receive alimony. The marriage is again a matter of determining the position of right.
- A widow is entitled to succeed the share of her husband's "Aungsa," but gets forfeited on consummating sexual relation with any person. The marriage and sexual relations are prescribed as fundamental elements of women's personality. These elements remain as "condition precedents" for acquisition and exercise of rights over property. The traditional concept of kinship is the fundamental basis of the gender biased property law jurisprudence of Nepal. The Hindu societal value system recognizes only sons having capacity for continuity of ancestral lineage.

Hence, daughters are seemingly secluded from having "kinship" relation with the natal family. Fictitiously, daughters are supposed to constitute "Kinship" with the ancestors of husband. The "Ancestral kinship" is taken by the property law of Nepal as a "primary source" of any rights relating to identity and property, which, together with right to contract, constitute the 'legal personality' of every individual human being.

Ancestral kinship is, therefore, the most fundamental

element qualifying an individual for the membership of the given family. For daughters are considered as having no attachment of "ancestral kinship" with natal family, they are supposed to be disqualified to obtain the membership thereof. The marriage is taken as an instrument to create their kinship with filial family. Hence, gender based discrimination in the Nepalese society begins at this point-kinship which is unavoidable qualification for family membership is obtained by son through birth, whereas the same is obtained by daughter through marriage. Obviously, a daughter is a liability of the parents until she gets puberty. At the moment she achieve puberty, she is given away for marriage. This defective value system is pervasive in property and family law of Nepal. The following examples will abundantly explain the statement:

- Not the mother, but the father is a source of nationality of the children. (Section 3 of Citizenship Act, 1964 and Article 8 of the Constitution of the Kingdom of Nepal, 1990)
- Marriage of girl at 16 years is valid irrespective of their consent.
- Parents can very much decide who should be her husband.
- Since parents can decide on her marriage, her right to remain unmarried and qualify herself as coparcener to the family property is easily evaded.
- The divorce, extramarital sex and sexual relation of widow terminate the martial relation and thus the right to obtain "Aungsa" from husband, but such incidents do not bring her back to station she was at while before the marriage. She remains in a "kinshipless" state. In this state she remain with greatly "deformed" personality. Being having been denied the "natal kinship" and consequential rights and interests, a girl child forced to face several disadvantages and difficult circumstances. A few instances can be cited as follows:
- For not being taken as members the family, daughters are simply considered to be the liability of parents. Hence, investment on their education and other development opportunities is something like 'watering the neighbor's flower plant'. Rampant ignorance and illiteracy is

therefore the result of defective societal value system. The ignorance subjects women to vulnerability of exploitation of all forms. Trafficking has stroked roots in the defective value system and flourished as a formidable for women's sexual exploitation.

- 16 years as minimum legal age for marriage, is desperately awaited by parents to reach. The marriage being unavoidable religious and moral obligation of parents, it is a chance not to miss. Hence, child or early marriage is common phenomena. Such marriages lead to early pregnancies, leading to birth to unhealthy children and larger maternity death. Hence, denial of property rights has direct bearings on health of women.
- Uneducated wives are virtually enslaved, and taken as "machine" to procreate children for husband.

Right to Contract

Right to contract is one of the basic rights associated with "personality" of individual. Defects on rights to contract seriously impair the personality. Generally, the right to contract is expressed in the form of "power to agree or disagree" to something. The "marriage and associated matrimonial relations" like divorce, extramarital relations, and judicial separations etc. fall within the scope of right to contract. However, women in Nepal are effectively subject to inferiority in exercise of the contractual rights, leading to serious impairment in their "right to identity." The situation is expressive in the following circumstances:

- Choice of husband is something not exercised by women, but imposed by parents. A woman is competent to make independent to take decision on marriage when she reaches 18 years of age. She has been considered adult at 16 years, old considered adult at 16 years, and so is thought fit for legal marriage. However, she is not permitted to consummate marriage by independent decision of her. Parents can give her away for marriage, but the same is not recognized if it is consummated by the woman herself. This provision of law is not based on any rationality. Of course, this provision of law is an obvious infliction on right to contract of women. To give in marriage without absence of women's consent virtually amounts to a "sell" if she is considered incompetent to express independent consent for marriage of choice before 18, how she can be thought to be competent "doing the same" when marriage is arranged by parents. The marriage arranged by parents is, therefore, an involuntary marriage imposed on women seriously impairing they're right to contract. Independent consent for marriage of choice.

– Husband is empowered to consummate the marriage with other women if first wife is not able to procreate the children. However, the women is not empowered to the same if the husband suffers infertility. If the woman marries to other man, she gets forfeiture of the right to "Aungsa" from the former husband. Empowering a person breach the trust of marriage on the ground of infertility, is explicit violation of the right to contract.

– Under the succession law of Nepal, husband and wife are competent to inherit each other. However, the husband can, without any legal constraints, consummate the marriage after the death of wife, and can inherit the property of wife too. The same privilege is not granted to widow. For succeeding and enjoying the property of husband, she should remain as windows through out the life.

In practice, there are several other restrictions on performance of contract by women. For instance, a woman is not granted the passport without concurrence of her father of husband. This result is an implicit ban on travel by women independently. Similarly, a woman is denied to sign a contract of employment with a company outside of Nepal independently. In many property matters, women are restricted to perform independent disposal rights. Lack of control over family resources is an outcome of inability for exercising the right to contract.

It is interesting to mention that the legal principles in law books (statutes) used to define women are related to marriage and sexual relations. Women characterized as "kanya" (virgin), bihe nagareko (never married), bihe (married) "lyayeko"(brought as wife but nor formally married). "bahira rakhako" (kept informally outside the home),"santan hune and nahune" (with or without children) and "bidhawa" (widow).

These terms are derogatory of the personality of woman in themselves. But they also denote inferiority in competency to contract relations with men.

Imperfections or limitations imposed upon these three rights virtually render the "status of women as subjects to men's control. "Control over sexuality" is the main purpose of limitations on women's personality. The existing legal system, despite the constitutional guarantee of equality of sex and safeguard against exploitation, maintains the men's control over female sexuality basically through the following instruments:

— Restricting women from transmitting her identity to children. The implication of restriction extends to ban on transmission of mother's nationality to children.
— Restriction on birth relation of women to their fathers' ancestors. The implication of restriction obliges women to consummate marriage mandatory, and to accept the family lineage of husband. The system of acquiring family lineage of alien family through the institution of marriage, disqualifies women to entertain rights over natal property.
— Recognition of law for prevalence of parents' decision on matters of marriages of daughters, virtually converts the marriage into an institution granting to husband the full control over sexuality of women. The implication of the practice renders the women's right to property dependent on their "sexual behavior."

These three instruments maintain full domination of men over women's position in the Nepalese society. They also help in the elaboration of sets of rules to be adopted or practiced by women folks in their general life, are as follows:

— Girls should be educated to behave well to their husbands, and should remain always sexually faithful them.
— Sooner the marriage, better chance for settled life.
— Women should not interfere in public affairs.
— Girls should learn domestic chores since early age by helping mothers in those affairs.
— Education has no meaning for women, as procreating and rearing children is their natural obligation.
— A woman unable to have a child, or having childless, is

unlucky and abnormal.

The social taboos and milieu based those indoctrination are responsible to:

- degraded social status of girl children, and their Commodification;
- seclusion of girl children from the mainstream development;
- deprivation of girl children from investment on education and mental development;
- depersonification of women;
- emergence of a sex market, where men can buy "sex" through bodies of women.

Ignorance, illiteracy and exploitation of girls and women are therefore outcomes of the defective value system inherited and zealously protected by the Nepalese society with the help of archaic laws.

The lack of State's (three organs plus political parties) commitment to bring about changes into laws discussed above, has nullified the potentiality of the constitution's scheme of equality of gender. The State has virtually failed to understand the role of empowered women in the development of family and society at large. It is interesting to note that a woman who is constitutionally capable of becoming a Prime Minister of this country but she is not capable of transmitting nationality to her child.

The World Health Organisation (WHO) has reported that the preconditions for a severe AIDS epidemic are present in Nepal. The Government established its first AIDS Prevention and Control Project in 1987 and, one year later, the first AIDS case was diagnosed. Taking into consideration the long asymptomatic phase of the disease and the lack of active surveillance, by 1993 it seemed likely that between 3,000 and 5,000 Nepalis may have been HIV positive. The National Centre for AIDS and STD Control's update for November 1998 reported a total of 1,175 HIV/AIDS cases, yet it is and unofficially estimated that between 20,000-25,000 Nepalis are now infected. Under-reporting of HIV/AIDS in some areas has concealed the true levels of infection and has made it difficult to predict the future of the pandemic. However, Asia has been described by the WHO as the "Sleeping Giant" of AIDS and it has been suggested that an HIV epidemic would have a devastating impact.

Nepal has links with both India and Thailand and the effects of a pandemic in either of these countries, particularly in India, are likely to impact Nepal directly. Relevant factors which will influence the characteristics and pattern of widespread HIV/AIDS in Nepal include increasing population density, "rural-urban-rural" patterns of movement and migration related to employment needs, the open border between Nepal and India, widespread STD infections and low condom usage rates. Economic conditions, health status, gender and sexual relations, and the political and cultural dynamics of the Nepali state will all determine the ways in which HIV/AIDS affects the people of Nepal.

In Nepal, as elsewhere in the world, acknowledgement of the potential danger of AIDS has led to the growth of an NGO industry and, to a much lesser degree, Community Based Organisations (CBOs) focusing on HIV/AIDS related programmes. These have developed in response both to perceived need and to such externals forces as funding, multilateral agencies' initiatives, and changing local political contexts. Whether Nepali NGOs have the capacity to adapt to and address the complexities of HIV within an epidemic situation remains to be seen.

The advent of HIV/AIDS has both constructed and interacted with the discourses of many Nepali NGOs previously working on gender issues. At times, it has led to the conflation of three distinct fields: that of 'girl trafficking', the "flesh trade", and that of HIV/AIDS. NGOs operating in the discursive field of HIV/AIDS retain significant conceptual links between these three fields, and indeed, create categorical confusion among them. This confusion informs the production and reproduction of discourses related to 'girl trafficking', prostitution and HIV/AIDS. There is commonly little distinction between the two distinct categories of 'girl trafficking' and prostitution, with the NGOs and media creating an ambiguous and blurred field that encompasses all forms of exploitation of women and the 'girl-child.'6

NGO Programmes have focused on a range of connected projects such as AIDS 'awareness' rallies and meetings, women's empowerment projects, trafficking 'prevention camps', income generation and micro credit schemes, condom distribution projects and various "training" classes where young women are taught the 'skills' of painting tablecloths and knitting as an unquestioned escape to a life of prostitution.

The NGOs are not alone in their conflation of HIV/AIDS and prostitution, as is evidenced by the official government reactions when a coalition of NGOs repatriated some 120-130 Nepali women from Bombay brothels in mid-1996. At this time, HMG ministers and officials accused the NGOs of "making Nepal a dumping site for AIDS".

Amongst migrant laborers returning to Nepal, STDs are referred to as "Bombay diseases", and in Nepal, prostitutes may be crudely described as "bhiringi girls" - bhiringi being a disease usually translated as syphilis and particularly associated with illicit sexuality. In HIV/AIDS discourse, both in popular culture and scientific representations, prostitutes have been variously described as a "risk group", "a reservoir of HIV infection", and "a bridge". Rather than presenting women in prostitution as links in broader networks of heterosexual HIV transmission, they have been described as infecting their unborn infants, their clients, and, indirectly, their clients other female sexual partners, as though HIV originated among them. Similar representations underpin much discussion of HIV/AIDS in Nepal. The virus penetrat[ed] Nepal's hinterland through prostitutes returning from the AIDS-ridden brothels of India.

A study by a Kathmandu based NGO on the status of Nepali women in Bombay brothels, while stating that the defining causes of prostitution are "illiteracy, poverty, social unconsciousness and lack of employment opportunities," describes the women in these terms: "above 30% of girls involved in commercial sex business at Bombay have now been converted into reservoir of HIV". The image of prostitutes as a "reservoir" of infection seems to have a particular salience and recurs in various research studies.

In the Nepali context, "prostitute-branded women" are placed in the lowest and most profane position. Cultural ideals and values defined by the fields of gender, caste, class and ethnicity produce a stereotype which often reflects an elite ideology, stigmatising women who engage in sex work as poor, ignorant and naive, or wanton. A soft-core public discourse emerges, utilising familiar tropes of prostitutes as "sad, mad or bad", framing "the prostitute" as a deviant woman, rather than a woman performing wage labour, and therefore vulnerable to interventions for the public good. Additionally, with the advent of AIDS, medicalising discourses have entwined with seemingly natural categories such as sex and prostitution, opening a moral space in both public health and the public sphere which is at once prurient yet safely anaesthetised and sterile.

Due to the Nepali state's emphasis on development and the high profile, action-oriented input of NGOs and INGOs into health issues, much of the Information, Education and Communication (IEC) material and strategies on HIV education and prevention have been imported from the West and directly translated and applied. This has fostered incongruous scenarios in which local middle class and 'respectable' women may be employed by NGOs to interview sex workers for "baseline surveys" on their sexual practice, mixed-sex groups blow up condoms as "icebreakers" in "sexuality trainings", local newspapers print articles on sex workers' places of work and lifestyles which incorporate photographs of the workers, lodge, or cafe phone numbers and moral education and the Nepal Contraceptive Retail Sales (CRS) Company FM Radio show simultaneously advertises the CRS hotline as an HIV/AIDS education program and an "exciting" popular show.

Prostitution, both as a category and an identity, has multiple social and historical constructions. Discourses on prostitution reveal not a singular, nor constant, "prostitution" extant through time and space but, rather, a range of possible prostitutions mediated by historical and cultural context. Prostitution was, for example, a regulated and contained activity in classical Athens, the European Middle Ages, in classical, mediaeval and contemporary India, and within nineteenth century British Empire outposts from the Raj to the Outback. However, the forms that regulation and surveillance took in each of these societies varied. Rather than speaking, then, of "prostitution", a social constructionist view would suggest we speak of "prostitutions", thus allowing for social, cultural and historical specificities. This view is particularly apposite when examining the sex industry of Nepal, in which widely differing prostitutions co-exist.

The sex industry in Nepal has been neither fully measured nor researched. However, increased donor funding of AIDS prevention has created an opening for research into STDs and CSWs as part of the development paradigm in Nepal. The 1990s has seen the rise of Knowledge, Attitudes and Practice (KAP) studies, but there has been little in-depth qualitative research. Much of the work has focused on issues derived from the paradigms of biomedicine and epidemiology: "risk groups" such as CSWs and migrant labourers, STDs, number of sexual contacts, condoms neglected, and so on.

The terrain of sexuality in Nepal, as elsewhere, is both highly contested and obfuscated, idealised and fractured. The localised dichotomies which position women in this world are mediated through ideal representations of moral worth, honour and purity, creating a dyadic fracture between good women and bad or dangerous women.

The National Centre for AIDS and STD Control differentiates between women who have become HIV positive as either "Housewives" or "Commercial Sex Workers" in a classic contrasting of mothers and whores.

These ideals continue to resonate in public discourses yet are at times destabalised by conflicting views of gender and sexuality. For example, at a mid-1998 Kathmandu seminar at which a prominent lawyer presented a set of proposed amendments to the current Trafficking Control laws, many of the women present contested his basic assumption regarding women who engage in sex work "willingly" or "voluntarily", arguing that no woman could possibly take up such work voluntarily and if there were such exceptional women they should be "punished". Taking into consideration such variables as lack of education and economic status, up to 3 years of gaol term was suggested.

By somewhat circular logic, it is argued that no (good) woman could possibly do such work, so of course she must be "rescued" and "rehabilitated". Therefore, any women doing sex work without overt coercion must be "bad" women and thus in need of regulation, surveillance and the discipline of the moral order and the state. For these "lost" women seen to be working in the sex industry "willingly", there is little support, funding or attention ; only a minority of NGOs are prepared to work with them on health issues and human rights or to involve the concerned sex workers in programmes which are directly aimed at them.

Most of the NGOs working directly or indirectly with sex workers prefer to engage with those women who can be represented as exploited victims, thus pandering to elite notions of appropriate female behaviour and denying or glossing the agency and choices and, indeed, life realities, of women who enter the sex industry. The punitive responses and proposed strategies aimed at addressing those women on the borders of the gendered moral landscape are predicated on the assumptions underlying the primary discourse on trafficking as described above: that victims must be rescued and redeemed, whilst "willing" or even potentially "willing" women require containment and punishment. Thus, "trafficking prevention camps" in which girls "in danger of being trafficked" can be educated and given "income generation skills" have been established in perceived danger areas such as Sindhupalchowk and Nuwakot Districts. At the 1998 seminar mentioned above, surveillance of households, a registration system of young girls and women, and a system of "spies" working with the police were outlined.

In a similar vein, at an "Awareness Raising Seminar" in early 1996 jointly organised by an NGO and the Planning and Research Division of Police Headquarters, Kathmandu, and held at Chautara, the District Headquarters of Sindhupalchowk, local elite participants such as school teachers and social workers suggested punitive measures for those women who "willingly" entered prostitution. Ideas presented included anonymous "criminal cards"; introduction of a registration and identity card scheme for all women aged between 12-35 years to allow monitoring at a village level; that the laws be amended so that those women leaving "willingly" could be prosecuted; that village authority be strengthened to allow punishment of "frequent comers"; that the property of returnees should be confiscated as a deterrent measure and, finally, that teachers organise students to collect data on returnee women who are HIV positive. These responses suggest a climate of "moral panic" and may be seen as attempts to discipline female bodies without reference to the wider cultural and structural positioning of these bodies.

While little qualitative data as yet exists on sexuality, sex work or sex workers in Nepal, preliminary research suggests that there is a "a vigorous sex industry". As with street children, the imperatives, discourses, and programmatic limitations of INGOs and NGOs have categorised sex workers in Nepal within several discrete fields. These categories of sex work, as described in NGO pamphlets and INGO texts, are as follows: those "trafficked" from the country, either willingly or unwillingly, to the sex industries of India and other neighbouring countries; those "local women" active as Commercial Sex Workers within the country; and those women working in the "traditional" prostitutions of Nepal, within practices said to be based in religious and cultural customs.

In effect, these three basic categories emerge in the Nepali discourse on prostitutions, all of which may be placed under the explanatory rubrics of modernity/poverty, religion, and culture. Terms such as "comfort women", Hidden Sex Workers, Women at Risk, and Identified Sex Workers have also been constructed by various NGOs, in addition to the more common Commercial Sex Worker, to further depict empirically separate categories of prostitution. However, the basic category is a reified one, in which women who engage in acts of sex on a transactional basis are essentialised by and through their work alone.

It is rarely mentioned that differing life experiences and, more particularly, divergent class, ethnic, caste, age, and geographical factors mediate the choices, negotiation abilities, and agency of women working in the sex industry. Indeed, if sex workers are allowed the problematic attributes of individuality, choice, and agency, it is difficult to engage in polemics based upon the familiar imperatives of rescue, rehabilitation, and redemption which may be traced back to similar moral discourses on prostitution prevalent during the late nineteenth century.

Girls and women do indeed get trafficked. Working in brothels in Bombay and Calcutta is hard work, yet the complexities and nuances of women's lives may be overlooked and denied within a reductionist framing of sex work in foreign brothels. For example, women such as Mïnu, a 22 year-old chhetri woman from Biratnagar who left school after class 5 and worked in a massage parlour in the Kathmandu tourist area of Thamel, become invisible within this narrow representation. Minu chose not to stay in her village and work in the family home and fields but kept in close contact with her family and was saving money, an option not open to her in the village. Her earnings as a sex worker have allowed her to support herself well in Kathmandu and enabled her father to have necessary medical treatment. She may be seen as an example of the fluid identity of some women who work as sex workers; she will possibly move in and out of sex work and eventually have an arranged marriage. Her family is unaware of the nature of her job. Indeed, if they knew she would be seen as "ruined" (bigriyo) and her family status (iijjat) would be lost. However, she regularly travels home for festivals, weddings and other family occasions. Minu has moral distaste for the nature of her work but has few employment options with her level of education and lack of skills.

In this context, to talk of choice and agency is both abstract and ambiguous. Yet representations of women within NGO discourses need to be teased out and seen as only partial truths premised upon an elite understanding of gender, ethnicity, caste and class. The NGO publications and the foreign journalists' accounts, well meaning in terms of advocacy, do a disservice to the women they are representing by distorting their lives in uncritical accounts filled with unreliable statistics which undermine the specific realities of exploitation. The construction and (re)production of their lives as a tabloid tale elides the very real pain which many women may have experienced.

"Traditional" prostitutions are practiced primarily in the Mid-Western and Far- Western regions of Nepal and include women who are Deuki, similar to the Devadasis in India: women who are offered as acts of merit to temples. In addition, there is the sex work of the Badi caste, which has been described both as a "cultural" and "traditional" form of prostitution.

Over the last decade, reportage on the Badi has escalated,

both in the national and international media, in NGO publications and academic studies and reports. The imperatives of international funding are such that, inevitably, a film on communities engaged in sex work will have a more compelling, if not titilllating, effect than a film depicting the lives of agricultural workers. However, the ethics of INGOs who are currently funding projects in these communities and filming marginal and sexually stigmatised women and children as a fund raising exercise remain unaddressed.

In many ways, the Badi have undergone a process of "hypersexualisation". Nina Kammerer has suggested that "hypersexualisation symbolizes and sustains social boundaries and inequalities". She further argues that hypersexualised images, as documented in her case study of the Hmong in North Thailand, "have the power in social life to both mask and maintain real economic and political inequalities". In the case of the Badi, this status as sexual "Other" created by representations which emphasize their deviant sexuality and deviance from ideal Nepali norms and practices, is further grounded by their positioning as a dalit (oppressed) or "untouchable" caste. A fetishising gaze rests upon the Badi, filtered through the dark lens of authorial representations, caste and class stereotypes and the gloss of moral knowledge. Local discourses on "girl trafficking" and prostitution have conflated a range of representations to create a generic image of "social evil" or "social perversity" that is detrimental to images of national honour. Within this context, the practice of sex work by the Badi is constructed as a "prevailing evil tradition".

Gender discrimination and "torture of women as sorcerers" are linked, with prostitution, as a "chain of perversities" which are "contrary to human civilisation" and seen as "manifesting hurdles in the healthy development of nationality". Trafficking of women in particular is seen as having "tarnished our glorious national image". The development discourses thus also come into play, contrasting a modern culture with the residue of perversities and superstitions from the "traditional" past, at odds with both national honour and development. In these discourses, elite, brahmanical views on caste and identity portray low caste people in a manner which collapses several fields such as "backwardness", poverty, and awareness into a complex image of caste status based upon such referents as dress, immorality, alcohol-use, violence and hygiene.

Rather than focusing on embedded structural inequalities, the prevalence of "lack of education and lower social awareness" have been pinpointed, with poverty, as causative factors in the "flesh trade". Homogenised representations of the Badi draw on these understandings of development, morality and caste. Quotes from three different people from bahira samaj ("outside society" - the term used by the Badi to denote wider society) in the village of Dhampur, all incidentally from the high-caste brahmin and chhetri groups, illustrate the narrow range of representations and thought on the local Badi populace.

A local businessman and landowner waxed eloquent in describing the Badi as "poor, oppressed and backward people - in need of education, support and upliftment." In contrast, a local schoolteacher angrily accused the Badi of laziness and unwillingness to work like other people. He added that as boys and youths visit the community they are "ruined" and this dishonors their families. His solution was to "break and scatter" the community to other places. A policeman stationed at the VDC (Village Development Committee) headquarters described prostitution as the caste occupation of the Badi but also posited "poverty" as the reason for their sex work. These depictions form a continuum with poverty as the central reference point - from the deserving poor to the undeserving poor. Yet poverty is socially constructed, produced and reproduced by the socio-cultural dynamics and political economy of a larger world. Indeed for the Badi, over the last fifty years, class and caste positioning have produced such gendered strategies as migration and sex work.

Prostitution as it is called within the community, is not perceived as a caste occupation by the Badi community in the sense that the other "occupational" castes are aligned with jobs such as leather-work or tailoring. Their caste profession was entertainment, and members of the musical and dancing groups were respected for their skills and called to perform at celebrations by elite castes.

Although pesaa takes place in many Badi communities,

there are also households and communities in which there is little or no pesaa. As one Badi NGO worker poignantly noted "nobody talks about the Badi marriage system - they always talk about prostitution." In common with some other caste groups in Nepal, such as the Magar, Gurung, and Thakuri, the preferred marriage system for the Badi was one of cross-cousin marriage, with males marrying their mother's brother's daughter (MBD) and women marrying their father's sister's son (FZD). This preferred pattern is still in place, to a certain degree, but has fractures for two reasons. Firstly, if women are practicing as sex workers, they generally reside in their natal home, with their sons, who are therefore living beside their potential marriage partners, that is, their MBDs.

Consequently, it is common for the girl-cousins to give tika (in the ceremony of bhaai tika in which sisters give tika to their brothers) to the boys they have been brought up with, and as they are then in a symbolic 'sister' position, marriage is impossible. Secondly, if a young woman was doing pesaa, it would be unthinkable to marry her to a young son as she is considered bigriyo (ruined). Nonetheless, several Badi males in their mid-twenties and working in NGOs have married their actual or classficatory MBDs whilst in Dhampur, eight of the households have members married in this pattern, showing that this marriage preference is still relevant for many in the generation under 30 years of age.

The notion of women who have become bigriyo underlines the fact that, while the Badi practice of sex work subverts Nepali norms of ideal behaviour, this praxis is enacted within the context of those norms, and non-virginal women are evaluated by according standards of purity. Therefore, while sex work is certainly a social norm in some Badi communities, it is not a moral norm, since moral knowledge is still in line with the Nepali moral order. In Dhampur, there are several categories of sexually mature women: young women who are virginal and attending school, young women doing pesaa and hence bigriyo, mature married and/or retired unmarried women and young daughters-in-law. With this last category, in-marrying young women, it is also possible to see the normative moral field and the hegemonic social order at work.

There are seven young women, aged less than 25 years, in this category in the community, some with arranged marriages and some with "love marriages." By caste affiliation, they are primarily Badi, with one Damai teenager. All were married at approximately 15-16 years and have young children or are pregnant. In relation to social and behavioral roles, they are lowly placed in the hierarchy of the family, as has been described for other Nepali young women in this positioning.

Women doing pesaa occupy an anomalous space, being bigriyo on an ideal level but also acting as a primary source of family income. The notion of bigriyo acts then, in practice, as a categorical sign and.there is no particular moral censure as such within the community. However, as noted above, these women are not considered as pure as a virginal women, and would not be thought of as potential brides for sons, although an elopement or love marriage is always possible. In such a case, all informants within Dhampur stated that the woman would cease doing pesaa as married women do not do pesaa.

In discussions with educated male Badi NGO workers in their mid-twenties, it emerges that they are particularly conscious of, and concerned with, presenting an image of middle-class mores through such key cultural markers as dress, language and personal presentation and behaviour. This image, for both men and women in the Badi community, stands in sharp contrast to representations of the stereotype of lower caste action and behaviour in general, and of the Badi caste in particular. For those contesting both the stigmatised status and the structural positioning of the Badi, a re-imaging of ascribed identity is thus constructed, inscribed, and maintained corporeally. The representations of the Badi in public discourses produce images of fear and distaste, albeit at times tinged with desire and titillation, and informants have noted that they would not want a Badi household next to their home or want to have Badi in their workplace as co-workers. In terms of employment, unless a programme of affirmative action or a quota system that reserved jobs for the wider dalit population were developed, young and unskilled Badi men seeking wage labour will continue to migrate to sites in India and Nepal and women will continue working from home as sex workers. Discourses on the Badi refract upon young women, both corporeally and in the social world, with all Badi women perceived to be prostitutes, a profane and deviant positioning in Nepali culture. Schooling offers an alternative identity and possibilities, albeit at the cost of adopting elite behaviours and worldviews.

Individual achievements in the fields of employment and education however will have little impact on the structural poverty and powerlessness of the wider Badi community, which is founded on historical and cultural disenfranchisement. While representations of Badi women fall at one end of a continuum of hypersexuality, all women who practice sex work are culturally positioned within images of deviance, danger and desire, with the possible exception of those women granted the one dimensional graces of innocence, naivity and "backwardness".

Since the commencement of HIV/AIDS prevention projects, there has been an increasing escalation of reportage and programmatic focus on prostitution and sex workers in Nepal. Much of the discourse on prostitution is reliant on images constructed by INGOS, NGOs, and the media, and this discourse reflects dominant ideals derived from cultural and development domains. At this point in time the exigencies of the advent of HIV/AIDS have been a contributing factor to the opening of a space in public and institutional discourses for debate regarding prostitutions and sexualities.

2

Education and Employment

In Nepal, crystallization of educational started formally in 1950 when the Nepal National Educational Planning Commission was formed. The report of this Commission clearly identified education as a factor to prepare people to be receptive to new developments which call empower them to progress rapidly towards consolidating the democracy gained at that time. It also reiterated that it is one of the basic lights which each individual child is entitled to possess. However, this report seemed to lack ally cleat. direction about girls' education. Consequently, educational development in Nepal got lopsided with a distinct tilt towards the promotion of male dominant sociocultural values, until the National Education System Plan (NESP) came to the rescue by giving a strong thrust towards promoting and expanding access of girls to education. Within the last two decades, global cognizance of the importance of women's roles in the development process has brought women's issues to the fore-front of the governments, academics and activists.

Among those approaches were the ones followed at the government level in terms of educational policy and planning, the ones inside it the international level in organizing global seminars and conferences and also the ones followed both at the national level as well as international levels in terms of various multi-pronged programs. Both private and public sector organizations were involved in initiating innovative programs for- promotion of girls' education.

The international conferences and seminars have led to a greater commitment on the part of HMG/Nepal and the international donor agencies. A large number of creative projects were launched and treasures like EGWN (Education for

Girls and Women in Nepal), Cheli Beti Program (Education for Rural Development, Seti Project), Basic Primary Education Project and others were taken by the government in Nepal.

The Donors

More than 10 multi-lateral and bilateral donors like World Bank, UNICEF, UNESCO, UNDP, Asian Development Bulk, Danida. JICA, and many other Northern NGOs like, Save the Children US, Save the Children UJK- ('are Nepal, Action Aid, Lutheran World Service, World Education, PACT are active in promoting girls' and women's education in Nepal.

Institutions actively involved in NFE/Literacy Activities for Women are:

- NGOs like PACT, SCF/UJSA, SCF/Japan, SCF/UK Action Aid, Plan International, GTZ, Care Nepal, Lutheran World Service, World Education and many other.
- More than 11000 local NGOs
- Ministry of Education and other line ministries
- Basic and Primary Education Project/MOE
- CERID, Tribhuvan University (provides support system to NFE workers in Nepal)

A study report of CERID (Research Centre for Educational Innovation and Development), A Profile of Non-formal Education Organisations, has shown that ,more than 80 % organizations offer. programme for, women and children.

More than 90% participants in literacy classes were female. Still there seems to be a widening gap between the literacy percentage of male and female.

Table 1
Literacy Rates between Male and Female

Census	*Male*	*Female*	*Both*	*Male/Female Differentials*
1971	23.59	3.91	13.89	19.68
1981	33.96	12.05	23.26	21.91
1991	54.10	24.73	39.74	29.37
1997	66.00	30.00	48.00	36.00

One of the studies conducted by CERID, Gender and Secondary Education, has revealed that, although there are some government policies to increase the girls' and women's participation in education, there is a wide gaps in implementation of those policies. Girls and women are still facing a lot of problem in participating in education.

A recent study entitled NMIS (1995 May-July) pointed out some specific characteristics of a girl as compared to a boy in terms of participation in education.

A girl child, compared with a boy child of the same age, is:

- 2.6 times more at risk of being kept out of school,
- 20% more at risk of having to repeat a year,
- at age 6, at twice the risk, of repeating the year,
- 89% more at risk of dropping out, and
- 2.3 times more needed for house-hold chores.

All the efforts that has been made towards the increment of girls and women education deserves a great appreciation in these two decades. As ally other efforts, there are some critical issues that persisted or developed over. time. These issues can be broadly categorized as:

- Socio-cultural practices
- Government policies
- Literacy program level

The status ot female members in the family has a colitinuum from ultra-liberal to the most conservative from one community to another due to their religious and social values, a factor which seem to make a great impact oil educational participation.

1. *Social Values*: Girls are often considered as only temporary residents in their natal homes. They eventually go to join their-in-laws where there house hold skills are more valued than education. With good intention to make their daughters' life a real success, parents tend to focus on equipping their daughters with skills that can make them adept in household chores. In some communities, parents have to pay more dowry if the daughter. has some level of literacy, as it apparently involves taking away their time for learning to read and write from household chores. On the other hand, if a son is literate /educated, his family can demand more dowry. There are some interesting case studies, documented by Concerned Center for Child Workers in Nepal (CWIN). Among them is a case from Sarlahi district where parents thought that it involves

double expenses for the parents to send their daughters to school.. Importantly, they mentioned that they have not seen ally instances of the education of girl, in whose community the leading members have helped in decreasing the bride money. Another worth mentioning case study was from Rautahat district where a woman told her story that she married her daughters off before they were twelve in order to evade their having to pay a high dowry price. However, responding to a new trend to educated girls, she sent her youngest daughter to school. She passed the primary level of education but cannot continue her further studies because the higher level school is located far from the walking distance, and it is not proper to send an adolescent girl to a distant place. Now when she wants her daughter, to get married, but due to her education her dowry charge has accelerated. Thus, she was regretting that she considered to educate her daughter.

2. *Religious Values*: Nepal is also a country where various religions co-exist, although it is a Hindu State. With this religious diversity, varieties in sociocultural characteristics is prevalent in communities. Manu Smriti says that if a girl remains unmarried after reaching puberty, the 'father' has failed in his duty towards her. Therefore, child marriage is also one of the social practices which may hinder the girls educational participation. According to UNICEF data given in CWIN journal, Nepal has the highest percentage (40%) of girl child (under 15 years of age) marriage compared to other countries in South Asia. Demographic Sample Survey, 1986/87 shows that nearly 7% of girl children were found to be married before reaching the age of 10. CWIN source also reports that the mean age at the marriage of girls in Terai, Hills, Mountains and Kathmandu Valley are respectively 15.2, 18.0, 18.5 and 18.8.It is customary that girls do not continue their schooling after marriage, especially in rural communities rather than for reasons of religion or for belonging to certain ethnic groups. Similarly, Muslims have their own system of educating their children along with some extra rules for girl children. Madrassa, Muslim educational

institution, is spread all over the world hi which Nepal is not an exception. Field observation showed that male and female children study together in Madrassa up to 5th grade. However, after 5th grade, ladder for girls to climb up in education in Madrassa system in Nepal seemed to be lacking. There is hardly any correlation between the curriculum of Madrassa and that of general schools.

Parental Attitude

3. *Parental attitude towards girls' education*: With this glimpse of sociocultural context, parental attitude towards girls' education is obvious which seems to testify the responses of the head teachers who were interviewed for- NMIS (Nepal Multiple Indicator Surveillance Cycle 11) - May-July 1995. The study made by Stri Shakti, mentioned earlier, reported that the attitude towards the level of education for boys and girls by rural /urban sites is different. According to their data, 24.5 percent parents hi rural areas said that they would like to give education to boys as much as the family can financially support while in case of girls, parents said that they will give education to girls as long as the girls want. They do not show any seriousness on the girls' education.

Despite all the efforts the government of Nepal has been making in the field of girls' and women's education, here are still some important issues that needs to be addressed by the government. Some of them are as follows:

1. *Lack of infrastructure to support the female literacy program in the community level*: Although gender is one of the major issues in the expansion of female education, government has not developed strong infrastructure for tackling the program. Ministry of Women and Social Welfare is established in the central level, but there is still no channel connected from center to the community level to supervise and monitor the girls' and women's education programme. For example, there is no special unit in the district level and beyond to deal with the issues related to female. Female education has been treated simply as just general education program whereas, due to sociocultural practices, it needs to get preferential treatment. It is specially necessary in rural communities.

2. *Lack of supporting programs for government's policy*: Government has set a policy to increase the enrollment of girls in the schools and to make education accessible to girls, and women who do not have access to formal education by providing non-formal education. A policy was made to recruit at least a female teacher in each primary school. This policy has not been really successful in rural communities, due to lack of female teachers in the local communities and female teachers from outside the community are reluctant to go to these schools as there is no incentives for them. Partly because, women find it very difficult to leave the house for the job, women teachers do not seem to spread in the rural communities. Another government policy to give scholarship to the girls, are so little that it is not significant enough to make any impact. The facilities like free textbook, uniform and mid day snack are also more like jargon than really making any impact.
3. *Lack of alternative programme for school incompleters*: Many girls children from disadvantaged groups drop out from the school as they grow up to be all adolescent. Girls get married and the boys go to earn. As there is no alternative program for them to continue to study and get through SLC (School Leaving Certificate), their investment in formal schooling gets relapsed into illiteracy. On the other hand, there is a dearth of female teachers in primary schools, specially in rural communities. If there is all alternative system to encompass these immature school drop outs to lead them to SLC test, there is a big chance that female teachers call be easily available in rural communities, too.

Literacy Programmes

Literacy programmes for girls and women has been organized by many national and international organizations in Nepal. It has helped immensely to bring quantitative development in the country and some definitely oil quality, too. However, these are some issues which needs attention. They are as follows:

1. *Logistics of the program operation*: Literacy programs, not only for women, in general are running as a "second class

education", which is very discouraging to the participants. One of the studies on out-of-school children program have shown that one of the reasons, children aspire to choose school over the literacy classes in rural areas was the venue of the class. Literacy classes, mostly, run in all open space, some one's porch or even in cow-shed, whereas all the schools, at least have a building and a secured room for children. Although similar situation is true with the adult literacy classes, there has not been any study to see how adult literacy learners feel about it.

Literacy classes are run in non-formal system, however, participants have access to that class only in certain two-hour time of the day/evening. Anybody cannot make oil that time, are left out. These participants, by nature, need more flexibility in many things including time. Unless there is a fixed place or system, which runs as a drop-in center, these educationally disadvantaged girls and women will still be out of the education loop.

2. *Textbooks*: Most of the women's literacy classes use the Naya Goreto. Some NGOs are starting to develop literacy materials, like Women's Rehabilitation Center (WOREC) and HEAL Project of World Education Nepal. Women Education Program (WEP) of BPEP have developed three primers and a supplementary book for the facilitator for providing three levels of literacy classes. Supplementary materials to make learning interesting and provide a continuum for]earners are still missing. One of the surveys done by CERID to identify the literacy materials in Nepal showed that there were 43 major organizations who have been producing literacy materials. Altogether 350 were counted. Among them about 70 of them were developed for women. As MOE has recently produced a blue print for literacy program, there is no systematic grading in these materials and going in every direction.

   Languge Issue in Textbooks: Textbooks assume all learners speak Nepali in all parts of Nepal, while the census shows that there are more than 30 different language spoken mother tongues. Language issues becomes more acute as one moves into the rural and poorer community where the formal school cannot even reach. Those are the places where the disadvantaged groups as well as more illiterate women are concentrated. They may need materials which is developed based oil local context and their local language as a budging course from their everyday life to literacy classrooms. However, the ultimate goal of the literacy class is to make them functional literate in Nepali language. Thus, reaching Nepali as a second language is also a necessary approach the material developers as well as the facilitators need to be trained in.

Centrally Developed Textbooks: All 2800 WEP classes are using the same textbooks all over the country. One of the important difference of NFE from formal education is flexibility and local adoption according to the need of the learners. Local adaptation of the centrally developed textbooks or development of textbooks in the local level is a quite challenging task. Thus, in order to serve this flexibility, training has to be provided to the personnel in how to develop participatory curriculum.

Thus there are a number of issues that need to be addressed in the textbook development for women and specially for those who do not speak Nepali as a second language.

3. *Training package is lacking gender sensitivity*: Training at this moment is more focused in using the primer rather than raising, awareness on gender issues that is existing in the sociocultural practices in the communities. Training should not be just focused for the facilitators, it should rather be focused for all the personnel who are connected with and women's education programme from central level to community level.

4. *Lack of effective monitoring and supervision system*: Regular supervision of the classes are done by local supervisors, but these supervisors are not trained to deal with the problems of women. Supervision has to change its model from "police" work to counselor" work to the facilitator. This requires training from DEO level to local supervisors so that the paradigm of supervision and monitoring call be changed. Separate training packages have to be developed for DEOs (District Education Officers), Resource Persons, and Local Supervisors.

5. *Evaluation System still based on formal system*: WEP tests are still like the one that is given to children in the primary classes or in out-of-school children's program. As these are grown up women learning to read and write, a separate system for evaluating their achievement should be developed.
6. *Lack of research on real issues of female*: Very few researches has been done on the real issues of women and the disadvantaged groups on the reason for their low participation in the literacy classes. Many innovative ideas are going on in the country, however, disadvantaged groups of people are still not able to participate in the programs. Thus, programs like, "POP" (poorest of the pool) are still suffering from appropriate level of participation.
7. *Focus of women's only in practical needs than in strategic needs*: Income-generating programs designed for women are mostly in sewing and knitting, or some local based skills. This type of program has been in a big fad for agencies who are doing women's program. The products of these income-generating programs either lack marketable quality or become too expensive for the local market. Thus, it needs to be evaluated seriously.
8. *Backlash of the income-generating activity*: A case study in a typical village in suburban area in Nepal, has; demonstrated an interesting issue. Income generating activities are being a pet program for- most of the program implementing organisations, who believe empowerment of women lies in economic development. Thus, loan for women program was launched in a village to give women access to income-generating, activities. Women raised cattles for milk. As there is a division of labour in every family, male members went to market to sell the milk. They made more money. Families were able to buy more cattle, which yield more milk. However, as the cattles increased in number, they needed more food for the cattles. Usually, women manage the food not only for family but also for the animals. Thus, they have to spend more time to bring food to the cattles. They needed more human resources. As practice in the families, girls

get to help their mothers in this mission. Families got more attracted in economic progress they were making.

Ministry of Education, other government organisations, national and international non-government organisations have been making abundant efforts to increase the female participation in education, through literacy classes, income-generating activities and loan programs. Still the gap between the literacy rate of male and female is widening. The reason for this is because there are some apparent causes and some real causes. Apparent causes for less girls in the school may be loaded household works, poverty and geographical distance, but the real cause is lack of acute sensitivity to towards female of the parents and the authorities in the political hierarchy.

3

Social Status

The United Nations has defined the status of women in the context of their access to knowledge, economic resources, and political power, When Nepalese women's status is analyzed in this light, the picture is generally bleak. In the early 1990s, Nepal was a rigidly patriarchical society. In virtually every aspect of life, women were generally subordinate to men. Women's relative status, however, varied from one ethnic group to another. The status of women in Tibeto-Nepalese communities generally, was relatively better than that of Pahari and Newari women. Women from the low caste groups also enjoyed relatively more autonomy and freedom than Pahari and Newari women. The senior female member played a commanding role within the family by controlling resources, making crucial planting and harvesting decisions, and determining the expenses and budget allocations. Yet women's lives remained centered on their traditional roles—taking care of most household chores, fetching water and animal fodder, and doing farm work. Their standing in society was mostly contingent on their husbands' and parents' social and economic positions. They had limited access to markets, productive services, education, health care, and local government. Malnutrition and poverty hit women hardest. Female children usually were given less food than male children, especially when the family experienced food shortages. Women usually worked harder and longer than men. By contrast, women from high-class families had maids to take care of most household chores and other menial work and thus worked far less than men or women in lower socioeconomic groups.

The economic contribution of women was substantial, but

largely unnoticed because their traditional role was taken for granted. When employed, their wages normally were 25 percent less than those paid to men. In most rural areas, their employment outside the household generally was limited to planting, weeding, and harvesting. In urban areas, they were employed in domestic and traditional jobs, as well as in the government sector, mostly in low-level positions. One tangible measure of women's status was their educational attainment. Although the constitution offers women equal educational opportunities, many social, economic, and cultural factors contributed to lower enrollment and higher dropout rates for girls. Illiteracy imposed the greatest hindrance to enhancing equal opportunity and status for women. They were caught in a vicious circle imposed by the patriarchical society. Their lower status hindered their education, and the lack of education, in turn, constricted their status and position. Although the female literacy rate has improved noticeably over the years, the level in the early 1990s fell far short of the male level.

In the early 1990s, a direct correlation existed between the level of education and status. Educated women had access to relatively high-status positions in the government and private service sectors, and they had a much higher status than uneducated women. This general rule was more applicable at the societal level than at the household level. Within the family, an educated woman did not necessarily hold a higher status than her uneducated counterpart. Also within the family, a woman's status, especially a daughter-in-law's status, was more closely tied to her husband's authority and to her parental family's wealth and status than anything else. Women constitute more than 50 percent of the population of Nepal. However, they are far behind men in all aspects of life. There is a wide gender gap in the social, economic, administrative, political and legal fields, primarily because of the patriarchal social system that confines women within the home and places men in control of all resources.

Preference for Sons

The Nepalis prefer sons over daughters. A son guarantees that the family line will continue and the parents will have a blissful path to heaven. According to religious tradition, when the parents die it is their sons who are entitled to carry out the different rituals ensuring their passage to heaven. Therefore, in many families the mother must continue giving birth until a son is born. On the other hand daughters are considered a great burden to the family. Since they have to leave their father's home after marriage, from birth they are already thought of as the property of someone else. That is why the majority of poor families don't spend more to improve the health, nutrition and educational status of a daughter.

Discrimination against daughters begins even before birth and continues into adulthood. Women are seen as weak and dependent on men, and derive their status-including inheritance rights, ritual status and access to property-from their fathers, husbands and sons. Most families do not provide any concrete economic security to daughters. Apart from shouldering her marriage expenses and giving her dowry in the form of some jewelry and clothes, most parents do not give anything to their daughters. Thus, a woman never takes part in decision-making, depending solely on her father before marriage, her husband after marriage and her sons in old age. The absence of property rights hinders the economic development and empowerment of women. A Nepali woman cannot inherit family property of ancestors and forefathers because only sons can do so.

The Constitution of the Kingdom of Nepal, drawn up in 1990 after the restoration of democracy, carries special provisions that are meant to make women legally equal to men and to ensure their social and economic development. Article 11 states that every citizen is equal before the law, and no citizen shall be deprived of the protection of law, nor be discriminated against because of religion, color, sex, caste and ideological faith. The government's ratification without any reservation of the Convention on the Elimination of all Forms of Discrimination Against Women (CEDAW) is also an encouraging step for securing the rights of women.

Many organisations have examined the significance of this state of affairs and clearly observed that the absence of equal property rights is the main root of the varied problems that women face. Voices from various social sectors have been raised to amend this situation since as early as 1975 with the declaration of the international year of women. However, to date most of the existing laws are discriminatory and their implementation is arbitrary and biased. Legal provisions relating to the inheritance of parental property, divorce, citizenship, tenancy rights are a few such examples which violate the letter and spirit of the Constitution.

Constitution of 1990

The Constitution of 1990 states, "The laws which conflict with the Constitution will be inactive after one year of the establishment of the Constitution." Article 88 states, "If any law conflicts with the country's main law (constitution), any Nepali citizen has the right to appeal to the Supreme Court for its abolishment and the court can use the same right to inactivate the law."

On the basis of this, two women lawyers filed a writ with the Supreme Court in May 1994 seeking to amend the discriminatory provisions in the Code of the Country, concerning the property rights of women in Nepal. After many postponements the Supreme Court finally gave a verdict in January 1996, directing the government to bring forth new legislation which is not gender-biased or discriminatory towards women within a period of one year.

The Supreme Court's verdict opened up avenues for women's organisations to advance the movement for improving women's economic status and identity. Several NGOs working for women's rights got together to formulate appropriate strategies for drafting the proposed bill on pro-women legislation and also for lobbying and conducting advocacy programmes for the promulgation of the bill. At the initial stage, the proposed bill on property rights was drafted with inputs from organisations working on the issue and public opinion collected from various districts.

Since early 1996 intensive lobbying activities have been undertaken among parliamentarians, leaders of various parties and concerned government officials for the proposal to be taken up and passed. Organisations conducted workshops, seminars and interaction programmes with people from various walks of life for lobbying purposes and to assess the negative and positive impact of the bill and formulate joint strategies to advocate for it. Awareness-raising and advocacy programmes were conducted by women's organisations throughout the country. Such programmes included rallies, demonstrations, street plays, publication of reports and articles in the newspapers, radio and television programmes, distribution of posters, advertisements, etc. Other organisations who did not have any specific programme on property rights also started integrating the issue in their ongoing programmes such as nonformal literacy , door-to-door campaigning, legal awareness, women's empowerment, counselling, training, etc.

Women's organisations met with all political parties to garner support for the bill. However, though almost all the parties agreed, none of them actually did so during the Parliament sessions. Thus, the bill that will provide equal property rights to women still remains frozen in the human rights committee of Parliament with little chance of actually being revived in the near future, especially with all parties busy campaigning for the elections in May. Meantime the concerned organisations must sit together and review the past weaknesses and strength of the movement, and ensure that votes in the election will go to candidates who will speak for the equality of women in every sphere.

Work Load

Women in Nepal work for longer hours than men, have much lower opportunity to gainful employment and possess extremely limited property rights. As in most of the world, women in Nepal precariously juggle themselves among the three principal work regimes, reproduction, house-holding and income generation. The work burden of women in Nepal, however, is much higher than the global average for women.

81% of women are confined to self-employment in the agricultural sector where their productivity is low and even high productivity is not properly recognized. Only 4% of women are involved in self- employment outside agriculture.

Low income earning opportunities together with absence of right to property has limited the role of women in the decision-making about the allocation of household income.

For Nepalese women, independent decision-making is highly restricted. Lack of decision making power has deprived women more than men of the basic elements of a decent life such as food and nutrition, education and skill development and health and family planning. This has ultimately undermined their access to gainful employment opportunities and participation in professional jobs. Womens role in Nepalese society appears to be changing in the cities but it is only a surface change. There are a lot of facilities available to expand people's minds and involve women in different areas they previously did not have access to. Women are receiving more education and are there for able to find employement. The respect they receive in this employement is still in question. The attitude of male domination is the underlying foundation of Nepalese society.

Unfortunately the majority of women are living in the rural areas of Nepal and do not have access to any of these facilities. 93% of Nepal is rural, and here change is coming at a painfully slow pace. They are raised as a burden to their family, although they will run the household and work in the fields until they are married, at which time they will become a burden to their husbands' family. The sons, being educated will be the ones to leave the village and go to find work, leaving their new wife with all the responsibility of raising their family and at the mercy of her new parents. The rural women have little or no self-confidence and do not consider themselves on par with men. The village womens life is nothing more than that of a servant or a possession of the family.

Marriage

In Nepal, marriage has an overwhelming importance in a woman's life. The event of marriage determines almost all her life options and subsequent livelihood. According to Hindu tradition, marriage is essential for all, whether man or woman. While a man's life is not considered complete without a wife, a woman has no option but to marry. In the Indo-Aryan culture, in particular, girls are encour-aged to marry in their early teens or even earlier by their parents. Early marriages are rooted in both the concept of purity of the female body and the need for helping hands in farm households in general. Marriage is a social contract between two clans rather than the personal affair of the bride and groom. Women and also men rarely have any role in the choice of their own life partners. In addition, polygyny, though outlawed, can be still observed especially in the rural areas of the Terai. Thus the majority of the population is dominated by patriarchal value systems that accord overwhelming importance to early marriage and male children. The overwhelming majority of both men and women are married before they are 25 years old. In 1991, more than 86 per cent of women and 61 per cent of men were married before that age. In the Indo-Aryan community, women are tied for life by their marriage bonds. Hence, a woman's power to accept or reject marriage partnership is evidently an index of the degree of freedom she exercises in the management of her own life, and thus also of her status. In the non-Aryan communities, they may enjoy greater freedom of divorce and remarriage, but they face the risk of being left with young children without assets or helping hands to provide for them.

The mean age of marriage for women in Nepal has increased significantly from 15.4 years in 1961 to 18 years in 1991, indicating a slow but steady change in social perceptions about the institution of child marriage. The change is most pronounced for young girls. In 1991,.7.4 per cent of females in the 10-14 age group were reported to be married, compared with 24.9 per cent in 1961.There are significant differences in the mean age of marriage between rural and urban women, among women of various ecological zones, and between educated and non-educated women. Urban women marry later than rural women do. From an ecological zone perspective, a higher proportion of females is married at an earlier age in the Terai than in the hills and mountains. Early widowhood with little possibility of remarriage, particularly in the Indo-Aryan culture, is another curse upon women. More than 1.6 per cent of the female population—i.e. 7,000 women—were already widowed by 29 years of age in 1991.

The risk of widowhood tends to increase with age. Only a small proportion of women are divorced or separated in Nepal. However, this rate has shown an increasing trend. Divorce rates also increase with age. While a higher proportion of divorced women may indicate the increased determination of women to escape from oppressive marriages and situations of polygyny, it may also indicate increasing abandonment by men.

Even today, women who are divorcees are stigmatised in the Hindu tradition. Thus, a divorced woman has little chance of remarriage within her own socioeconomic group if she comes from a high caste/class Hindu family. In a patriarchal society, women derive social status primarily from fertility as carriers of "clan seeds" and mothers of the male progeny. But they have little control over their own fertility or children. In the Hindu tradition, women are worshipped for their fertility, in the exalted status of mother goddess, while infertility is considered a curse. On the other hand, childbirth and lactation force women to withdraw from active economic work, thus making them dependent on other members of society. Frequent pregnancies impinge on their health and sometimes even on their lives. Therefore, one of the most important indicators of women's empowerment is control over their own fertility.

Poor Health

However, Nepalese women and girls at large still suffer from poor health compared with their male counterparts, due to lack of adequate health services, general poverty, and, in some cases, the sociocultural preference for male children. Women suffer from lack of medical facilities in case of pregnancy complications, malnutrition, anaemia, and many other diseases related to their reproductive functions.

Although nationwide data on anemia are not available, the Department of Health, based on small hospital surveys, has estimated more than 50 per cent of women in 15-49 age group to be anaemic. It is estimated to be more than 60 per cent among pregnant women. Risk related to pregnancy and child delivery is the largest killer for women. Although maternal mortality rate (MMR) has fallen to 539 per 100,000 live births today from the figure of 850 reported during the 1980s, this is still high even by South Asian standards.

Doctors and nurses assisted only nine per cent of mothers during delivery. Village health workers (VHWs), mother and child health workers (MCHVs), etc., assisted another 1 per cent. Over 90 per cent of women deliver at home and only 5 per cent of rural women delivered at a health facility in 1996. Even in urban areas, this proportion is below 50 per cent. Antenatal care is rare, with only 2.8 per cent of mothers receiving it. Seven per cent of women were chronically ill. There is a large discrepancy between urban and rural women in terms of their access to health services.

The high incidence of malnutrition and a lack of health awareness lead to much sickness in children and to high infant and child mortality rates. The difference in male/female immunisation rates is not significant either in urban or rural areas. However, according to NLSS, the Terai and hill populations show higher differences in male/female immunisation rates than the mountain population. Similarly, the middle two income quintiles (3rd & 4th) show much larger gender gaps in immunisation rates than the top and bottom two quintiles. This indicates that gender discrimination is not directly linked to economic status.Infant and child mortality rates are important indicators of women's status for two reasons. First, they reflect social attitudes towards male and female children. Second, they also throw light on the health situation of women as mothers. A comparatively higher female infant and child mortality rate signifies social neglect of female infants and children. At the same time, a high infant and child mortality rates force women to multiple and wasted pregnancies, thus depleting their strength. The infant mortality rate in Nepal is high even by South Asian standards. Male/ female IMRs do not indicate any discrimination towards female children. The most recent NFHS reports IMR at 102 and 84 for males and females, respectively. Thus, the strong preference for sons reported in various studies is not reflected in the IMR. On the other hand, gender discrimination in the family behaviour towards male and female children is captured distinctly by the gender difference in child mortality rates. Contrary to the scientifically proven fact that female children are stronger than male children during their infancy and early childhood—resulting in higher mortality rates worldwide for male infants and young children—the under-five child mortality rate is still higher for girls than for the boys in South Asia.

In Nepal, 125 per 1,000 boys under five die each year, compared with 139 per 1,000 girls. Overall, a higher proportion of women than of men dies each year in Nepal. Consequently men live longer than women do. This is contrary to the international trend, and even the South Asian trend, which indicate higher mortality rates among men. The higher mortality rate of women in Nepal is attributed to higher female child and maternal mortality rates.

Universally, a larger proportion of women than men survives to old age. Consequently, there are more women in the world than men. However, in South Asia, the economically more backward countries such as Nepal, Bangladesh, and India used to have opposite overall sex ratios due to the socioeconomic discrimination against female children and against women in general. In Nepal, however, while the overall sex ratios observed in 1971 and 1981 were in favour of males, the 1991 census shows a slight dominance of females.

Educational Opportunities

Women have made substantial gains in literacy over the last 25 years, partly due to vigorous government programs for girls' education starting in the early 1970s, including the training of female teachers from backward areas. The female literacy rate (six years and above) increased from a meager 4 per cent in 1971 to 25 per cent in 1991. A recent survey 13 reports literacy rates of 57 per cent and 27 per cent, respectively, for males and females over six years of age. Likewise, two recent surveys (NMIS and NLSS, 1996) reported adult female literacy rates as being between 19 per cent and 23 per cent.

Despite the gains in overall educational opportunities, however, the level of literacy is still low, and the gender gap in the literacy rate remains enormous. The gender literacy gap has in fact been expanding. However, the good news is that in the younger 10-14 age group, the gender gap is declining 14. The Kathmandu Valley has the highest female literacy rate and also the highest female/male literacy ratio. There are 68 literate adult women to 100 literate adult men in the valley, while there are only 34 literate women to 100 literate men in rural areas. Similarly, this ratio is associated positively with income.

The compelling factor hindering women's education in general is the fact that girls are transferred to their affiance households after marriage, with the result that parents have no claim on their work or income as adult women. When parents are asked in surveys why they are not sending their girl children to school, one of the often-repeated answers is that "they will go to other people's houses. Poverty, workload, and cultural perceptions are the major factors hindering female education. High fees in the private schools and the emerging dichotomy in the private and public education systems are other major issues. Girls and children from poor households have much less access to private schools. Social factors aside, the lack of physical facilities (such as toilets and hostels) and a lack of trained teachers (especially female teachers) are considered to be major constraints in increasing girls' enrolment in secondary education.

For those who attended school, according to NLSS, the mean number of years of schooling (primary + secondary + higher secondary) was uniformly lower for girls by about one year, with little difference according to socioeconomic variables, such as ecological zone, rural or urban residence or consumption levels.

As a result of discrimination in educational access, women are much more disadvantaged educationally than men. In addition, although there has been a significant improvement in female educational achievement at all levels, the higher the educational level, the lower the female representation.

Violence against women takes various forms, ranging from verbal "eve teasing", physical/sexual abuse within the household, to rape and trafficking. All these cases are widespread in Nepal, but lack of comprehensive data and people's awareness of these issues, as well as a lack of law enforcement, has left these cases almost untouched. According to SAATHI and the Asia Foundation, 95 per cent of the women and girls surveyed reported first-hand knowledge of violence, of which 77 per cent was from their own family members. Such violence was reported across all ethnic, caste, and income groups.

According to the ERA report, however, one of the major causes of women leaving the married household has been polygyny and subsequent violence against one of the cowives. Alcohol-related violence in the domestic arena was reported high all over Nepal and across all communities. Incidents of dowry-related violence are reported to a lesser extent. This could be due to lack of information collection and reporting, and the myth that traditionally a dowry system has not existed in Nepal. In Western hills and in some Indo-Aryan communities, however, a "bride price" system, similar to the dowry system, is prevalent.

In the Maithili communities of Western Terai as well, a system called a *Tilak* has been widely practised under which a bride's price is negotiated and received by the groom or his family before marriage. Traditionally, a milder form of dowry has been also prevalent among the Brahmins, Chetris, and Newars in Nepal's hill areas. The dowry usually consists of bed and bedding and some utensils.

Following are the issues in gender-based violence:

i) lack of reliable data and under-reporting on violence, especially domestic violence.

ii) lack of bargaining power of women, dowry, polygyny, and alcoholism as underlying causes of domestic violence.

iii) trafficking of women widespread across all ethnic groups/ castes.

iv) poverty and lack of access to economic resources for women outside marriage as causes of women entering into commercial sex work.

v) inadequate legal framework and general law enforcement on gender-based violence larger dowry are considered to have been rising, adding further psychological pressure on women.

Extreme cases of stove-bursting and women's "dowry death" have also been reported. The old tradition of nominal dowries is being converted into a new channel for accumulating business capital and acquiring modern goods, such as motorcycles, televisions, furnishings, freezers, etc. In the SAATHI and Asia Foundation survey , knowledge of violence related to dowry was reported by 38 per cent of respondents in Banke, a western Terai district with a predominantly Muslim population.

In other districts in the sample—which included Jhapa, Kanchanpur Kathmandu, and Nuwakot—much lower proportions (26 per cent, 18 per cent, 11 per cent, and 7 per cent, respectively) of respondents reported such knowledge. Lack of women's economic and bargaining power in the household is an underlying cause of domestic violence. As the report notes, "women's economic dependency on the spouse and extended family was identified as the primary reason (73 per cent) for women not reporting incidents of violence against them, followed by lack of education and the need to keep the family intact due to children (49 per cent).

Violence

The extreme forms of violence include rape, trafficking,

and forced prostitution. Prostitution by choice and trafficking are distinct but related problems. Women may be forced into prostitution in the later stages of their lives to earn a living after having earlier been raped or sold.Modern consumerism and drug use among youngsters have also lured young women of even middle class families into prostitution, as evident from the fact that the CSWs are not necessarily illiterate or from poor family backgrounds.

Violence against girls and women on a large scale by husbands and other members of the affiance household, as well as occasionally by natal relatives – particularly uncles, brothers, and aunts – and members of the community especially, was identified as a major cause pushing women into prostitution, especially for those in low-caste households. Trafficking of children for sex work also appears widespread. Most of the children involved are either sold forcibly or duped into the trade. According to the New ERA survey, almost 48 per cent of the total 196 CSWs interviewed entered the trade between the ages of 10 and 15. Of these, more than 13 per cent started sex work between 10 and 13 years of age, while 4 per cent started even earlier, between 10 and 11.

According to the interviews with Nepalese CSWs in India, more than one fifth of girls trafficked to India are currently between 12 and 15 years of age.

Some groups of children, e.g., those whose mothers and sisters are CSWs, who work in *bhattis* (local pubs), lodges, and restaurants, and domestic servants, orphaned and low-caste children seem to face special risks, as most of CSWs seem to come from such groups. *Bhatti pasal*s, hotels, restaurants, and lodges play the key role as places for soliciting sex work, *dalali* (pimping), and trafficking. Owners/workers of these places, drivers, and professional pimps are reported to be the groups most heavily involved in *dalali* and trafficking.

Government Policies and Laws Against Gender-Based Violence Government policy and the legal framework for gender-based violence in Nepal are far from complete. The area in which most progress has been made is girl trafficking, for which the Government initiated a new policy in 1997. The policy lays down that the Government will:

i) initiate an extensive campaign against girl trafficking;

ii) promulgate laws to end discrimination against women;

iii) strengthen cooperation with non-government organisations (NGOs) and international non-government organisation (INGOs) to implement programs for controlling trafficking; and

iv) initiate cooperation with other countries at bilateral and multilateral levels to control girl trafficking and acquired immune deficiency syndrome (AIDS).

In addition, the Government committed itself to further actions, including increased compensation for the victims of sexual exploitation, the creation of a national commission on girl trafficking, and the building up of consensus among all political parties on the issue of girl trafficking, and on adopting appropriate measures for alternative employment. The Government has also promised the creation of family courts to resolve family disputes.

Nepal also has adequate laws on trafficking, but this is the only area for which an adequate legal framework exists among all other gender-based violence issues. Human trafficking, particularly among minors, is punishable by up to 20 years of imprisonment. However, the punitive provisions of the law on rape are not considered to be equal to international standards. For example, the rape of girls below 14 years of age is punishable by imprisonment of 6 to 10 years while, in the case of women above 14, by imprisonment of 3 to 5 years. The punishment provisions for rape criminals are considered to be insufficient, and accordingly, amendments for more strict treatment have been introduced in the Parliament. The bill proposes imprisonment for 10 to 20 years in the case of victims below 10 years of age, 7 to 14 years in the case of victims being 10 to 16 years of age, and 5 to 10 years in the case of victims being above 16 years old 22. Violence against women both in the domestic and public spheres is hardly touched by current laws.

The strategic issues which are preventing women from economic participation are:

i) women's limited access to productive assets reinforced by unequal inheritance laws and by social norms that confine women's resource base only to marriage.

ii) lack of information on women's employment and wages, and under-reporting or "invisibility" of women's economic activities.

iii) concentration of women in low-productive, subsistence agriculture.
iv) concentration of women in low-wage, low-skill, menial jobs in the agriculture and non-agriculture sectors, due to lack of education, training, information, and bargaining power.
v) high and increasing work burden without concomitant increase in access to resources.
vi) the "feminisation" of the self-employed sector.
vii) poor working environment and the gaps between law and practice.
viii) difficult environment for women entrepreneurs.
ix) child labour.

Lack of access to, and control over, productive resources is one of the major factors that hamper women's equal participation in economic activities and the decision-making process. While Nepal's 1990 Constitution provides equal rights for women to property inheritance, there have been no specific laws in Nepal to enforce this. On the contrary, family laws in Nepal that govern marriage, divorce, property rights, and inheritance reinforce the patriarchy and put severe limits on women's command over economic resources. For example, the National Code of Nepal *(Mulki Ain)* of 1963, which codifies the inheritance system, derives from the Hindu system of beliefs emphasising patrilineal descent and a patrilocal residence system. Some of the provisions severely limit economic options for women. Attempts at integrating women in development programs and projects tend to have been hampered by these sociolegal constraints. According to the National Code, as amended in 1975, a woman shares equal rights of inheritance to her husband's property with her sons. She is also an equal copartner (one who may claim a share) in the ancestral property if her husband is not alive, provided she is at least 30 years old and/or has been married for at least 15 years.

Inheritance

However, she is entitled to equal inheritance rights with her brothers in her parental household only if she is unmarried and is at least 35 years of age at the time of the division of the property. The property she receives as the marital household is conditional on her remaining faithful to her husband and his clan even if he is dead. She loses all rights to his property upon marriage to another person or divorce. She has no claims on even maintenance after five years of divorce. A woman inheriting property in her parental household must return this property to her brothers or their direct male descendants if she marries afterwards. On the other hand, a woman has absolute rights over *stridhan* – a type of property that originates from her own earnings, and from gifts from her parental household, her husband, his household, or from any other sources. *Stridhan* is the only property upon which a woman can freely make legal contracts. Nonetheless, family laws stipulate that the husband has the right to decide the place of settlement, and a wife must receive her husband's permission to work outside the home, thereby limiting her opportunity to earn her own income.

The new law, when approved, would remove the age limits for women to inherit property both in the natal and marital households; ensure property rights of divorced women until she remarries; make girls eligible for adoption; and strengthen preventive measures against polygyny, child marriages, and rape. However, her right to inheritance would remain conditional on her marital status. On marriage, a daughter would still forfeit all her rights to inheritance in the natal household.

Woman's common property rights have also been limited in that a wife can only exercise them if her husband does not abandon her. Under the common practice of polygyny, however, this is not guaranteed: if a husband marries another wife and subsequently leaves her – which is highly probable in the average woman's life – she loses all access to community property as well. Such processes are hard to capture in data, since no data are collected on polygyny, which is technically illegal.

Recorded data, therefore, need to be analysed with much care to identify the symptoms of inequality in access to resources. Two major indicators of such inequality are women's limited access to credit and the increasing involvement of women in commercial sex work for survival.

Women's access to credit is limited because both formal and informal credit institutions cater to property owners who can provide collateral. All formal credit institutions seek tangible collateral for loans. Hence, women are effectively excluded from institutional credit since women have little access to inherited property. Village moneylenders are also more interested in earning high interest or in acquiring the debtor's property than in financing people in need.

The *Nepal Rural Credit Review Study* (NRCRS) by the Nepal Rastra Bank in 1991/92 revealed that, of the total number of female-headed sample households, almost 35 per cent borrowed from one or other sources compared with 39 per cent of male-headed households. However, among borrowing female-headed-households, only 15.4 per cent borrowed from institutional sources such as the Agricultural Development Bank and commercial banks, and 84 per cent borrowed from non-institutional sources. Almost 40 per cent borrowed from moneylenders.

In Nepal, the problem is complicated further by varying definitions of economic activity rates among various censuses. In spite of these shortcomings, a fairly high proportion of women are reported as being economically active in Nepal. Moreover, the sex composition of the economically active population shows an increasing proportion of women in the labour force.

From the gender perspective, one notable aspect is that, while male economic activity rates fell significantly between 1981 and 1991 due to definitional changes 25, female rates remained almost constant. This could be due to a more accurate recording of economic activity rates. It is quite possible that, in earlier censuses, all males were recorded as economically active, irrespective of working months, age or work status, while women were mostly recorded as homemakers. In 1991, the definitions may have been more accurate.

Women participate in the production of goods and services for the market and household consumption, in agriculture, food production, or family enterprises. Though included in the United Nations system of National Accounts and, therefore, in international standards for labour statistics, this unremunerated work is often undervalued and under-recorded. Nepalese agriculture is dominated by small-scale subsistence farming. The majority of households (66 per cent) have less than one ha of land on average. More than 40 per cent have less than 0.5 ha. The size of land holding is smaller in the Terai but much less productive in the hills and mountains. Hill agriculture has come to be primarily dependent on women due to male migration from the hills, leaving women to operate most of the farms. In the Terai, the majority of women, especially in smallholder agriculture, also contribute substantially to agriculture, both in terms of labour input and decision making.

Role in Agriculture

Women also play a major role in the livestock raising. Overall, women contribute 70 per cent of the labour and up to 26 per cent of the farm level decisions in the livestock sub-sector. Care of livestock stall is primarily an activity of women, while boys and girls are engaged in herding activities on a large scale. Only in the case of the big herds in the mountain areas, which require seasonal movements for grasing, are men engaged on a large scale. Men are also involved in animal care and herding as hired labour, while mainly women are hired for fodder collection. According to the Agricultural Perspective Plan (APP), women were also found to be more knowledgeable in treating sick animals. Following are the issues of women in agriculture:

i) "Feminisation" of agriculture.
ii) Women as unpaid family workers in subsistence agriculture.
iii) Low level of technology and primitive farming practices
iv) Long work hours; carrying the double burden of work in the family and farm; their contribution to income and economic well-being of the family is not recognised

Agriculture is becoming progressively feminised. Many women engaged in family farms are still reported as economically not active as discussed above. Nonetheless, even according to census figures, the proportion of female labour force in agriculture increased from 30.4 per cent in 1971 to 36.4 per cent in 1981, and to 45 per cent in 1991. Although the employment of women is increasing in nonagricultural occupations, they form the largest sectoral share only in agriculture. On the other hand, the share of agriculture in GDP is declining perceptively. Following are the issues of employment manufacturing sector:

i) More women entering this sector due to poverty
ii) Concentration of women in low-skill, manual, repetitive jobs
iii) Lack of education, training, and mobility are major reasons for women staying in the lower hierarchy large are being left out of structural changes in the Nepalese economy, further contributing to women's economic marginalisation.

In the nonagriculture sectors, by industry, personnel and community services are the leading sources of employment for both men and women. The next largest group of women is in the commerce sector. Manufacturing occupies only a remote third position for employment for both men and women.

While women appear to be engaged in large numbers in tourism (e.g. hotels, airlines, restaurants and travel and trekking agencies) and other tourist related services very little information is available on the extent of their involvement. The Nepal Rastra Bank study of the tourist sector 36 shows that 20.6 per cent of the employees in tourist and related industries were women. The carpet industry had 66.4 per cent female employees. With regard to the levels at which women worked, the distribution of female employees was more or less even in tourist industry but, in related industries, they were concentrated at the lower levels.

Relatively few women seem to have been employed in garments, probably because it was overwhelmingly dominated by immigrant labour.The overwhelming majority of the employed are self-employed, but proportionately more women are self-employed than men and more women work in agriculture than men both in wage and nonwage employment. The percentage of self-employed workers, which remained more or less constant at about 86 per cent between 1971 and 1981, had decreased to 75 per cent in 1991. Males mainly account for this decrease. In other words, a larger proportion of women is self-employed than men. There is a slow but perceptible change taking place in the employment status of the population.

The proportions of both male and female employees in the population are increasing, while those of the self-employed and unpaid family workers are decreasing. This may indicate a positive or negative trend, depending on whether those who move out of self-employment are getting better jobs or moving out simply because of impoverishment caused by competition from factory produced goods. The flood of plastic goods in the market, for example, has ruined many traditional craft workers. Women received lower wages than men. A lesser proportion of women than men was reported to be unemployed. The Constitution guarantees equal pay for men and women workers for similar jobs. General working conditions are governed by the Labour Act and the Trade Union Act, both promulgated in 1992 and replaced old acts that had placed restrictions on the freedom of association. The Labour Act, which replaced a 1959 Act, incorporates provisions for job security, minimum wages, environmental health, security, welfare measures, a code of conduct and penalties, consultative and cooperative management, and labour courts for dispute settlement.

Trade Union Act

The Trade Union Act is primarily geared at maintaining industrial peace while, at the same time, protecting the constitutional rights of workers to organise for collective bargaining and to redress their legitimate demands according to ILO standards. This Act has no gender-specific provisions. The Labour Act and the Labour Regulations formulated under the Act have provisions specifically relevant to women.

As social custom restricts women's role to the household, they are mostly involved in home-based industries, such as food processing, garments, hosiery, and crafts. However, these industries are gradually closing due to competition from imported products, or are being replaced by organised formal units. On the one hand, the displacement of traditional crafts by light industry is causing the replacement of female workers by male labourers. On the other, women are also being converted into wage labourers in such industries as the carpet industry.

However, women function as managers, supervisors, entrepreneurs, and even as skilled workers in home-based craft enterprises. As industrial activities become increasingly commercialised, both male and female workers lose control over the production process and become transformed into wage labourers. In this process, women are affected more since newly emerging organised industries not only need more capital but they lay more emphasis on educated and mobile labourers.

The managerial class in these industries, which is dominated by the Indo-Aryan and western concept of gender specialisation, reinforces its own biases in hiring and firing. Furthermore, the few women who remain proprietors face severe problems of access to capital, institutional credit, marketing networks, marketing information, and appropriate business training and education. They also lack self-confidence and risk-taking capacity as they have access to very little capital and may face family problems in their enterprise.

Following are the problems faced by women entrepreneurs:

i) low access to credit and marketing networks.
ii) lack of access to land and property and reduced risk-taking capacity.
iii) lack of access to modern technology.
iv) lack of personal security and risk of sexual harassment.
v) severe competition from organised units both in the domestic as well as the international markets.
vi) low level of self-confidence.
vii) social and cultural barriers such as exclusive responsibility for household work, restrictions on mobility, etc.

There is little evidence to indicate that there are more women than men among the poor or that female-headed households are poorer than male-headed ones. However, female-headed households are more vulnerable to external shocks and lack adequate resources.In addition, in Nepal, 'feminisation' must be analysed in the context of the feminisation of agriculture, concentration of women in low wage jobs, more girl child labourers than boy labourers, more workload for men than women, and women's lack of assets and resources.

Since the early 1990s, there has been a major concern over the "feminisation of poverty" the world over, linked to a perceived rise in the incidence of female-headed households. "Feminisation of poverty" is also used to indicate a hypothesis that (i) there are more poor women than men, and/or (ii) increasingly more women than men are becoming poor. In the case of Nepal, despite the many disadvantages women face in access to resources, employment, and income, recorded data do not indicate comparatively disadvantaged positions for women or female-headed households in terms of poverty status.

With financial problems in the household, girls are forced to begin working earlier than boys. Children work mainly on farms, as does most of the population. Certain industries, however, employ a high proportion of child labourers, notably carpets, tea estates, brick factories, stone quarries, and the service sectors. The working conditions in these industries are often appalling. Young girls are also recruited into forced prostitution on a wide scale. Poverty, family disruption, parental illiteracy, and agrarian relations forcing families into bonded labour are the major causes of child labour. Legislation against child labour, although adequate, is rarely enforced. Child labourers face long hours of work in unhealthy environments, low wages, and hazardous conditions of work. This leads to various diseases among child labourers and denies them access to educational opportunities. Moreover, employers do not devote any resources to improve the situation.

The main challenge is how to improve the situation of child labourers and increase their access to education and better opportunities without stopping their sources of income. Many families are too poor to support their own children, others have abandoned them. A third group of child workers are orphaned, with no relatives to bring them up. The current Constitution, as mentioned earlier, recognises the socioeconomic disadvantage faced by women, and incorporates specific provisions to provide some political support to women. The Constitution specifies that all political parties must have at least 5 per cent female candidates in the election to the House of Representatives, the Lower House, and at least three women in the Upper House.

The Constitution guarantees equal rights to all citizens, but the Citizenship Chapter of the Constitution and the subsequent Act discriminate against women. First, they do not recognise maternal descent for natural citizenship rights and, second, they accord unequal treatment of the foreign spouses of male and female citizens. Equal property rights to earn, enjoy, and transact wealth are guaranteed to all citizens within the laws, which themselves are discriminate against women.

The system of development administration is

decentralised to the VDC and municipality levels, which comprise several wards. VDCs consist of nine wards, while the number of wards in the municipalities depends on the population and area under their supervision. Each ward has an elected ward committee of five persons chaired by the elected ward Chairperson. According to the Ordinance, later passed as the Act on Election to the Local Institutions, each ward must have at least one woman on the ward committee. All ward members constitute the VDC assembly, while the ward chairpersons constitute its executive committee, which is responsible for day-to-day operations.

At least one woman is nominated to each VDC or municipality executive committee. Further, VDC chairpersons and vice-chairpersons, parliamentarians elected from the districts and six nominated members, including one woman, constitute the district assembly, and they elect the DDC chairperson, vice-chairperson, and members of its executive committee. Each DDC also must have at least one woman nominated to it. Women's political participation and representation at decision-making levels are two different issues. Participation is a necessary but insufficient condition for representation because representation does not flow automatically from participation. Women all over the world have participated widely in political movements in times of crisis but, once the crisis is over, they are relegated again to the domestic arena.

Women's participation as voters and their awareness about their own rights have increased in general. Their willingness to participate in the political process has increased in the last decade. Rural women who knew about women's organisations increased from 4.7 per cent in 1978 to 15 per cent in 1992. The proportion of women in Parliament in 1996 was actually smaller than in the 1989 Panchayat parliament. Similarly, the representation of women at VDC and district levels had not changed much until 1996. There are no women mayors or DDC chairpersons even now. Only recently has the situation changed substantially at the grassroots level. The Act on Local Election required all political parties to field at least one candidate at the ward level. Representation of women is also mandatory at VDC and DDC levels. Among the nominees there must be at least one woman.

Following are issues on Women's political participation and representation:

i) Broad-based political participation of women not being translated into representation

ii) "Mandatory" female representation at local level a good start but women rarely in executive positions

iii) Further sensitisation on women's issues necessary level elections as candidates and more than 36,000 have been elected to the village assembly.

Even though participation at the initial stages may be taken in certain places, it is generally expected to work as good schooling for women political activists. The main issue now is to sensitise these women and their political counterparts on women's agenda.

Without a woman's agenda, the gender situation will not improve very fast. Women's participation may improve, but without addressing any of the gender discrimination issues at local and national levels. Women's representation in government administration is increasing only slowly, both at the gazetted (officer) and non-gazetted (non-officer) levels: for example, from 3 per cent in 1978 to 5 per cent in 1997, and from 2.8 per cent in 1978 to 3.5 per cent in 1997, respectively. But the level of representation itself is low for both positions. There are only three "special class" women, the highest position in the decision-making echelons of government service. The revisions to the Civil Service Act in 1998 are expected to facilitate the entrance of women to civil administration. These include revisions to facilitate the regularisation of personnel who have been working for a long time in projects such as Production Credit for Rural Women (PCRW), and to increase the maximum age limit for entry to government services to 40 years; and certain other preferential provisions for women.

In Judiciary

The participation of Nepalese women in the judiciary is also negligible. Women constitute only some 4 per cent of the judiciary's decision makers. There was one secretary, two women judges, and a district judge as of 1997. In spite of the independent Judicial Commission and the Act for Judicial Service, which provide more scope for recruitment and promotion than the Public Service 49 Those that received at least 3 per cent of the votes cast in the 1994 parliamentary election. Following are the special facilities to women in public administration:

i) The maximum age for entry has been set at 40 years for women and 35 years for men.

ii) The maximum age for lateral entry in second and first class posts has been set at 45 years.

iii) No maximum age limit for those already in public service.

iv) A one-time waiver of the maximum age limit for sitting in Public Service Commission examinations has been provided to those women who have been in public service without a break for last five years.

v) The time limit for probationary periods has been set at six months for women and one year for men.

vi) Efforts have been made to transfer husband and wife to the same district when both are in government service.

vii) Women become eligible for promotions one year earlier than men.

Women's political participation and access to positions of power are restricted for several reasons. Women's mobility is restricted; they have fewer opportunities to mix with those in power; they have the sole responsibility for household maintenance and child care activities; and they face a political nepotism that favours men.

The Nepalese political and social life is primarily dominated by the Hindu religion, which divides Hindu society into four varnas, namely, Brahmins, Kshatriyas, Vaishyas and Sudras. Casteism developed a rigid hierarchical society with the purity and pollution of castes. In this manufactured caste hierarchy, Brahmins lie at the top, and Sudras, or Dalits, lie at the bottom of society. The word dalit literally means "a person immersed in a swamp." Traditionally, Dalits have been treated inhumanely as "Untouchables." Although untouchability was abolished by the New National Code of Nepal in 1963, its practice still continues. The people belonging to this community are living in a swamp of illiteracy, exploitation, marginalisation, absolute poverty and, above all, caste discrimination. Dalit women, however, are triply oppressed:

(1) oppressed by the so-called high caste people, which equally affects both male and female Dalits,

(2) oppressed by the design of the Hindu patriarchal system and

(3) oppressed by Dalit males.

The Dalit community constitutes 20 percent of the total population of the country, or four million people, and that the population of Dalit women is half of this figure, i.e., two million people. In general, Dalits are characterised as being illiterate, unemployed, landless, poor, ignorant, exploited, docile, unhygienic, dirty, sick and ignored by the rest of society.

The Dalit community has lost its self-respect and dignity as a result of centuries of social discrimination, oppression, exploitation and suppression. Despite being marginalised, Dalits are skilled artisans. However, statistics have revealed that Dalits are far behind in the development process compared to other caste groups. Unlike other ethnic groups, Dalits are scattered throughout the country. In today's context of the globalisation of women's issues, Nepalese women from different segments of society are also raising their voices against discrimination and exploitation. The government has already established the Women Development Ministry to monitor national and international women's issues, which can be viewed as a good initiative.

Unfortunately, the Dalit women's issue has not been recognised yet as a national issue. In addition, the so-called "mainstream" women's movement, led by high caste women, ignore Dalit women and their concerns. In general, the status of women in Nepal is very low, like in other South Asian countries. Among them though, Dalit women face the worst conditions and oppression. Dalit women are living a history of pain, agony, sorrow, misconduct, maltreatment and suffering. They are not only the victim of gender discrimination but also the victim of casteism.

Moreover, the lives of Dalit women are spiralling downward from bad to worse. There is no controversy among development planners and workers that there has been very little impact on raising the status of Dalit women from the development initiatives implemented thus far in Nepal.

The difficult lives of Dalit women are perhaps best revealed by studying the social, economic, educational, health and political conditions of Dalit women, which are outlined below.

Social Condition

Though outlawed since 1963 and made punishable by the Constitution of the Kingdom of Nepal in 1990, untouchability is still practised. Thus, Dalits are treated as socially untouchable even in a democracy. This can be observed around the periphery of the Kathmandu Valley and in the rural areas. Even in public places, such as schools, Dalit students face discrimination. The entire Dalit community is exploited and discriminated on the grounds of caste, but women, as noted earlier, are further victimised.

Untouchability related to women is practised in many ways that affect all Dalit women every day. For example, when Dalit women fetch water from public water taps, wells, etc., they suffer from mental as well as physical assaults.

Moreover, by traditional cultural practise, women usually are the member of the family that worships in the temple; but in Nepal, Dalit women are not allowed to enter the temples nor are they allowed to enter the house of upper caste people.

Meanwhile, intercaste marriage is socially disapproved, and Dalit women are the principal victims of this system. If a girl from an upper caste family marries a lower caste boy, for instance, then she is accepted by the boy's family.

However, when a marriage takes place between an upper caste boy and a lower caste girl, problems occur as she is not accepted by her husband's family. Subsequently, she is mentally and physically abused and abandoned in many cases.

Economic Condition

Most Dalits have their own traditional occupation, but they are economically exploited. It is estimated that more than 50 percent of the total population of the country lives below the absolute poverty line. Dalits, due to their history of discrimination, exploitation and abuse, constitute a large proportion of this number-approximately 90 percent of the total Dalit population of four million people. Since women have no economic power in the family, it clearly indicates the economic condition of Dalit women. These women have to work hard as labourers to earn a living, but they receive very little in return. Moreover, payment is mostly in kind, and their pay does not justify the intensity of the work. There is no doubt that Dalit women are more economically exploited than their upper caste women counterparts.

Education Condition

The literacy rate of Dalit women is very low in comparison with high caste women. The present literacy rate of men is 66 percent, and the education rate for women is 30 percent. However, the literacy rate of the Dalit community is 16 percent; and for Dalit women, the literacy rate is only 7 percent. Among two million Dalit women, there are hardly 10 to 15 graduates and postgraduates. Ignorance, absolute poverty, caste and gender discrimination can be considered as the explanation for such statistics.

Health Condition

In Nepal, the life expectancy of women is lower than that of men (Nepal is one of the three countries in the world where women live less than men). Compared though to the so-called "upper caste people," the health condition of Dalits is very miserable. For example, a very backward Dalit caste-the Mushar of Terai -has a life span of 42 years against the national average of 55 years.

Moreover, gynecological diseases, like a prolapsed uterus, are very common among Dalit women. They do not know much about birth control and spacing and become pregnant every year. Furthermore, because of illiteracy and ignorance, they live in filthy and unhygienic conditions which further deteriorates their health. The children of Dalits are also severely malnourished.

As Dalits do not have easy access to clean drinking water in most places, they are compelled to drink polluted water and thus suffer from various gastrointestinal diseases. In this environment, both the mortality and fertility rates are high.

Political Condition

Nepalese society is patriarchal, and the involvement of women in public life is not encouraged. This social prohibition applies to politics too. Thus, although Nepali women comprise 52 percent of the country's population, their representation in politics is among the lowest in Asia, i.e., as low as 5 percent. This is in spite of the 1990 Nepalese Constitution in which there is a mandatory provision that 5 percent of all candidates put forward by the country's national parties should be women.

However, there were no mandatory rules for women to be represented in local government. In 1997 though, 5 percent of the seats were reserved for women in local government, and yet this rule cannot embrace Dalit women.

Dalits are about 20 percent of the total population, but Dalits are not represented in national-level politics. Presently, there are four nominated parliamentarians in the National Assembly, but there is none that have been elected to the Lower House of Parliament. If the representation of men is so negligible, then one can easily imagine the political participation of Dalit women.

Sexual Exploitation

Because of poverty, ignorance and illiteracy, Dalit women and young girls are compelled to be involved in prostitution. One of the Dalit castes-Badi-is regarded as the prostitute caste. In addition, there is the trafficking of girls. Most of the Dalit girls taken by the brokers are trafficked to Indian brothels. In addition, many women working in carpet factories, hotels and government and private offices are sexually harassed and exploited.

Because of the untouchability problem related to caste, Dalit women are deprived of the opportunity of working in the moneymaking professions, i.e., opening teashops and restaurants. Their time is spent on earning subsistence wages, and they do not have time to think about improving their condition.

Very few efforts have been made by the government of Nepal to eradicate the problems of Dalits in general and of Dalit women in particular. In recent years, particularly after the restoration of multiparty democracy, the women's movement has gained momentum with the emergence of many women's organisations and leaders. Unfortunately, none of these women's organisations have taken the issues and plight of two million Dalit women seriously. This is why we established an organisation dedicated to the rights and emancipation of Dalit women.

There is a serious lack of consciousness among the entire Dalit community about their fundamental human rights. Therefore, they accept all forms of discrimination and exploitation as God's grace to them. Meanwhile, the outside world has been silent about caste exploitation and discrimination. In recent years, a few educated Dalit women, have come forward to move the issue forward. Theu intend to influence the government, donor agencies and international non-governmental organisations (NGOs), enabling them tc realise the harsh reality of Dalit women and to direct resources for the upliftment of these downtrodden women. They also planned to agitate at the local level against caste discrimination and violence and to join hands with other like-minded organisations.

The vast problems of Dalits and Dalit women cannot be solved through the efforts of one or two organisations though. Therefore, we strongly feel that all national forces should join hands together. In this spirit, they would like to offer the recommendations below.

(1) Various programmes should be launched to uplift the living conditions of two million Dalit women.
(2) Scholarships should be provided from primary to higher education to all Dalit girls.
(3) The practice of untouchability in all public places, like schools, water sources and teashops, should be punished with immediate effect.
(4) All laws and acts which discriminate against Dalits and Dalit women should be rescinded immediately, and a law should be formulated and enforced to discourage the practice of untouchability.
(5) Intercaste marriage between Dalits and non-Dalits should be promoted and protected.
(6) There should be reserved seats for Dalit women in appropriate constitutional bodies, and these seats should be reserved for Dalit women in elections from the local to the national level.
(7) The government should abide by the U.N. International Convention on the Elimination of All Forms of Racial Discrimination
(8) Dalits and Dalit women should be represented in the National Human Rights Commission.
(9) A separate commission at the national and the international level should be formed to identify the problems of Dalit women and to make recommendations

to resolve these issues.

As for national and international NGOs, it is recommended that they consider the steps that follow.

(1) A series of in-depth studies should be undertaken about Dalit women.

(2) All NGOs should declare Dalits as one of their target groups of development and should formulate specific programmes to improve their lives.

(3) All human rights organisations should network with Dalit organisations and expose the human rights problems of Dalit women at the national and international level.

(4) The government of Nepal should be pressured to implement all of the U.N. conventions on human rights.

(5) International NGOs especially should give priority to Dalits and Dalit women in employment and involve them in the formulation of plans and programmes for the Dalit community.

Empower Dalit Women of Nepal

'Empower Dalit Women Of Nepal' is a small grassroots organization, dedicated to enable Dalit (low-caste) women and all disenfranchised people in Nepal to fight for their human rights. Through education, literacy training and empowerment groups, 'Empower Dalit Women' aims to foster a measure of economic independence, to boost self-esteem, and to instill solidarity and a sense of national pride.

Much of Nepal's population has for centuries suffered under the caste system, an integral part of the Hindu religion, which determines an individual's occupation, status, access to land etc. Nepal is home to 5 million Dalits, a term used to describe the lower rungs of the caste ladder. Although illegal, caste discrimination is deeply ingrained in Nepali society and widely practiced, especially in rural areas.

Dalits and women in particular, are mostly illiterate and have no advocates within the Nepali high-caste establishment. They suffer discrimination in innumerable ways, notably in terms of access to education, health care and jobs. They are shunned by the rest of society, abused and humiliated in untold ways. They are barred from entering the temples and forbidden to use common water sources. Lower-caste people and lower-caste women in particular, suffer greatly from lack of self-esteem and have no tradition of solidarity. Dalits often do not even consider themselves citizens (of Nepal). Women and girls from all of Nepali society are often subject to physical and emotional abuse even in their own families and communities, due to ingrained religious and cultural bias against women. An estimated 50.000 Nepali women and children, a large percentage of them Dalits, have been trafficked to Indian brothels. Women are economically completely dependent on the men in the family, and can not inherit property. Boys get the more nutritious and plentiful meals, are more likely to be sent to school and to receive medical treatment. The literacy rate for women is half that for men.

'Empower Dalit Women of Nepal' was founded in 1996 by Bishnu Maya Pariyar (then 20 years old). Born to a family of low-caste subsistence farmers in a remote village in Western Nepal, she had to overcome remarkable obstacles to become a social worker. Ms. Pariyar is currently in the United States to expand her education and to find sponsors for her organization.

'Empower Dalit Women' focuses specifically on low-caste women in inaccessible communities, largely overlooked by the established development community and off the beaten path of trekkers.

A group of Nepali and American volunteers in Boston have recently formed an American arm of EMPOWER DALIT WOMEN.

As a member of a savings and loan group, each woman must contribute 10 or 20 rupees (15-30 cents) at the mandatory monthly meetings. From the growing pool, the members can borrow money for small enterprises, such as buying and raising a goat, buying inventory to start a small store etc. At the meetings, the members repay their loans with interest. The group may also lend money to the community at large. Once a group is established, it is self-sustaining, and only accountable to the members.

Literacy as Key to Empowerment: After motivation and trust building in the community, literacy training is the first step towards creating a savings and loan group. A volunteer teacher, generally someone from the community, must commit to teaching every night for two hours. After three months, most of the women are able to read a simple text, to write and to do of the women are able to read a simple text, to write and to do simple math necessary for accounting.

Empowerment and Social Benefits: Besides the obvious economic gains, belonging to a group gives a woman status and a measure of independence. The groups foster a can-do attitude in their communities, and have initiated community improvement projects, such as clean-ups. In many cases, the groups have successfully fought against domestic violence, which is often entwined with alcoholism and gambling. In cases of medical emergencies, the groups have enabled individuals to be brought for treatment. In a variety of situations, the groups give emotional support to the individual. The groups vigorously encourage schooling of all children.

*Breaking down the Caste Hierarchy*In some groups, women of higher caste have been admitted as an experiment. It has resulted in new relationships across caste lines and improved understanding on both sides of the divide. Within such groups, women from different castes can now drink from the same water source, a revolutionary development.

Low Cost and Sustainability: EMPOWER DALIT WOMEN provides new groups with seed money to get the fund started, and cover cost of literacy material and a lantern. Women from established groups are helping to create new groups in other communities as well as in their own. Men, initially hostile to the idea, have replicated the idea and started their own savings and loan groups.

A scholarship program for low-caste children is currently supporting over 200 elementary school children, 20 high school students and 10 young women in college, who are pursuing careers as teachers and health care workers. As a pilot project in community partnership, EMPOWER DALIT WOMEN is starting a fund to enlarge and upgrade the overcrowded and dilapidated school in Taklung, Gorkha. EMPOWER DALIT WOMEN will cover the cost of materials, the community will provide the labor.

4

Discrimination Against Women

Discrimination against women is based on dominance, rather than distinction, and the key to understanding male dominance lies in the social construction of sexuality. Women, through male eyes is a sex object, that by which man knows himself at once as subject. Objectification of male sexuality is a material reality of women's lives, not just a psychological, attitudinal or ideological one. Nepalese legal system and practice is based on patriarchy. The women and the girls are mostly subjected to discrimination and exploitation of various forms. The gender-based discrimination against females originates at home, and is institutionalized as a part of culture. Girl children are known as others belongings so the parents do not want to invest for their upbringing. Not only the society but also the law is equally responsible for not providing the equal protection to men and women.

1. Slavery Convention Jan 7, 1963(a)
2. Supplementary Convention on the Abolition of Slavery, the Slave Trade and Institutions and Practices similar to Slavery. Jan 7, 1963 (a)
3. Convention on the Prevention and Punishment of the Crime of Genocide Jan 17, 1969 (a)
4. International Convention on the Elimination of all forms of Racial Discrimination Jan 30, 1971 (a)
4. International Convention on Economic, Social and Cultural Rights May 14, 1991 (a)
6. International Convention on Civil and Political Rights May 14, 1991 (a)
7. Optional Protocol to the International Convention on Civil and Political Rights. May, 1991 (a)

8. Convention on the Elimination of all forms of Discrimination Against Women April 22, 1991
9. Convention Against Torture and Other Cruel Inhuman or Degrading Treatment or Punishment May 14, 1991
10. International Convention on the suppression and Punishment of the crime of Apartheid July 12, 1977 (a)
11. International Convention Against Apartheid in Sports March 1, 1989
12. Convention on the Rights of the Child Sept 14, 1990
13. Convention on the Political Rights on Women (11) April 26, 1966 (a)
14. Convention on the suppression of immoral trafficking and protocol 25 December, 1995

The Above-mentioned international instruments directly or indirectly prohibit discrimination against, and exploitation of women and girl children.

The Treaty Act 1990 provides that the provisions of such treaties or agreements are enforceable as the law of Nepal, Similarly, the provisions of law that are inconsistent with such treaties or agreements become null and void. The Treaty Act, however, is almost proved weaker in terms of enforcement.

Convention on the Elimination of all kinds of Discrimination Against Women (CEDAW)

After the declaration of Women's Year 1975, CEDAW was adopted on December 18, 1979, and was enforced on September 3, 1981. It became a mainstream of the commitments to develop consensus and implementation strategies for eliminating all forms discrimination against women in the world. The convention states that the discrimination against women, violates the principles of equality of rights and human dignity, and is an obstacle in the participation of women, on equal terms with men, in the economic, social, political and cultural life of the countries.

Under the clause 15 of Part 4 of this convention states:

1. State's parties shall accord to women equality with men before the law.
2. State's Parties shall accord to women in civil matters, a legal capacity identical to that of men and the same opportunities to exercise that capacity. In particular, they shall give women equal rights to conclude contracts and to

administer property and shall treat them equally in all stages of procedure in courts and tribunals.

3. State's parties agree that all contracts and all other private instruments of any kind with a legal effect which is directed at restricting the legal capacity of women shall be deemed null and void.
4. State's parties shall accord to men and women the same rights with regard to the law relating to the movement of persons and the freedom to choose their sentences and domicile.

Nepal has ratified the CEDAW without any reservation in 1991 and became a responsible state party to fulfill the commitments of the convention. But there have been many laws that are manifestly discriminatory to women.

Legal Framework in Nepal

Nepalese legal system, is generally based on Hindu Legal System that prevailed in the Indian sub-continent. The Basic norms of the Hindu legal system were developed from two different schools, namely the Mitakshara and Dayabhaga. The Mitakshara School is considered relatively conservative to gender issues. According to the Mitakshara, women and children have no rights or claim to the property owned by the father. Although the Dayabhaga School urged that wife and sons had independent personality in matters of property, it failed to recognize the equal status of daughter, and obviously denied defining daughters as heirs or co-parceners to the property of the natal family.

In Nepal, the Muluki Ain (Code of the Country) was promulgated in 1963, It was more like a Hindu religious book rather than the code of conduct. The whole social order was based on the cast system. However, the Muluki Ain was based on the Mitakshara school, the wife and sons had been defined as heirs and co-parceners of the father. The daughters were excluded from becoming heirs or co-parceners. In 1950, the Rana rule was overthrown by a popular movement and then the New Muluki Ain. was formed This code was relatively better but daughters were again denied recognition as sons. The New Muluki Ain still prevails as a general law. It has been amended any times. After the women's year 1975, the sixth amendment on New Muluki Ain in 1976, brought a little improvement regarding women's property rights and some other women's issues. For example, before this amendment, under the partition provision even 35 years old unmarried daughters were not entitled to have an equal share of parental property as their brothers. Likewise, the New Muluki Ain has defined women's exclusive property given by parents and in-laws' relatives as "Daijo and Pewa" respectively. Provisions of New Mulluki Ain are applicable merely as common law, and as such cannot overrule the application of a specific statuette promulgated in matters of family property, succession, adoption, incest and other matrimonial relations. There are very few specific acts relating to the protection of women in the Human Trafficking Control Act, 1977, Children's Act 1992 etc. Domestic Violence Act and Family Court Act have been drafted and are in the process of submission to the parliament. Many NGOs and academicians are working hard to have adequate laws relating to women.

Constitutional Framework

In 1947, the Rana regime had promulgated a law called" Nepal Sarkar Baidhanik Kanoon 1947. However, the law was most favorable to Ranas, there were few good provisions about fundamental rights like free education and equality before law. But Ranas didn't practice and follow the norms. After having democracy, the Interim constitution was promulgated in 1951 it was committed about the gender equality and also held directive principles favorable to women and children.

The first constitution of the Kingdom of Nepal was promulgated in 1958. Although, the constitution guaranteed the equal protection of the citizens, discriminatory provisions continued to exit in the Muluki Ain. In 1962, that is, two years after the introduction of the partyless Panchayat system a new constitution-"Constitution of Nepal" was promulgated. It had also guaranteed the rights to equality for all citizens irrespective of their sex, race, caste, tribe or any of them. But again the New Muluki Ain, like the previous one, could not bring any significant changes in the position of women. The popular movement restored democracy again; and after the promulgation of "The Constitution of the kingdom of Nepal, 1990", repealed the previous Constitution of Nepal. With regard to women, the existing constitution contains negative and positive provisions, which go a long way in securing gender justice. Part II of the Constitution has the provision for citizenship. Under the article 9(2) of the Constitution, no child can obtain citizenship of Nepal by virtue of descent, if his/her father is a foreign national. The mother's nationality thus can not be a valid ground for a child to acquire Nepalese nationality. In fact, this has been a defect placed by the Constitution and the Section 3 of the Citizenship Act 1963. This provision clearly discriminates against Nepali women and thus is inconsistent with the CEDAW and International Convention on Civil and Political Rights. Although the Supreme Court repealed the writ petition by saying that the citizenship issue is a special provision, which is entirely different from fundamental rights.

Similarly, under the Article 9 (5) of the constitution, a woman of foreign nationality who has a matrimonial relationship with a Nepalese citizen may acquire the citizenship of Nepal. A petition was filed against this provision for not providing even the residential visa to a foreign man who had the matrimonial relation with a Nepali woman.

In this regard, the Supreme Court gave a very positive verdict announcing the clause 4 of the regulation, inconsistent to Article11 and issued the mandate to the immigration office to provide the visa.

Fundamental Rights

Even though, all the fundamental rights continued in part III, Articles 11 to 23 are applicable to all the citizens irrespective of sex, certain fundamental rights contain specific and positive laws to protect the rights of women.

Rights of Equality

Article 11 of the Constitution guarantees right to equality before law. Article 11 (2) of the Constitution stipulates that no citizen can be subjected to discrimination on the ground of religion, race sex, cast, tribe or ideological conviction or any of these, in matters of general application of laws. Likewise, Article 11 (3) prohibits the state from discriminating among citizens, on grounds of religion, sex, cast, tribe or ideological conviction or any of these. Similarly, Article 11 (5) provides for safeguard against discrimination with regard to remuneration of men and women for the same work.

Positive Discrimination in Favour of Women

Article 11 (3), of the constitution also has the special provision to protect the women, children, aged or the physically or mental incapacitated people, or economically, socially or educationally backward class people. In other words, the state is empowered to make any such provision and it shall not violate Article 11 (3). The State can positively discriminate in favor of women to make special provisions in order to have the gender equality regarding the social, economic and political justice. These provisions could be seen in the sphere or political reservation for women, in both the Parliament and also the special quota for women in the local bodies. This measure is towards correcting the gender injustice. The provision of the positive discrimination is also the reflection of the spirit of the directive principles of state policy contained in part IV of the constitution.

Article 26 (7) (9) directs the state to make a policy to support the female population and the helpless women.

Right to Freedom

Although, Article 12 of the Constitution has guaranteed the personal liberty of the citizens stating that no person's individual liberty shall be encroached upon. Women are far from enjoying these provisions.

Right to Property

However, Article 17 (1) has granted the right to all citizens (men and women) to earn property, to use it, to transfer and enter into other property -related transactions under the law of the land. There are many provisions prevailing in laws against Nepalese women.

Right Against Exploitation

Article 20 of the Constitution specifically prohibits trafficking of human beings, slavery, and serfdom or forced labor in any form. Even though, on the strength of this article, slavery is abolished by law; and for the protection of women, there are many laws, still slavery is existing in the society. Bonded laborers and domestic servants are the example of human rights violation. Similarly, women are being abused in many aspects.

Gender Discrimination and Legal Rights

Although, gender discrimination in any manifestation are prohibited by the international instruments and the constitution, a number of laws prevailed are manifestly discriminating against women. Women are legally marginalized in terms of acquiring fundamental rights, some provisions could be seen as follows:

a) No. 1, 2 of the chapter on Partition (Aungsabanda) of the Muluki Ain restricts daughters from sharing the parental property. They are not even recognized the members of the natal family.

b) No.10 of the same chapter is given silent for the maintenance of daughters. However, in the case of Ms. Jagat Maya vs Ms. Shanu Khadgi 3 the Supreme Court decided to give maintenance rights to an unmarried daughter who had not yet reached the age of 35 years, this ruling has yet to be amended in Muluki Ain.

c) According to No. 10 (a) of the partition, if a women who has been married at least for fifteen years and who has at least reached the age of thirty five, can separate herself, having received, a share in the property of her husband, if she likes. But if the wife has been driven out of her home, by her husband, together with the in-laws or by the husband alone or if she is frequently made to suffer by being beaten or if the husband has brought or kept another wife, then such a wife can have her share separated from her husband's share in property. If that wife dies or elopes, then the property left after being used by her for food and clothing will go to the heir. In a situation where she has been driven out of home by the in-laws only, she should be provided with food and clothing according to the means and social standing.

d) Under No. 12 of the same chapter, a widow, without sons, who is living together before the partition of property has taken place, can not receive her share in property and live separately until she has completed the age of thirty years as long as the heir living together, provides her with food and clothing and with the means for religious offering. If the heir does not fulfill these conditions, she is entitled to receive her share in property and live separately even when she has not reached the age of thirty.

e) Under No. 2 of the same chapter on "Women's Property" of the Muluki Ain, an unmarried woman, one having a husband; or a widow who has been separated can use all the movable property of their share and up to half of the immovable property of her share without anybody's consent. An unmarried woman can, by the consent of her father, if he is alive, and a widow with the consent of their grown up sons if they exist, can use even the immovable property as she likes. In this way, the women are restricted from independent use of their property.

f) Under No.6 of the same chapter widow forfeits her property received from her husband or her family, if she is found sexually disloyal to her deceased husband.

g) No. 2 of the section of the Inheritance (Aputali) of the Muluki Ain states that if the deceased has sons or son's son, the daughters shall not be entitled to inheritance.

h) Although the fourth amendment in 1996 of the Act Concerning Land, 1964 provides tenancy rights to daughters and daughter-in-laws, there are discriminatory conditions for daughters. According to the amended provision only 35 or above aged unmarried daughters are entitled to have the tenancy rights.

i) No. 2 and 9 (a) of the chapter related to Adoption cautions the provision that the wife can not adopt a male or female child as long as the husbandis alive whereas the husband can adopt one without seeking his wife's consent.

j) According to No. 8, the chapter on Marriage, if a women having a husband or a widow, gets herself married deceptively giving false statement that she is unmarried, she makes herself liable to punishment. The marriage consummated thus is annulled, but the restriction is not applied to husbands however. Likewise, the husband can divorce if the wife has had sexual relationship with another man, however, there is no provision that the wife can divorce if the husband has had the same sort of relationship with another women.

k) In the provision of Transaction (Len Den) and Partition (Aungsabanda), women are not legally recognized as the chief of the house in terms of transferring the property.

l) No. 9 of the chapter on Marriage, provides many grounds for a man to keep more than one wife but as far as women are concerned, the law is silent.

m) Under Clause 7 of the chapter on "Rape of the Muluki Ain, any person who has sexual intercourse in any manner with a prostitute without her consent, or through the use of force shall be fined up to rupees 500 or imprisoned up to 1 year. This shows a prostitute is not treated as a human being and she does not have the right to say no to sex. This provision is not only based on gender discrimination but also the word "Prostitute" is against of women's chastity and dignity. From this provision mainly the women who are cheated in the name of religion and tradition like "Badi", "Deuki", "Jhuma" are being sexually abused. They don't report due to these shameful discriminative legal provisions and there is also a big risk of being re-victimized from the law enforcement agencies.

Besides the above mentioned provisions, the gender discrimination could be seen in any other legal provisions in Muluki Act-1959, Foreign Employment Act-1985, etc.

Gender discriminative provisions are inconsistent to the Article 11 of the constitution as well as the Article 15 of the convention on the Elimination of All forms of Discrimination against Women. The reason behind the gender discrimination is the defective value system, which is deeply rooted in the society. The law markers are also in touch with this negative value and due to poverty of great thinking the law is biased on the "Doctrine of sons."

Abortion Laws

Nepal is one of the few countries in the world where abortion is illegal. Unsafe, illegal abortion is a major cause of maternal death in Nepal. 'The medical complications of improperly performed illegal abortions are now reaching epidemic proportions in many parts of the world, and represent a leading cause of death of women among childbearing age.

The abortion issue has never been perceived as a health issue for the people who are in government and people who make policy. Even feminists and activists in Nepal had not raised abortion as a woman's health issue. Although some concerns have been raised by the medical community from time to time during the last twenty years, it was only after ICED and the Beijing conference that this issue began to gain momentum among women's activists in Nepal .

Millions of women around the world risk their lives and health to end an unwanted pregnancy. Every day, 55,000 unsafe abortions take place, 95% of them in developing countries, which lead to the deaths of more than two hundred women daily. World-wide, the percentage of maternal deaths due to unsafe abortions is 13%, but in Nepal this figure rises to 50 percent.

From the medical point of view, abortion is the termination of pregnancy and is "legal under some circumstances in nearly all countries of the world: 96 per cent of countries recognise a threat to a mother's life as legal basis for stopping pregnancy". Nepal is among the those 4 per cent of countries where abortion is illegal even if pregnancy is a threat to the mother's health or life. That is why no hospitals in Nepal perform abortions even as a medical procedure and for this reason women are forced to seek other methods.

Historically, women have performed abortions in villages in Nepal to regulate their fertility. Many village women know some kind of traditional medicine to abort the foetus in the first 2-3 three months of pregnancy. Many village women seek the help of old women to get rid of pregnancy or go to the "village doctor", who may be male or female. Most of the time, pregnancies are terminated in the villages in a very brutal manner. A stick with mud or cow dung and even sometimes poison grass is inserted inside the vagina to induce the contraction of the uterus and cause the foetus to be expelled. Sometimes the abdomen of the pregnant woman is massaged with the hand or with the feet so that the foetus is expelled.

Nepali laws are especially harsh to women who try to abort their foetuses. In addition to imprisonment the sentence may also include the confiscation of all the woman's property. This is a provision which makes woman particularly vulnerable to false charges from greedy in-laws or other relatives. Because of these laws an estimated two thirds of the women in Nepalese jails are convicted of garbhapat (destruction of life), which is a term applied to abortion, infanticide and attempted infanticide through abandonment. Sapana Malla, a young lawyer, clearly states what Nepalese law says about abortion and infanticide. Abortion and infanticide is a crime against the state, dealt with under the homicide chapter of Muluki Ain, the Civil code of Nepal. In the case of abortion, penalty for the termination of a 6 month pregnancy is 2 years imprisonment and for pregnancy above 6 months it is 3 years imprisonment. The punishment for infanticide is life imprisonment and confiscation of property'.

Ironically, not a single man has been punished for abortion in Nepalese legal history. Society has forgotten the fact that men are equally responsible for the pregnancy of women. Male sexuality is never have been challenged or even questioned by the society, religion or culture and that very 'non-challenge' is reflected in the law and practice.

Thousands of Nepali women suffer every year from dangerous back-street abortions. According to one study done by the Maternity Hospital of Kathmandu, from May 15, 1995 to August 31, 1996, 1,961 cases of abortion complications were registered. According to the history given to the doctors by the patients, only six percent of those were induced abortions but the condition in which they were brought strongly suggests more than 50 % was induced.

One gynaecologist working in the hospital said, "Most of those cases which have come to the hospital with abortion related complications, most of them done by quacks. Many come to us in a very bad condition." When asked if she reported the cases to the police, the doctor replied, "We should have, but we did not do it. We don't report it to the police because sick women would have been arrested and that would add insult to injury".

Dr. Renu Rajbhandari once told the authour personally, "6 years ago, I was working in Bharatpur Hospital. One woman was raped by a village man while her husband was away and she got pregnant. She went to a quack and something was put inside her vagina. After two days the foetus was expelled. She dug a hole and put the foetus inside it. Three days after the abortion she developed a fever, started bleeding and came to the hospital while I was on duty. By this time, a neighbour had already complained to the local police that she had an illegal abortion. The police came to the hospital and brought the woman to me and asked me to write a report stating whether she had undergone abortion or not. I talked to the woman and found out the whole story. In order to save her from the police and to save her family life, I gave the report that there had been no abortion and she had very bad infection which required hospitalisation. Of course it was not true medically but I do not feel guilty about it, because if I had not written this report the police would have taken her and her life would have been shattered."

A 20 year-old woman with two daughters, aged 3 and 1 in Butwal, a small city in the southern part of Nepal, became pregnant. She was harassed by her in-laws that again she would have a daughter. Due to this harassment and her fear of having another daughter, when she was 5 months pregnant she went to a private gynaecologist. The doctor told her that it was dangerous to have an abortion after 4 months. She was desperate to abort the foetus so she went to a woman who was notorious for performing abortions. This woman put something inside her vagina and the following day, after painful contractions, she aborted the foetus. Bleeding began and lasted for three days and thereafter she was taken to the hospital. Unfortunately, because of septicaemia and severe anaemia, the doctors could not save her. The hospital record stated the cause of death as septicaemia caused by induced illicit abortion. Before she died she told her husband about the abortion, but the family was unable to take any action, as they did not have any witnesses.

In Nepal maternal death is one of the highest in the world 1500/100000: half of these are caused by illegally induced, back-street abortions. But women's lives are not the only cost of unsafe abortions. "Between 10 and 50% of all women who undergo unsafe abortions need medical care for complications. The most frequent complications are: incomplete abortions, sepsis, haemorrhage and abdominal injuries, such as puncturing or tearing of the uterus.

Unsafe Abortion

Long-term health problems caused by unsafe abortion include: chronic pelvic pain, pelvic inflammatory disease, tubal blockage and secondary infertility. Other possible consequences of unsafe abortion are ectopic pregnancy and an increased risk of spontaneous abortion or premature delivery in subsequent pregnancies. Such problems can limit women's productivity inside and outside the home, constrain their ability to care for children and adversely affect their sexual and reproductive lives."

There is a tremendous impact on the public health system by illegal abortions and the resulting abortion related complications. The treatment of such complications often requires several days of hospitalisation, staff time, as well as blood transfusions, antibiotics, pain control medicines and other drugs. The provision of this care depletes funds and medical supplies needed for other types of treatment. As much as 50% of hospital budgets in some developing countries are used to treat complications of unsafe abortion."

One prominent lawyer describes the situation as follows: "I know that in Solukhumbu District (in eastern Nepal) five out of nine women in prison have been prosecuted for/ are serving sentences related to infanticide. One specific problem related to women in prison charged with infanticide is that there is no medical investigation system in Nepal to determine if a woman was really pregnant or not, whether she had a normal delivery, abortion or forced delivery. For this reason, many women are in prison. Secondly, men are in the most cases outside judicial action.

Feminists and activists in Nepal are working toward legalising abortion from the perspective of health and justice for women who are forcibly jailed for abortion. A bill has been drafted and put through parliament. The women's movements are trying to raise this issue in connection with Beijing Conference which was signed by our government. The Fourth World Conference on women recommended that countries "consider reviewing laws containing punitive measures against women who have undergone illegal abortion."The bill's recommendations include legalising abortions carried out by registered physicians in the first 12 weeks of pregnancy and thereafter in special cases like rape, incest, life-threatening situations and where the foetus is diagnosed as being severely handicapped

Proposal for Reforms

The proposal for reforms is based on three realities. First, it responds "to the limits of public tolerance and public opinions in Nepal. Second, it responds to the increased awareness of women's rights and the growing concern about the victimisation of women in abortion matters. Third, it accepts modern evidence that legal abortion is significantly safer than its frequent social alternative. The bill contains these major characteristics: Abortion at an early stage of pregnancy will be legalised. Medical doctors will perform the operation. Services will be more assessable to women early, thereby reducing the duration of pregnancy at the time of abortion. Proper information will be given to women".

Despite the fact that suggests many reforms, much work is still needed. The proposed bill does not look at abortion as a 'reproductive right' issue and does not consider male responsibility. There has been a great deal of discussion regarding this bill, and in February 1997, another bill was introduced which addressed a number of issues relating to women's rights including property inheritance, rape and a proposed amendment to the abortion law.

Unfortunately, the parliament was dissolved in 1996 as result of a political crisis, before legislative action was taken on this bill and only now is the bill under discussion again. 'According to a survey done by Family Planning Association of Nepal, 74% of members of parliament are in favour of legalising abortion, as are 94% of gynaecologists'. The idea of legalizing is not without obstacles.There are some Hindu religious groups that want to continue to make it illegal. Though they are not a very strong force, they have had an impact. At the same time some members of Parliament are not keen to raise the issue of abortion as they do not think that it is an issue which should be dealt in the discussion. Nevertheless, women's voices, which equate legalizing abortion with women's political empowerment, have already made some changes.

Nepal Medical Association of Nepal has forwarded a program in which it has clearly suggested to the doctors conditions under which abortion can be performed in hospitals. Though in the lawbooks it is illegal to perform an abortion, in some parts of our country doctors in hospitals do perform abortion if mothers health is in risk, or the fetus is severely damaged. It is an open secret that the government is aware of.

But it is not done in every hospital and not on the request of the mother.

We cannot hope that the legalization of abortion in Nepal will automatically guarantee access to safe abortion for all segments of the population. In a developing country like Nepal, merely the fact that abortion law is liberal does not and cannot gurantee that women have access to legal abortion facilities. There are too many constraints, including the lack of human resources such as doctors and nurses in many parts of Nepal, lack of confidence of women and financial obstacles. Activists and medical professionals should be aware that "legalising abortion is thus only the first step in making safe abortion a real option."

In countries like India, where abortion is legal, incidence of illegal abortion is still very high. "In India at least 10 times as many illegal abortions are carried out as legal ones and ar least 80 per cent of women admitted ot hospitals with complications have had abortions performed by unqualified people". So we have to work to make sure that people have equal access to safe abortions. "properly performed, abortion is a woman's safety net and one of the most important reproductive rights of all".

The government will have more responsibility to ensure that abortion is available to all who need it after it is legal. In order to reduce the current heavy toll of abortion-related maternal death and morbidity, governments, international agencies, women's groups and non-governmental organisations (NGOs) must take steps: ensure universal access to family planning; increase the availability of safe abortion services to the extent allowed by law; improve the quality and accessibility of post-abortion care; educate their communities about reproductive health and unsafe abortion; and work for changes in policies to safeguard women's reproductive health. A high priority should be given to the prevention of unwanted pregnancy through comprehensive client-oriented reproductive health services.

Non-judgmental attitudes, confidential counselling and quality family planning information and services should be universally accessible to all women, including emergency contraception where feasible and appropriate. Quality Services should be safe and available to the full extent allowed by law, particularly in rural and impoverished areas. Service providers must be carefully trained to offer high quality services and compassionate counselling. The providers must be well informed about the legal status of abortion and protocols for providing services so that eligible women can access them quickly and without unnecessary delay or bureaucratic procedures. The available services should be publicised within the community and links should be strengthened with women's groups, health centres and related organisations thus ensuring that women who need services are informed about where and when to seek care.

Property Rights

The Nepali laws of succession are based upon traditional Hindu kinship, i.e., joint, multi-generational family groups of partilineally related males. A young bride who has left her parent's home to live with her husband may find him living with his parents, brothers, the brothers' wives and children and the unmarried (and possibly widowed) sisters.

If a woman's husband dies before she has given birth to any sons, then until she reaches the age of 30 she is entitled only to claim maintenance from his family, assuming he is still living jointly with his parents and brothers. If the marriage fails in such circumstances, then a woman's rights to demand partition of her husband's portion of his father's property are unclear. In cases where the husband has separated from his father and brothers, if the husband dies then his property goes in equal shares to his widow(s) and any sons. Likewise, if the marriage fails after the husband has separated from his father and brothers, a woman seeking separation and partition from her husband is legally entitled, provided she has been married for 15 years and is at least 35 years old, to a share equal to that retained by her husband and each of their sons and co-wives and any co-wives' sons.

Until fairly recently, even where there were no sons in a family, when a father died his daughters did not inherit his property. Rather, the daughters had to look to their husband or future husband for support and the father's property passed to his brothers and their sons. Under prevailing law these are two situations, where the law does provide for inheritance of a father's property by a surviving daughter.

One such instance involves a daughter who remains unmarried beyond the age of 35. Such women will inherit paternal property even if they have brothers. Prior to the 1975 amendments to the Mulki Ain they inherited only half of the share inherited by their brothers. Now they inherit a share equal to that of their brothers. The second situation in which a daughter may inherit paternal property is that in which a deceased father is not survived by his wife, a son, or any sons of his sons. In general, however, these exceptions to the rule point out that women's family property rights usually depend on the social fact of marriage, whereas men's property rights spring from the biological fact of their existence.

Even after property has passed to a woman, except in the case of her strıdhan (i.e., her daijo and pewa and any property which she has earned or bought with her earnings from her own employment), there are restrictions on her use of such property. For example, the law provides that a girl, married woman or female who is living separately may dispose of all of her movable property as she wishes, but of only one half of her immovable property. For the rest, she must first gain the consent of others such as her father, or her adult sons. In the case of a married woman living with her husband, the law forbids her to enter into any financial transaction or contract on her own, because no such contract by a woman would allow a creditor to reach her husband's ancestral property.

The practical result of this is that only those women who have sufficiently documented daiio or pewa or other exclusive separate property may obtain credit. The question of what amounts to sufficient documentation has been addressed in a well known Supreme Court case that arose under the 1974 Evidence Act. That act provides, in part, that in the absence of proof to the contrary, any property registered in the name of an individual is presumed to be joint property of that individual's coparcenary.

Thus, unless a woman has uncontrovertible proof that property which is registered in her name is her stridhan, she may have to share it with her husband and his family. This may often prove difficulty, since it is not common practice to maintain written records tracing the origin of property, especially in the rural areas of Nepal. Thus, in practice even a woman's stridhan may not be hers to dispose of as she wishes.

Two women advocates filed a writ in the Supreme Court against unequal rights to parental property in May 1994 demanding that No.1, 2 and 16 of the chapter on Partition (Aungsabanda) of the Muluki Ain are contrary to the Article 11 of the constitution of the Kingdom of Nepal, 1990. Although the Supreme Court gave a verdict in August 1995, directing the government to bring new legislation which is not gender discriminatory towards women within a period of one year. The verdict was not as positive as expected, that gives the long explanation about the patriarchal society and the marital status of women.

The ratio of the verdict could be seen as follows:

> "Taking into consideration the social condition of men and women the Nepalese law has provided only some different process of getting partition share. Instead of depriving a daughter of the right to get partition share or making discrimination against her, the right of a daughter to get partition share has only been managed in a slightly different manner from that of a son, taking into account the social status of the women. For instance, according to No. 16 of the chapter on Partition, an unmarried daughter should attain the age of 35 years in order to get partition share, while even a married daughter should attain the age of at least 35 years and a period of 15 years should have been spent from the date of marriage to get partition share. In regard to the process of getting partition share son gets partition share at his birth, but a daughter should fulfill some terms to get the same, which cannot be disregarded. Before declaring No. 16 of the Chapter on Partition unconstitutional and making provision as to the same entitlement of a daughter to partition share as that of a son, the negative sides of thereof or its implications on the society should also be taken into account. This has a great impact on the structure of the patriarchal society like ours, handed down from ancient times. A daughter may not be compelled to get married and go, to her husband's

house after marriage, while on the other hand, declaring No.16 of the Chapter on Partition unconstitutional and making provision entitled to get partition share from the properties of both he father and husband and a son will be entitled to get partition share only from the property of his father, in regard to the right to obtain more partition share that a son's right to obtain partition share thus, creates conditions discriminatory against son. This affects all the laws of the country made in regard to the property right.

Therefore, declaring clause No. 16 of the Section on Partition void and making provision entitling a daughter to get partition share as of a son is not a solution to the problem. In making sudden changes in traditional social practices and in matters of social norms pureed by the society since a long time ago, the society happens to become unable to adopt several matters, and if so happens, a different situation beyond perception would emerge. Therefore, before reaching a decision all of a sudden, a just provision should be made by holding wide and extensive discussions and deliberations taking also into a account the constitutional provision vis-à-vis equality. As the family law, relating to property is to be wholly considered, this directive is hereby issued ordering that His Majesty's Government introduce an appropriate Bill in Parliament within one year of receipt of this order, by taking the necessary suggestions on this matter from the recognized women's organizations, sociologists, the concerned social organizations and lawyers as well, and by studying and considering also the legal provisions made in the constitutions of other countries in this regard.4 After the order issued by the Supreme Court, many programs had been launched by GOs, NGOs and other interest groups. After a long time, the proposed bill has been drafted and submitted to the Parliament. But again the Bill has failed to create an equal right that defines the marital status of women, and provides the limited right to daughter. Under the proposed amended Bill, the daughter has to return the share of the parental property to the natal family after the she gets married.

There is one landmark precedent is established by the Supreme Court in the case of Bhishma Kumari Maharjan.5 In this case, the Supreme Court held that "the law does not restrict granting of property to a daughter before reaching age 35 years if all co-partners are willing to make partition including such daughter as a co-partner of the property.

The Constitution of the Kingdom of Nepal, 1990, under chapter 3 guarantees "right to equality" to all the citizens as a fundamental right. It states that the State shall not discriminate amongst citizens on grounds of race, caste, and sex. It also states that the Constitution is the fundamental law of Nepal and all laws inconsistent with it shall be void.

However, discriminatory laws against women in relation to property right still prevail. Nepal has also become a State party ratifying the CEDAW on April 22, 1991, without reservation. Mandatory country report was submitted after a delay of 6 years. The State has made no deliberate effort to eliminate de jure and de facto discrimination against women in accordance the spirit of CEDAW.

Evidence of discrimination and disparities are as follows:

a) A daughter is denied from equal inheritance rights,
b) Daughter is denied the right to maintenance,
c) Discrimination in the line of succession (The line of succession gives a right to inheritance to the daughter only after mother and brother),
d) Discrimination on dolaji property,
e) Discrimination against Married Women to get the Property,
f) Divorcee Woman without Property Right (only conditional maintenance right),
g) Unfaithfulness looses the right in the husband's property,
h) A victim of rape is considered as ex wife by the law,
i) Discriminatory Property Right of a Widow,
j) Discrimination on tenancy right,
k) Discrimination on Transaction, and
l) Consent needed to dispose off immovable property.

Barriers to guarantee equal Inheritance right for Women are as follows:

i. Lack of Women in Decision-making Bodies,

ii. Lack of Political Power or Political Commitment,

iii. Deep Rooted Gender Discriminatory Value System,

iv. Beliefs Reflecting the Derogatory Attitude Towards Girl Child/Women including the following:

– Dhilo paye, Chhora paye ("Let it be late, but let it be a son");

– Chhora paye swarga jaane ("The birth of a son paves the way to heaven");

– Chhori ko janma hare ko karma ("A daughter is born with a doomed fate");

– Chhora paye khasi, Chhori paye Pharsi ("If a son is born, it is celebrated by sacrificing a goat, if it's daughter, a pumpkin is enough");

– Chhora bhaye sansar ujyalo, Chhori bhaye bhanchha ujyalo ("Son brightens the whole world, whereas a daughter brightens only the kitchen");

– Kanya Daan ("a daughter should be given away as a gift");

– Mare paap, pale punya ("It's a sin if the groom kills the bride, charity if nurtured");

– Srimati bhaneko paitalako dhulo ho ("Wife is the dust of the foot");

– Chhori mari, thulo ghar pari ("If a daughter dies, we can say she has been married into a rich home");

– Pothi base ghar mahscha ("A woman ruled house is sure to be destroyed"); and o Swasni mancheko buddhi pachhadi ("Women are always shortsighted").

Holding of such traditional values by both the lawmakers and many common Nepalese people have been detrimental for the realization of equal rights for both sons and daughters. Majority of the population is still exposed to such values because of lack of access to modern education. Negative Campaign in the Media have had the following messages:

– The Nepalese society is not yet prepared to embrace equal property rights.

– Nepalese social structure would be badly disturbed by equal property rights.

– Hindu religion would be wounded if equal property right is given.

- The Bill would destroy the prevailing harmonious family relationships. There already exists many court cases among brothers relating to property rights and equal property rights would only result in increasing their number, as there would be cases among the brothers and sisters as well.
- Brothers would no longer show respect and fulfill their responsibilities to their sisters.
- Equal property rights leads to land fragmentation.
- Equal property rights in Nepal and prevailing discrimination in neighboring country India Daughters may refuse to get married since they would be economically independent after getting equal property rights.
- A woman would be entitled to dual property, one from her father and the other from her husband.
- If wife is uneducated, her husband and his family might misuse her property and then throw her out of the house.
- Domestic violence would go up because of conflict of interest between the husband's family and the natal home.
- Equal property rights would trigger divorce.
- The number of spinsters, polygamy and abortion would increase if women get equal property rights.
- If daughters should get equal property rights, aged and/ or disabled parents would be deprived of care from their sons o Property right is a non-issue in a country where the majority of the population lives below poverty line.
- What is important to girl child/women is access to education and opportunities and not property rights.
- In the Hindu tradition, a woman is entitled to her husband's property making equal property rights irrelevant.

Effects of disparities in relation to unequal inheritance on women is envisaged to be deep-rooted in their life cycle in various aspects which have impaired their overall self-development as well as their capability in family, community and national development.

The lack of equal inheritance right to women has disabled (without power) them in various fields. The affects in various aspects of a woman's life can broadly be categorized as follows:

Economic Dependency

– Due to economic dependency, women have to face problems like domestic violence, psychological domination, polygamy, no decision making power in the family, harassment for dowry which in many cases, leads women to accept prostitution as a way of life. They have to bear all these problems as they are denied any financial security. They have hardly any choice during their marriage, which in many a cases, results in unequal or child marriage. As a daughter is taken as an obligation and a liability only, there is also no expectation from her, hence priority is given to male family members, as they are expected to take care of the family.

– *No independent identity*: The fact that women have no independent identity, can be seen from the discriminatory provisions in the Citizenship Act, 1963,and Constitution of the Kingdom of Nepal where father is the natural guardian of children. As a woman does not have an independent identity, she can not transfer citizenship to her children and husband, hence she is not recognized as an independent citizen of the country.

– *Low social preference*: As women do not have any inheritance right, they face discrimination right from childhood in matters of nutrition, health, education and distribution of family resources.This discrimination continues against them all throughout their life till death. Hence one can firmly say that women face discrimination arising out of unequal right to inheritance which affects various aspects of a woman's life which ultimately hinders their overall development.

Lack of Equal Inheritance Right to Women

State has made commitments to guarantee right to equality to both man and women in all sphere of their life including right to property in different policies, plan, constitution and international conventions which can be seen from the matrix below.

One of the initiatives taken by the government is the Country Code (11 th Amendment) Bill 1997. Its major features are as follows:

Progressive preamble: It is stated in the preamble of the Bill itself that the rights and interests of women in the existing Country Code require timely amendments. It further adds that the Bill was being proposed in view of the constitutional guarantees in favor of equal rights to women, Nepal's ratification of the United Nations Convention on the Elimination of all Forms of Discrimination Against Women and as per the Directive Order issued by the Supreme Court to His Majesty's Government to introduce an appropriate Bill within one year.

Daughters are recognized as heir of the family: It recognizes father, mother, son and daughter as equal co-heirs. Daughters are required to return the remaining property to the other co-heirs on their parents side, if they marry. Married daughters are not included while defining the co-heirs.

Court grants wife a share of husband's property before a divorce: It makes an attempt to eliminate women's unequal access to property by authorizing the court to grant a share of the husband's property (matrimonial property) to the wife before granting a divorce, as well as entitling the wife to a monthly or annual maintenance from the husband till the process of partition is complete. The wife is entitled to a share of her husband's property only if the cause of the divorce is the husband or if the divorce is by mutual consent.

Complete authority of widow in her property: The proposed Bill removes the age restriction placed on widows to claim property and live separately. It also entitles her to have complete authority over her property. However, she must return her remaining assets to the heirs of her first husband if she remarries.

Unmarried daughters are included in the line of succession: In the case of a woman's exclusive property, even though an unmarried daughter has been included, a married daughter has been placed last in the line of succession. A women's Daijo and Pewa, unless otherwise stated, must pass in the following order: son or daughter, husband, and then only to the married daughter. The Chapter on Succession also placed the married daughter last in the line of succession.

In the Initial Report submitted by Nepal to CEDAW, the Government recognized the legal discrimination against women prevailing in the country. It also accepted the fact that girls are assigned unequal legal status in comparison to boys, that the law is silent on the maintenance right of daughter and that in regard to property rights, a male child is entitled to inheritance right from birth while a girl child acquires such property right only if she remains unmarried until the age of 35 years. However, it has not specified initiatives and constraints to guarantee equal inheritance right to the daughter as well as fail to explain limitations of widows, wife and divorcee women to get a share of husbands property.

Political Commitment through the Party Manifestos on equal inheritance right All the political parties have been making various commitments towards women's upliftment and equality in their manifestos since the restoration of democracy. However, no substantially effective programs have been undertaken to bring about such reforms as yet.

The two communist parties, CPN (UML) and CPN (ML) both issued whips to their Parliamentarians to favor the Country Code (11 th Amendment) Bill in Parliament in 1998. Unfortunately, the whip could not be used for the desired outcome. The major political party, the Nepali Congress, which has been in the Government for the longest duration after the restoration of the multi party system, and other parties which have been in the Government, have not taken any initiatives or actions to fulfill their commitments under their political manifestos. Three major political parties, the Nepali Congress, CPN (UML) and CPN (ML) have pledged to bring about social, economic, legal and other reforms for women, in their party manifestoes for the 1999 general elections for Parliament. The two communist parties have made commitments for the equal inheritance rights of women. How much of these grandiloquent speeches and commitments are actually carried out by these political parties remain to be seen.

Besides their commitment in the election manifesto and being in the Government for the longest period, Nepali Congress has not taken any steps to fulfil their commitments except the submission of Country Code Amendment Bill. Voice of the women Parliamentarians has been marginalized. Similarly, UML, RPP and Sadhvana party's' commitments towards women's equality is not being fulfilled, despite them being in the Government. Women's participation in the cabinet is also very nominal.

Weaknesses in the Government Bill-Discriminatory inheritance provision in the Country Code (11 th Amendment) Bill, 1999 The proposed Bill accepted the daughter as an heir of the family. However, the married daughter has been excluded. If an unmarried daughter gets married after succession or partition, the remaining property must be returned to the maternal relatives.

A widow may undergo separation and take away the share of property she receives on behalf of her deceased husband if she so wishes. If she remarries, the remaining property must be returned to the heirs of her former husband. Married daughters are excluded from equal succession right. The proposed Bill provides that once a woman files an application for divorce, the court should direct partition and should provide one share of the family property to her but it applies only in cases in which the cause of the divorce is the husband.

The proposed Bill makes some effort to reform the discriminatory legal provisions. Accepting daughter as an equal heir as the son, increased punishment and unavailability of bail for polygamy, making abortion legal under certain conditions, etc. are some positive aspects of this Bill. However, it is still discriminatory against women as it fails to deal with the important issue of equality in relation to inheritance right and the problem of different forms of violence against women .

Thus, the proposed property Bill, rather than making women self-reliant, creates inequality between sons and daughters, making them dependent on the father until they marry, and on the husband after marriage. Granting women rights on the basis of their marital status is clearly against Article 1 of CEDAW.

The Court only declared that the existing provisions for daughters to inherit paternal property is conditional as a daughter has to remain unmarried until the age of 35 to do so, whereas son is entitled to inherit right after his birth. Thus, instead of declaring the laws void, the court passed a directive to the Government to introduce a Bill in the legislature within a year, reviewing laws related to property rights. At the same time, the court also asked the Government to take into consideration the patriarchal nature of the society, social structure, and fears of positive discrimination against men.

No serious efforts from the Government sector to formulate appropriate legislation were observed following the Supreme Court's verdict. Therefore several NGOs got together to formulate appropriate Bill.

NGO achievements include:

a. Directive Order of the Supreme Court to submit the Bill in the Parliament in regards to property right of women.

b. Despite the negative interpretation of this issue, the challenges against the existing laws has had a positive impact, as a result of which women have become relatively more empowered. Due to the court decisions in the inheritance right case, the entire society has been forced into rethinking about the patriarchal structure, male supremacy, and the status of individual freedom of women. Women have begun to be vigilant about the issues and link them with the broader issue of equality.

In spite of an increasing need for an amendment in the existing legal provisions in order to create a just and equitable society, there have been diverse views and opinions regarding the issue of granting equal property rights to women. Education, political participation, distribution of productive assets and income, employment, social, cultural, religious and legal situations have proved that disparities/ discrimination exists between man and woman in Nepal.

Economic and socio-cultural discriminations have an adverse affect on the lives of women, leaving them far behind men to compete or take part in national development. Various cultural, practical, attitudinal, conceptual, social and political factors have limited women from moving in equal footing with men. Economic rights are one of the measures by which both women and men can achieve self-development.

The majority of the Nepalese women are illiterate, have poor health, and are dominated by conservative social value system which makes them dependent on their fathers, husbands or sons, as well as easy victims of domestic and social violence. Thus, it is crucial to enact new legislation guaranteeing equal inheritance right for women to address the problem of discriminatory social and cultural practices.

There is a debate on the question of which should come first - the law giving equal inheritance right to women or an attitudinal change in the society in favor of giving equal inheritance to women? Review of the history of legal changes in Nepal reveal many instances where laws have preceded the change in social attitude and behavior, e.g. abolition of slavery, abolition of wife burning together with the dead husband (sati system), age of consent for marriage etc. This reinforces the fact that if the equal inheritance right law is introduced, it will gradually bring about positive changes in discriminatory attitudes and practices and there shall be an instrument to enforce the law.

There have been arguments that the Bill, if adopted, may upset the social and cultural milieu. It may be true that once the Bill is introduced some upheaval might occur in society as is inevitable with all kinds of changes and transition. Democracy was reinstated in the country in 1990 and even now the country is still undergoing a lot of instability and disorders. That does not mean we should go back to the period before democracy, or even further back to the autocratic Rana regime when there was no democracy at all.

5

Women's Participation in Government

The major issues related to women in the economic field include their limited access to productive assets—the land and property, credit and modern avenues of knowledge and information; concentration of women in low productivity agriculture and high and increasing work burden without concomitant increase in access to resources,child labor, lack of access to training, technology and education; concentration at lower levels jobs, poor working conditions and lack of child care facilities at work places; trade union's neglect of women's problems; risk to personal security and sexual harassment in the formal sector and low level of technology, limited market access, low income and progressive loss of proprietorship in informal sector. Women entrepreneurs face special problems of resources scarcity, low risk taking capacity and marketing access. Moreover, there is a severe dearth of information on women's employment and earning patterns, problems, grievances and aspirations in the formal sector including tourism and other services. The recorded economic activity rates under reports women's work and contributions to household survival.

Access to Resources

Women's access to land and property is derived through her marriage relationship. A married woman has no right in her parental property. She gets an equal share in the husband's property together with her son, if she remains faithful to him and his clan. This is server's limitation on women's access to all productive assets. Marriage becomes the overwhelming factor determining all her life options. This reinforced by all round social norms and legal structures, every thing else is secondary to marriage. Single women, even with many children are not given land in resettlement areas, even if such households may be among the poorest of the poor. They may not claim any tenancy rights.

Although many husbands may keep property in the name of wives, such women may not make any transaction in the property without the consent of her husband and sons, etc. This limitation is not applied to husbands and the sons. Households get access to community resources such as forests through household heads who are usually men. Women may have the derived user rights as long as her husband does not abandon her. When a husband brings another wife and leaves her, which is constantly recurring even in the Nepalese social milieu, she looses all access to community property as well.

Such processes are hard to capture by data, since no data are collected on polygamy. It is illegal to have more than one wife, but women get no property on divorce and so a access to resources. Two major indicators of such inequality are access to credit and increasing involvement of women in commercial sex work for survival. A detailed discussion of the second symptom is beyond the scope of this paper. Nevertheless it is pertinent to note that lack of alternative avenues of livelihood is one of the major causes why women get into commercial sex work, why parents sell their daughters into dubious marriages and sex bazaar.

Access to Credit

Women's access to credit is limited because both formal and informal credit institutions are geared to funding property owners. All formal credit institutions seek tangible collateral from loan and women are effectively sidelined from institutional credit since women have little access to the inherited property. The village moneylenders are also interested more in earning high interest or acquiring the debtor's property rather than financing people in need.

Women's access to institutional credit is further restricted by their confinement to household activities and lower level of awareness and educational attainment. As such they are more prone to fall prey to the exploitative conditions of the village moneylenders than their male counterparts.

Table 1
Borrowings from Formal and Informal Sources

Source of Credit	*All Households*	*Male*	*Female*
Institutional	29.7	30.4	15.4
ADB	15.9	16.4	4.9
Commercial Bank	11.6	11.9	7.4
Others	2.1	2.1	2.1
Non-Institutional	70.3	69.9	84.6
Friends & Relatives	24.5	24.2	30.5
Moneylenders	28.4	27.9	38.9
Landlords	0.9	0.9	1.0
Merchants Traders/Others	16.5	16.6	14.2
Total	100.0	100.0	100.0

Nepal Rural Credit Review Study (NRCRS) by Nepal Rastra Bank in 1991/92 revealed that of the total female headed sample households almost 35 percent had borrowed from one or the other sources compared to 39 percent male headed households.

However, among the borrowing female headed households only 15.4 percent had borrowed from institutional sources such as Agricultural Development Bank and Commercial Banks and 84 percent had borrowed from noninstitutional sources. Access to institutional credit in one of the major stumbling blocks for women entrepreneurs in all sectors including agriculture. Almost 40 percent had borrowed from moneylenders.

Economically Active Work Force

Accuracy of reporting on labor force participation rates in censuses and the definition of economic activity are some of the major issues, which concern women's right activists the world over. Many books and reports have focused on them. Several UN agencies have documented them in detail.

Accordingly united Nation's Conference on women noted in its Platform for Action that "Women contributed to development not only through remunerated work but through a great deal of unremunerated work. On the other hand, women participate in the production of goods and services for the market and household consumption, in agriculture, food production or family enterprises.

Though included in the United Nations system of National Accounts and therefore, in international standards for labor statistics, this unremunerated work, particularly that related to agriculture, is often undervalued and under recorded. On the other hand, women also perform the great majority of unremunerated domestic works and community work, such as caring for children and older persons, preparing food for the family, protecting the environment and providing voluntary assistance to unalterable and disadvantaged individuals and groups. This work is often not measured in quantitative terms and is not valued in national accounts. Women's contribution to development is seriously underestimated, and thus its social recognition is limited. The full visibility of the type, extent and distribution of the unremunerated work will also contribute to a better sharing of responsibilities."

In Nepal, the problem is complicated further by varying definitions of economic activity rates between various censuses. Inspire of these shortcomings of census data a fairly high proportion of women are reported as economically active in Nepal. Moreover, sex composition of economically active population shows an increasing preparation of women in labor force.

In the 1991 census tabulation, those who worked for at least three months and those seeking employment were classified as economically active while in 1981 census only those working for eight hours or more were classified as economically active. As such the economically active population of the 1981 census may not be comparable to the economically active population of the 1991. Only about 38 percent of the population were reported as having worked for eight months or more in 1991.

According to those statistics, gross economic activity rates of 1991 have apparently declined drastically compared to those of 1991. That could partially be explained by the demographic changes in favor of children, by the increased number of students, etc. as analyzed by Niraula. But fundamentally it much be a problem of definitions and its interpretation by the enumerators.

One notable aspect, from the gender perspective, however, is that while male economic activity rates have declined almost constant. That could be due to a more accurate recording of economic activity rates. It is quite possible that in earlier censuses, all males were recorded as economically active, irrespective or length of work house, age or work status while women were mostly recorded as home makers.

Table 2

Women in Labor Force (15-64 Age Group)

	(Percent in Total)	
Country	*1980*	*1995*
High Income Countries	39	42
Low Income Countries	40	41
South Asian Countries	34	33
Bangladesh	42	42
India	42	42
Nepal	34	32
Pakistan	39	26
Sri Lanka	27	35

Further, women's economic activity rates are estimated to be much more than what is reported in census data as analyzed below. The daily chores of family life in rural Nepal involve women in labor-intensive farm work and time consuming domestic work to provide fuel, water and food for household member and farm workers.

As per the 1991 census data, more than 36 percent of the female population were reported as home makers and so inactive. A scrutiny of the regional figure clearly indicates a persisting reporting bias in economic activity rates. While the overwhelming majority of Mountain (73.6 percent) and Hill (57.9 percent) women were reported as economically active, only about 27 percent of the Tarai women are thus reported.

The Status of Women report series has shown that women in the Tarai were equally active in the economic sphere, albeit invisible within the household production system e.g., in food processing and cooking for farm labor and village sweet shops, but such activities are not reported as economic. Another point of concern is the declining economic activity rate of women in urban areas, from 31.5 percent in 1981 to 20.3

percent in 1991. Decline of women's economic activity with the modernization process has been noted in other countries also. Nepalese economy predominated by households as unit of productions seem to be rapidly replaced by a system which separates households from economic activities limiting them to human reproduction and consumption activities. In this process women may be loosing their economic roles. This is also reflected in declining role of women in household decisions.

Women in Agriculture

The Nepalese agriculture is dominated by small-scale subsistence farming. Majority of households (66 percent) have less than on the average. More than 40 percent have less than 0.5 ha. The size of land holding is smaller in Tarai but much less productive in the hills and mountains. Although women contribute substantially to agriculture both in terms of labor input and decision making-women's access to land is limited due to the patrilineal inheritance system. Nevertheless, the hill agriculture is primarily dependent on women due to male migration from the hills, and women operate most of the farms.

Agriculture is becoming progressively feminized. Many women engaged in family farms are still reported as economically not active. Nonetheless, even according to census figures, the proportion of female labor force in agriculture has increased between 1971 and 1991. In 1971, women constituted 30.4 percent of the agricultural labor force. That increased to 36.4 percent in 1981 and to 45 percent in 1991.

Although female employment is increasing in the non-agriculture sector, comparatively a larger proportion of agricultural labor force are women. In 1981, more than 96 percent of the economically active women were involved in agriculture and forestry.

In 1991 this percentage has come down to 90 percent. Concomitantly, there has been an increase in the proportion of economically active population engaged in the leading sources of employment for both men and women. The next largest group of women is in trade sector. Manufacturing occupies only a remote third position in employment generation for men and women.

Occupationally, even in urban areas a substantial proportion of women are concentrated in the category of farm, forestry and fishery workers although the share of the non-agricultural sector in total employment has shown a substantial increase in 1991. In the non-agricultural sector, women are mainly engaged in services, sales and as labors in manufacturing, construction, transportation, communications and others.

Compared to 1981, a larger proportion of economically active women seem to have entered the group of professional and technical workers. Nevertheless, compared to 1981 now comprise lesser proportion of total number of professional and technical workers-indicating relatively lower access of women to education and knowledge.

Employment in the Organized Manufacturing

An increasing number of women are entering the work force in the formal manufacturing sector because of economic need. However, they are mainly concentrated in low-skill, menial and repetitive jobs and in the lower echelons of the industrial hierarchy in what is virtually an extension of their household activities. Lack of education, training opportunities, employer biases and limited mobility due to social responsibilities combined to keep them at lower echelons of industrial hierarchy.

In 1976/77, women had constituted 11.2 percent of the total labor force in manufacturing industries. That proportion went up to 17 percent in 1986/89 and to 23.0 percent in1990/91 but has slightly declined since then.

According to a survey in 1987, women's employment in industries in the organized sector depended less on type of industry than on its location, size of investment and degree of mechanization. More women workers were employed in manufacturing in the Hill region than the Terai. Female employment was concentrated in those industries where the fixed capital investment was the lowest. That meant that the majority of female workers received low pay. The majority of women in the formal sector worked as semi-skilled and unskilled workers. In virtually all food, drink, tobacco and match industries female workers were mainly concentrated in packing the finished product and in related processes. The large-scale textile factories are no exception. For example, at the Hetauda Textile Factory, with 50 percent women in the work force, there were very few women performing supervisory functions and none at all at the managerial level.

The concentration of women in low-paid, unskilled jobs may be attributed to low literacy, low skill levels and also to social bias regarding the appropriateness of employing female workers for certain jobs but not others. As per 1991 census 62 percent of female manufacturing labor force were married and 27 percent literate of which 6 percent had reached secondary education (8-10 classes) and only 4 percent had finished secondary and higher education.

A survey of 66 women engaged in nine industrial establishments located in the Kathmandu Valley indicated that almost 71 percent of women employees in these industries worked because of poverty. Almost 29 percent had no other breadwinners in their household.

About 52 percent of women engaged in such industries were illiterate, about 15 percent had completed school and about 11 percent had college education. About 64 percent were married or widowed and 29 percent were unmarried. More than 60 percent were between 20 and 34 years of age. About 12 percent laborers in 10-14 age group.

Working Conditions

Only scattered information is available on the working conditions in the industrial establishments. According to Basnet, only about 55 percent of women workers had permanent jobs, about 17 percent were temporary employees and 29 percent were casual laborers. Only 20 percent had been promoted to higher levels and about 29 percent believed that they were getting as much pay as male employees. They worked under difficult physical conditions and more than one-third of those interviewed said they had experienced some work related health problems.

Only about 33 percent of them received some facilities additional to wages. Less than one-fifth women laborers (14 percent) were trade union members while 17 percent were aware about trade unions. Other studies on working conditions depict no better situation. Even in the carpet industry, where it is a highly skilled job, women are still treated as unskilled and intensely exploited by the factory owners. Additionally, as international competition in such industries is very keen, wages are kept low.

According to Thacker, the carpet industry in the Kathmandu Valley had 66 percent women workers. Nearly 97.8 percent of these women were piece rate workers while only 14 percent of men were so. These women were overwhelmingly young (below 22 years of age) illiterate and worked for reasons of poverty. Cheating by the employers on payments of salary and wages was rampant. Women benefited little from industries, as men progressively took the mechanized jobs.

Women in the Tourism and Related Sectors

Women are believed to be engaged in large numbers in tourism (hotels, airlines and travel agencies) and other tourist related services such as restaurants, carpets and handicrafts manufacturing. As per the sectoral composition of labor force, after agriculture, commerce manufacturing and personal and community services have substantial proportion of female employees.

But very little information is available on women in tourist sector (hotels, airline travel and trekking agencies) per se. Nepal Rastra Bank study of the tourist sector showed that 20.6 percent of the employees in tourist and related industries were women. Carpet had 66.4 percent female employees. Distribution of female employees as per the level of jobs was more of less even in tourist industry while in the related industries, they were concentrated at basic levels. Relatively few women seemed to be employed in garments, probably because it was overwhelmingly dominated by emigrant labor.

Table 3

Women in Tourism and Related Industries (1988)

Subsector	*Overall*	*Level*		
		Top	*Middle*	*Basic*
Tourist	10.8	10.5	11.2	10.6
Related	48.6	4.6*	2.5*	61.3*
Total	20.6	9.6	10.8	25.2

Self-employment and the Informal Sector Workers

The overwhelming majority of workers are still self-employed or own account workers while less than one percent are employers. The percentage of self-employed workers, which remained more or less constant at about 86 percent between 1971 and 1981, has decreased to 75 percent in 1991. Males mainly account for that decrease. In other words, larger proportions of women are self-employed than men. There is a slow but perceptible change taking place in the employment status of the population.

The proportions of both male and female employees in the populations are increasing while those of the self-employed or unpaid family worker are decreasing. This may signify a positive or negative trend, depending on whether those who move out of the self-employment are getting better jobs or just moving out because of improvements caused by flooding of the market by factory produced goods. The flood of the plastic goods in the market for example, has ruined many traditional craft workers.

Most male and female unpaid family workers are below 20 years of age. The proportion of men and women working as unpaid family workers decreases with increase in age. In the higher age groups the percentage of the male; unpaid family worker is negligible. Furthermore, with an increase in age the percentage of male employers expands. That is also true of female employers although the increase is less significant. It should, however, be noted that most women portrayed as self-employed are actually working as unpaid family workers. Women working in household farms or other house-hold enterprises would not be perceived as unpaid family workers and reported so.

Lesser proportion of women reported unemployed than men and than women revived lower wages than men. Overwhelming majority of those employed are self employed, but proportionately more women are self employed than men and more women work in agriculture than men both in wage and non-wage employment.

Majority of the self-employed and unpaid family workers, both men and women are in agriculture. Nevertheless, there are numerous small, unregistered production entities engaged in the production of variety of products both for home consumption as well as for local sales and a significant proportion of manufacturing in Nepal takes place within the household. Also, the production of a few selected export products such as carpets is widely diffused. Their operations are generally restricted to offfarm hours and hence employment is only parttime. Units are widely scattered, but predominately located in the Hills and Mountains, along with major clusters in urban areas. Very few women are able to earn more than rupees 2,000 per month from such activities, even from fulltime employment.

Women Entrepreneurs

Since the social milieu restricts women's role within the household they are mostly involved in home base industries such as, food processing, garments hosiery and crafts. However, these industries are either progressively dying due to competition from imported products or being replaced by organized formal units. On the one hand, the displacement of traditional crafts by light industry is causing the replacement of female workers by male laborers. On the other, women are being converted into wage laborers in such specialized sectors as the carpet industry. Women have been functioning as managers, supervisors, entrepreneurs, and even skilled worker in home based craft enterprises.

As industrial activities become increasingly externalized, however, both male as well as female workers lose control over the production process and become transformed into wage labor. In this process, women are affected more since newly emerging organized industries need not only more capital but also lay stress on more educated and mobile laborers. The managerial class in these industries, which is dominated by the indo-Aryan and westernized conceptions of gender specialization, reinforce their own biases in hiring and firing.

Further a few women who remain proprietors face serve problems of lack of capital, access to institutional credit, lack of access to marketing network, marketing information, appropriate business training and education. Other constraints include limited access to modern management methods and technology; and high cost of production leading to uncompetitive pricing. They also lack self-confidence and risk taking and staying capacity as they have access to very little capital and may face numerous family problems in their enterprise.

Child Labourers

With the resource crunch in households, girl are forced to work earlier than boys. As per 1991 population census, there are about 532,000 economically active children aged 10-14 years. Relatively a much higher proportions of this age group of girl children are economically active (28.0 %) compared to male children (18.1). One study has reclassified the economically inactive children further into those in school and not in school and concluded that those not in school are also economically active. This classification puts boys' and girls' economic activity rates at 25.5 and 49.4 percent respectively. Girls in the poorer households have much heavier workload than boys of the similar age group. Children work mainly in agricultural farms as most of the populations do. But proportionately there are more child laborers in certain industries, e.g., carpets, tea estates, brick factories, stone quarries and the service sectors, particularly hotels, tea shops and restaurants, domestic servants and porters. Young girls are recruited into forced prostitution on a wide scale.

The working conditions in such in duration are often appalling. Poverty, family disruption, parental illiteracy, agrarian relations forcing families into bonded laborers, are some of the major causes of child labor. Legislation against child laborers, though adequate is rarely enforced. Child laborers face long hours of work in unhealthy environment, low wages and hazardous conditions of work. This leads to various diseases among child laborers and denies them educational opportunities. Employers do not devote any resource to improve the situation of child laborers. The girl labor rates surpass the boy labor rates in all 75 districts. For each 100 working boys there are 219 girls in the Hills and 177 girls in the Tarai are working. The gender imbalance ratio is higher in the Western Hill and Mountain regions, than in other parts of the country. The main issue is how to improve the situation of child laborers and increase their access to education and better future opportunities without stopping their sources of income. Many families are too poor to support their own children. Others have abandoned them. A third group of child workers, is orphaned with no relatives to care for them.

Problems of Employment

The Constitution of Nepal guarantees fundamental rights of speech, association and political participation without any discrimination on the bases of sex, ethnicity religion, etc. Economic rights include right to earn, enjoy, own and transact wealth within the laws. The guiding principles embodied in the Constitution make women's equality a priority issue.

Constitutionally women also enjoy equal rights to employment and equal pay for similar jobs. The Labor Act incorporates provisions of job security, minimum wages, clean and healthy working environment, security, and welfare measures, code of conduct and penalties, consultative and cooperative management and labor courts for dispute settlement. Together with the Labor Regulations formulated under the Act, they have some provisions specifically relevant to women.

- 52 days of paid pregnancy leave up to two pregnancies, replaceable in case of death of either of the previous children.
- Crèche facilities equipped with necessary toys and staffed with trained caretaker for babies and children of the women workers, in cases where the factories employ more than 50 women and necessary breast feeding time for women with breast feeding babies. $ Separate toilet facilities for women and men in factories employing more than 50 women.
- Working hours have been fixed at 48 hours per week or 8 hours per day including half-an-hour lunch break. Only 5 hours of continuous work is allowed.
- Overtime work is allowed only for hour hours per day, which must be paid at 1.5 times the regular rate.
- Women and under age children may not be generally employed outside 6 A.M. to 6 P.M. except in cases of special agreements between the management and the workers, and in hotel, travel, tourism and related business. In such cases women must be provided with necessary security.

- Individuals may not generally be required to carry loads larger than their own body weight, except in cases of adult male workers carrying pre packaged loads. An allowable load for girls of 16-18 years of age is 20 kg. Boys in the similar age group may carry 25 kg. Adult men and women may carry 55 kg. and 45 kg. Respectively.
- Government fixes equal minimum wages for agricultural and other sectors.

Thus, politically all rights have been guaranteed to women. But democracy has a severe problem of inclusion. Many of the groups who are socially backward or economically asset-less are unable to compete for their rights in public arena. In the case of women in Nepal, even legally laws apply to men and women in inheritance and ownership of property. Ownership of asset is one of the most important factors governing the distribution of resources in an economy. Lack of equality in inheritance rights, makes women a group disadvantaged in access to all productive assets.

Even legally marriage becomes the overwhelming factor in determining all her life options. This is reinforced by all round social norms and legal structures, every thing else is secondary to marriage. Single women even with many children are not given land in resettlement areas, even if such households may be among the poorest of the poor. They may not claim any tenancy rights. Although many husbands may keep property in the name of wives, such women may not make any transaction in the property without the consent of her husbands and the sons, etc. This limitation is only partially applied to husbands and the sons. Households get access to community resources such as forests through household heads, which are usually men, women may have the derived user rights as long as her husband does not probability event in an average woman's life, she looses all access to community property as well. Such processes are hard to capture by data, since no data are collected on such aspects.

For the analysis of division of labor within the household, access and control over household resources, mobility and male control over her sexuality, communities in Nepal were classified between two broad groups, Tibeto-Burman and Indo-Aryan by Acharya and Bennett. This classification is stall valid for intra-household analysis as illustrated by the recent ICIMOD publication of eleven case studies from different parts of the region, covering eight countries in the Hindu-Kush-Himalayas. However, when it comes to access and control over the public resources and public decision making processes, women in all communities face various levels of discrimination. Control over property and land is universally patriarchal in Nepal. Moreover because of the gendered nature of the modernization process itself, which is permeated by the capitalist, individualistic western value systems, gendered education system and gendered technology, women in all communities loose out in comparison to men. Such modernization process reinforces the discrimination against women in the gendered societies. In other less gendered societies, the modernization forces introduce gender discrimination by selective intervention in favor of men. How this happens is extensively recorded by now and needs no elaboration here.

On the positive side the modernization process could:

- Free women from the ardor's tasks of collecting fuel and fodder;
- Give a choice in her fertility decisions;
- Lighten her work burden by introduction of technology;
- Increase her mobility due to development of transportation; and $ Open up new opportunities of employment.

On the other hand the elements in the modernization process which reintroduce or reinforce gender bias include:

- Dichotomization of production and reproduction;
- Marketization and globalization of the production process;
- Male oriented technology;
- Gendered education system both in terms of access and the genders value systems;
- Privatization or public resources along the patriarchal lines;
- Gender institutions, both in terms of structures and value systems;
- Replacement of values of sacrifice and collective good by individual greed and consumerism; and

- Increased physical insecurity for women girls on account of commoditification of human body.

Recent economic policy initiatives in Nepal have focused on commercialization and liberalization of the economy, market friendly deregulation, development of infrastructure to facilitate foreign and local investment, downsizing of the government and privatization. The real sector liberalization has included all sectors, agriculture, forestry, the industrial and the financial sectors.

The GDP growth rate accelerated to about 5 percent annual on the average until early nineties. The share of agriculture in the GDP is declining perceptibly. Its contribution to GDP has come down by more than 10 percentage points between 1980/81 and 1998/1999. The role of manufacturing, trade, restaurants, hotels and constructions increasing proportionately.

The recorded manufacturing output has increased and its institutional structure is estimated to be changing substantially from home and village cottage industry based to factory based. Commercialization of agriculture is felt to be increasing slowly. Vegetable and fruit production, which is primarily for sale, has increased substantially, their production index going from 100 in 1984/85 to 168. in 1998/1999 the index had reached a height of 198.

The proportion of urban population increased by almost 50-percentage point in the eighties, from 6 percent in 1981 to 9 percent in 1991. With the construction of new roads, new townships are growing day by day and the process of urbanization is expected to continue.

There are some distinct indicators of decline of the household economy and increased commercialization in terms of income. The proportion of non-agricultural sector contribution to household income and the proportion of cash in the wage/salary income have increased substantially between 1984/85 and 1995/96. The proportion of non-agricultural enterprise contribution to the household income has almost doubled during the period under review.

How have these structural changes in the economy impacted on the employment opportunities and workload of the women in Nepal? Another fundamental problem is non-recognition of women's contributions to GDP economically and consequent devaluation of their social labor.

Changing Structure of Employment

Occupational structure is an indicator of employment opportunities, both for men and women. The 1996 NLSS has collected has been defined as primary if he/ she had devoted the most hours of work in the preceding twelve months to this activity. In case equal hours are allocated to two activities, the first activity has been taken as the primary one.

The increasing proportion of non-agricultural sector in the GDP should have expanded opportunities for non-agricultural employment, both for men and women. As per the census counts the number of women employed in the non-agricultural sectors had gone up from 64 thousand in 1981 to 249 thousand in 1991. Women's employment had increased significantly in personal and community services, in commerce and manufacturing, although relatively they were still concentrated in agriculture. But, a comparison of occupational distribution of the population, in the 1984/85 MPHBS and the 1995/96 NLSS, shows slightly higher concentration of both men and women in agriculture in the later year. Overall, the occupational employment pattern displays little change, either for men or women. Within the non-agricultural sector, particular declines are noticeable in the proportion of both men and women employed as ordinary labor and female workers in the category of production workers, that is, women working as skilled and semi-skilled labor in the manufacturing sector. What is surprising is the overall decline in the combined role of manufacturing and construction transport/communications sectors as employment generators in urban area as indicated by a decline in percentages of both men and women workers employed as production workers.

Table 1 summarizes the occupational information by urban/rural regions of the country. Most of the categories are self-explanatory and follow ILO standards. For example, the category of professional/ technical workers includes primary school teachers to professors in the universities, from doctors to assistant midwives in the health sector, etc. Service sector workers include cooks, domestic servants, barbers, caretakers as well as working proprietors engaged in sectoral work. The definition of the category of production workers includes workers with some skill in the manufacturing, construction, transport and the communication sectors.

Compared to urban Tarai, urban Hills indicate a much faster expansion of non-agricultural work opportunities for women. Employment opportunities for women seem to have almost doubled in the group of professional and technical category in the hills. Service sector opportunities have also expanded significantly. A declining trend is observed in the proportion employed in agriculture, as expected in the urban hills the role of production as an employment generator has increased for women as against a substantially declining trend observed in the case of men. In the Tarai even urban areas show increased concentration of women in agriculture and decreased proportion in production.

Table 4
Percent of Ten Years and Above Economically Active Men and Women in Selected Sectors of Employment (Primary only)

Sectors	*Male*		*Female*	
	MPHBS 1984/85	*NLSS 1995/96*	*MPHBS 1985/85*	*NLSS 1995/96*
Professional & Technical/ **Administration (All Nepal)**	**3.1**	**2.7**	**0.4**	**0.7**
Urban	7.9	9.9	3.2	7.7
Hill	11.1	10.7	3.5	6.9
Tarai	4.9	9.0	2.8	8.8
Rural	2.7	2.3	0.2	0.5
Mountain	3.5	1.3	0.1	0.4
Hill	2.9	2.7	0.4	0.4
Tarai	2.2	1.9	0.2	0.6
Clerical Workers (All Nepal)	**3.0**	**2.8**	**0.3**	**0.2**
Urban	13.8	17.9	3.0	4.9
Hill	17.4	21.6	3.6	6.7
Tarai	10.4	13.7	2.2	2.4
Rural	2.2	1.8	0.14	0.1
Mountain	2.3	0.9	0.0	0.2
Hill	3.7	2.5	0.1	0.1
Tarai	1.2	1.4	0.1	0.1

Agriculture and Forestry (All)	**72.9**	**78.9**	**86.1**	**93.7**
Urban	23.5	22.2	54.6	49.3
Hill	19.2	15.2	51.5	39.7
Tarai	27.6	30.2	58.9	62.1
Rural	76.6	82.8	88.3	95.3
Mountain	77.4	88.8	91.0	96.8
Hill	65.7	82.0	68.6	95.4
Tarai	81.1	82.4	89.0	94.9
Production (All)	**6.1**	**5.7**	**2.9**	**1.7**
Urban	20.2	18.4	9.5	9.8
Hill	19.6	13.5	12.3	14.9
Tarai	20.8	23.8	5.8	3.0
Rural	5.2	5.8	2.5	1.7
Mountain	3.6	4.9	1.4	0.6
Hill	7.6	5.1	3.2	1.7
Tarai	4.0	4.7	2.1	0.8
Sales (All Nepal)	**4.4**	**5.0**	**2.4**	**2.6**
Urban	16.0	20.4	8.4	18.0
Hill	15.4	24.0	8.8	18.7
Tarai	16.4	16.4	7.8	17.1
Rural	3.5	3.9	1.9	2.0
Mountain	2.0	0.9	0.7	0.2
Hill	3.9	3.5	1.9	1.8
Tarai	3.8	4.8	2.6	2.5
Services (All Nepal)	**2.8**	**1.9**	**1.3**	**0.8**
Urban	8.1	6.5	8.9	9.5
Hill	7.8	9.4	8.8	11.5
Tarai	8.4	3.2	9.0	6.7
Rural	2.3	1.6	0.7	0.5
Mountain	2.2	0.4	0.6	0.2
Hill	1.6	1.4	0.6	0.5
Tarai	2.8	1.9	0.9	0.5

In the rural areas, a positive trend is noted only in the slight increases observed in proportions of women employed as professional and technical workers in the Mountains. In the rural Hills, no change is observed in this respect. The proportion of population engaged in agriculture is increasing, both for men and women and in rural areas of all ecological regions. But this shift is more prominent for women than for men.

Given limited land resources, this may be construed only as a fallback strategy rather than as a conscious shift. The proportion of working women engaged as production workers has declined in all ecological regions. As a source of employment for rural women, even the trade and service sectors indicate declining trend. Thus, decline is observed in proportion of women and men employed in the category of production workers in general, with few exceptions.

This decline is larger for women (42 per cent) than for men (7 per cent). The trend may be attributed to the fact that the indigenous local cottage and household level manufacturing sector is disappearing due to the onslaught of mass produced goods, such as plastic products, aluminum utensils, textiles, ropes, even matting and furniture especially in rural areas. The service castes as a group are out of job on an extensive scale.

The increasing mountain tourism and trekking business do not seem to have compensated for the decline in local demand for such products in the rural areas of hills and mountains. Nor have services (including tourism) and trade been able to compensate for the declining role of manufacturing as a source of employment in rural areas. Rural Tarai also shows a proportionately declining trend of non-agricultural employment opportunities for women in general. The only exception is visible in the expanding of professional and technical workers.

Compared to 1984/85, a larger proportion of women are now employed in trading and as professional and technical workers, particularly in urban areas. But they are concentrated at lower echelons of power. For example, the increase in proportion employed as professional and technical workers is accounted for largely for lower. Compared to 1991 census, the 1996 NLSS indicates an increase in the proportion of women in all occupational groups, except among production and other workers. As per the NLSS, women now constitute 53 per cent of the agricultural labor force, 33 per cent among sales workers and 29 per cent among the service sector workers. The proportion of women among the production workers, however, shows a declining trend. All manufacturing and construction transportation/communication industries are included in this group and these are expanding sectors of the economy as evident from the structure of the GDP. But employment opportunities in this sector for both men and women seem to be declining more so for women than for men.

Trade and services are predominantly informal and often complement agriculture as a fallback strategy. Without a detailed analysis of these activities it is not possible to say whether the women's employment pattern is changing towards a positive or negative direction trend for women, as they own very little land and also because the productivity of labor in agriculture is relatively low. Overall, in 1995/96 women constituted about 49 per cent of the employed population.

Employment Status

As per the census figures, the overwhelming majority of workers are still self-employed, as account workers while less than one per cent are employers. But the percentage of self-employed workers, which remained more or less constant at about 86 per cent between 1971 and 1981, has decreased to 75 per cent in 1991.

In contrast to the increasing role of wage employment in the economy, as indicated by census trends, a comparison of the NLSS information with the 1984/1985 MPHBS one sees that the proportion of self-employed workers in the total employment is increasing during this period both for men and women. This may indicate decreasing wage employment opportunities greater self-employment opportunities or just a definitional problem.

In the rural hills women's concentration in self-employment has actually increased. Urban hills and mountains do show slightly decreased concentration in self-employment. This trend is true for the men as well.

With the decline of the role of the household as an organization of production, industrial activities become increasingly externalized and both male as well as female workers lose control over the production process as self-employed and become transformed into wage laborers. In this process women are affected more, since newly emerging organized industries need not only more capital but also lay stress on more educated and mobile laborers. In Nepal, the managerial class in these industries, which is dominated by the Indo-Aryan and westernized conceptions of gender specialization, reinforces its own biases in hiring and firing.

Wage Employment and Earnings

Most of the women are concentrated in agriculture, both as wage workers and self employed. Among the agricultural workers, almost 13 percent (out of the total 93 percent) are wage employees. They earn about 4/5 of what about men earn as wages. Only about seven per cent of the female population, as against 27 per cent men, is employed in the non-agricultural sector. Of this, wage employment constitutes a meager 2.6 per cent for women and 16.4 per cent for men, the rest are self-employed.

The NLSS data indicates some different in the pattern of wage/salary employment of male and female workers. Structurally, a larger proportion of working women is in the category of professional and technical workers and in the service sector, than men. However, both are primary manufacturing laborers. Within manufacturing, women are concentrated among spinners, weavers and tailors.

As compared to men, a smaller proportion of women is employed as ordinary laborers in the non-agricultural sector. This is quite in conformity to the tradition of hesitating to send one's own woman for employment as ordinary labor is socially degrading for a household. Urban/rural, or ecological, regions make no difference in the fact that the largest proportion of employed women outside agriculture work as production workers.

As for the women in each of the occupational groups; services and professional/technical worker groups top the list, in all areas except for the rural Mountains where the largest proportion of female workers are among clerical workers. Overall, women constitute 11.8 per cent of the total non-agricultural labor force.

Women, in Nepal, devote 6-7 hours per day to wage outside of agriculture. Generally they work lesser hours per day than men do in such activities. But women production workers work almost as many hours per day as men do.

Overall, women earn 12 per cent less than what men earn

as daily wages in the non-agricultural sector. In the total salary and wages, however, they earn about 97 per cent of what men earn.In a regional perspective, only the urban Tarai women seem to devote less than six hours per day to non-agricultural activities. This could be due to a lack of socially acceptable jobs for women in the Tarai areas. The Tarai women also work few days per year.

Considering only average daily wages, contrary to expectations, earning of women in rural areas are higher than in urban areas. Only the more competitive labor market in urban areas due to immigrant labor may explain this. In the total of wages and salaries, women in the Tarai and Mountains seem to earn almost 20 per cent less than the Hill women. Due to the price factor, which is much higher in the Hills and Mountain areas, wages are generally higher there. In this case, mountain women are disadvantage both because of the wage differential and the factor.

Ethnicity and Caste Factor in the Structure of Economic Activities

The studies in the series on Status of Women in Nepal concluded that in Nepal ethnicity/caste played an important role in the economic activity pattern of Nepalese women. The sample population in the above study, were classified in two broad ethnic groups - the Indo-Aryan and the Tibeto-Burman. From a comparison of their economic activity patterns, it was concluded that women from the Tibeto-Burman group tended to be more enterprising and more involved in economic activities in the market than those from the Indo-Aryan group. Those conclusions were derived from an analysis of 280 households, from eight villages from different parts of the country. The NLSS provides a larger data set, which is analyzed below by ethnicity/caste. Nevertheless, there is a large number of missing records on ethnicity/caste in the NLSS data set. The following analysis should be read with this limitation in mind.

On the basis of primary data on occupational distribution nine ethnic/ caste groups including others, were formed for further analysis. The category of others includes those not classified elsewhere and has been left out in further analysis. The grouping was necessary to expand the sample size in each of the occupational sub-groups for a meaningful analysis. In the current analysis, this tradition is broken because from the primary processing, Rais seem to be much more advanced occupationally and closer to Gurungs than Limbus.

Outside of agriculture, a majority of Newar, Gurung / Rai and Yadav/ Ahir women worked as production workers. Muslim women were concentrated among ordinary labor and almost half of Tharu women were concentrated in the service sector.

For Brahmin/Chhetri, Yadav/Ahir and Gurung/ Rai professional/ technical/ administrative/ managerial professions provided bigger job openings. Damai/Kami/Sarki women were almost evenly spread among professional/ technical/managerial/ administrative/ managerial administrative, agriculture/forestry, production and ordinary labor group.

Male/female composition of occupational groups by ethnicity/caste seems too erratic to lead to any firm conclusions . Only a few remarks can be made. Trading seems to be predominantly a female business among the Gurung/Rai. Women constitute the larger half among the service worker within the Tharu, Tamanag/Mager/Limbu and Damai/Kami/ Sarki groups/ The agricultural labor force has more that 50 percent women in all ethnicity/caste, except among the Yadav/Ahirs. Men predominate in all other occupational groups. Nevertheless, Gurung/Rai women constitute nearly 48 percent in the professional/technical/ managerial/ administrative professional group within this community.

Current findings partially support the thesis that women from the Tibeto-Burman group will be more attracted to outside income earning opportunities as services and trading sectors seem to be predominated by women among the Tamag/Magar/Limbu and Gurung /Rai respectively. The data on composition of the overall occupational groups on the other hand do not support this thesis, as proportions of women in the overall employed population of their respective groups are highest for Brahmin/Chhetris and Muslims. Other factors such as opportunities in the case of Brahnmin/ Chhetri, and poverty in the case of Muslims, may be playing more important roles in this respect.

As for employment status, both men and women

irrespective of ethnicity/caste are concentrated in self-employment, but proportionately more women than men are concentrated in such employment in all ethnicity/caste groups. This concentration, however, is lower for the service caste group, Damai/Kami/Sarki, both for men and women. Agriculture predominates as a source of self-employment both for men and women. Once again, proportionately, the degree of concentration of self-employed women in agriculture is more than that for men in all ethnicity/caste groups. Compared to the higher castes, a much larger proportion of lower caste women such as Sarki, Damai, Kami and Muslim are in wage employment, as expected. Next to them nearly an equal proportion of employed Yadav/Ahir women are engaged in wage work. Thus, a larger proportion of women form the Tarai are represented in wage employment than form other areas which may be explained by greater opportunities for wage employment in these areas or a higher level of poverty among the households of these caste/ religion groups.

Women's Entrepreneurial Activities

Most female-headed enterprises belonged to trade/hotels/ restaurants and manufacturing sectors. However, enterprises operated by the lower caste belonged primarily to the manufacturing sector, More than 66 percent of the enterprises operated by the disadvantaged ethnic Tamang/ Magar/Limbu groups and 54 percent of Newar enterprises also belonged to this sector. Thus, it seems that the more advanced of the ethnic groups, the Gurung/ Rai, and the "high caste" Brahmin/ Chhetri groups are primarily in trade and services.

Access to institutional credit is much more limited for enterprises run by female headed households (FHEs) than that for household enterprises headed by men (MHEs). In total, about 17 percent of the MHEs and 10 percent of the FHEs had borrowed. While male-headed enterprises from all ethnicity/ caste, except Gurung/ Rai, had borrowed some money from banks and financial institutions few female enterprises had borrowed from such sources. Women who borrowed from such sources were from the Brahmin/Chhetri households. Yet, only 5.3 percent Brahmin/Chhetri female entrepreneurs had borrowed from the bank and financial institutions. Male enterprises access to institutional credit ranged from nearly 48 percent in the case of the Newar group to 20 percent in the case of Tamang/Magar/Limbu groups. Overall, FHEs earn 2/3 of what MHEs earn. Female enterprises make much less in most ethnicity/caste groups. Education, training, capitals and credit are crucial factors in prompting women's non-agricultural activities. Women in educationally disadvantaged groups are usually unable to take advantage of the new employment and business openings. Low service castes have very little access to education. But within groups, women have less access to education than men do.

A large proportion of women's contributions to GDP and household maintenance activities are still not recognized in economic calculations. This makes women's labor contribution to social reproductions process and women themselves invisible in economics except as consumers. This issue has been raised by women activist world over since 1975 and some improvements are visible in economic definitions and concepts at the international level. Accordingly some improvements are being made in Nepal also. The Ninth Five-Year plan has recognized this problem of women's invisibility explicitly and promised to make amend the measurement methods as per international standards. Accordingly specific efforts are being made to expand the concept of economic activities in the forthcoming census.

United Nation's new manual on the system of national accounts makes a distinction between the general production boundary and the SNA production boundary .The general production boundary encompasses all production of goods and services as per the third person criteria. Only those activities, which can not be effectively performed by others for person are beyond the general production boundary.

The SNA production boundary, on the other hand, is limited to include production of goods and services for the market and production of goods for its own use by households. Services which includes all household maintenance activities including cooking and childcare are still out of SNA except when performed by paid domestic hands.

Market Production

The market production as defined in SNA comprises of all goods and services transacted in the market regardless of the institutional unit producing them. Therefore, the issue of whether the goods are produced in the formal or informal sector has very little relevance for GDP calculations.

It is more an issue of labor statistics. Many products generated by the informal sector activities may already be in the GDP, so far as they belong to the export sector (e.g. carpets, handicrafts) or are ancillary to the larger formal production units. The only issue here is the invisibility of female worker and not of the products themselves. Non-market production includes goods produced and consumed at home, non-financial corporations own use production and goods supplied by the government free or at non-significant prices. Production and processing of primary products for own use, production of other goods for own use and production of fixed assets for own use - all such activities, although facing numerous measurement problems, are conceptually within the current SNA boundary. Earlier, such product has lesser reflection in GDP. GDP also includes the imputed value of home ownership and goods produced and consumed in kind. Rest of the activities classified as services are beyond the current SNA boundary.

From the perspective of developing countries and gender, the new system is a definite improvement over the earlier ones as defined by the 1968 Manual. Many of the activities, previously classified of market and outside the National Accounting System, particularly processing of market goods for self consumption and water collection have been classified as productive. All production of goods in households, whether for market or consumption is now theoretically within the SNA.

Nevertheless invisibility of women in GDP calculations still remains as many of the activities and production thereof, which are classified as services, such as cooking care of the sick, the old and the children and the households, maintenance to presented to illustrate the problem and the amendments proposed so far.

In Nepal, presently the Central Bureau of Statistics (CBS) publishes estimates of GDP at current and constant prices annually by the International Standard Industrial Classification (ISIC). On the whole the estimates are based on the industry approach. No statistics are complied institutionally. Acharya analyzing the SNA of Nepal identifies the following items as most likely to be missed in such accounts.

- Small scale fodder collection and fetching water;.150 Gender and Democracy in Nepal
- Hunting and gathering for household consumption;
- Food processing for household consumption;
- Processing of primary and market goods for household consumption, e.g. weaving clothes, tailoring, knitting garments for household consumption;
- Domestic services by domestic servants;
- Rural tea/sweet shops, alcohol stops, overnight stops etc.; and Porter services supplied individually or by the informal-sector.

Contribution to the Social Production Process

An exploratory study was conducted by IIDS in 1994 to construct an accounting system including a satellite account on value added from household maintenance activities. This exercise was carried out for 1991, because of availability of Census data of 1991. Table 4 is subdivided in three parts. The second part of the table presents an estimate of the magnitude of production, which theoretically should but has most probably been not accounted for in the Nepalese GDP. This part amounts to 52 billion rupees, which is 45 percent of the official GDP of Rs. 116 billion in the year 1991. About 58 percent of those 52 billion rupees are attributable to female work. The third box is an estimate of the monetary value of household maintenance activities, which are outside the 1993 SNA production boundary. Women contribute almost 93 percent of such production.

The results obtained show that women contribute to family maintenance much more than usually perceived. Although the above statistics are presented only as methodological examples only, they do illustrate the magnitude underestimation of women's work and contributions to human well being.

The scheme described above serves several purposes simultaneously. It reflects human activities to a fuller extent than conventionally reflected in SNA and shows relative contributions of men and women to national production process and human welfare. Of particular interest for the developing countries, is the second box, which tries to capture that part of the production, which is theoretically within the SNA production boundary, but in practice may be excluded from GDP calculations in many countries.

Most important example of such activities could be food processing for self-consumption. Even by 1968 definition of SNA, processing of primary products was supposed to be included in SNA But whether it is actually included in practice needs to be examined on country by country basis. Value added from the processing of purchased goods for self-consumption and water collection has been outside the SNA, even theoretically until 1993. Further, historical records constructed according to this scheme would facilitate an understanding of the dynamics of market non-market interactions and its impact on various sections of the populations. Democracy is a necessary and not sufficient condition for making progress towards gender equality, given the initial situation of unequal and in-egalitarian social structures and gender relations. The modernization process some times reinforces gender subordination.

At other times new elements of discrimination are introduced in relatively egalitarian communities. The modernization process and the liberalization policies followed after the democratic changes in the country have provided some non-traditional employment opportunities to women, particularly in the carpet industries and the textile sector in general. But comparative to men their concentration in agriculture has increased.

As a result of interaction of complex social and economic processes, women in Nepal face several disadvantages in the economic field. Besides their limited access to productive assets - the land and property, credit and modern avenues of knowledge and information, other major economic issues include their uneven access to new avenues of employment and concentration of women in low productivity agriculture.

This has led to high and increasing work burden without concomitant increase in access to resources. Child labor, women's concentration at lower level jobs, poor working conditions and lack of child care facilities at work places are additional problems related to their formal sector employment. The trade union's generally neglect of women's problems. Women also face risk to personal security and sexual harassment in the formal sector. Progressive loss of proprietorship in the informal sector employment and generally lower level returns on their enterprise are women's additional problems. Women entrepreneurs face special problems of resource scarcity, marketing access, low level of technology and have low risk taking capacity. A problem to be noted is also the declining economic activity rates of urban women probably signaling the "domestication of women"

Despite of HMG's declared objectives of integrating women in development since Sixth Plan, a diaspora of micro-credit and small training programs for women, Proportion of non-agricultural employment opportunities for women and men is decreasing in the country. Agriculture is getting increasingly feminized. Women, in 1995/96, formed 53 percent of the agricultural labor force compared to 36 percent in 1981.

Individual examples of successes of women's income earning and forestry groups may abound. But such programs have not been able either to make dent in the traditional in-egalitarian socio-economic structures or to reverse the process of marginalization of women from social production, which is a special feature of advanced capitalism.

Wage Employment

The trends on wage employment opportunities are not clear. While the census information indicates an expanding trend in wage employment opportunities both in and outside agriculture, MPHBS and NLSS comparisons indicate a reverse trend. Relatively more women are concentrated in self-employment in comparison to men. Women wage-workers are concentrated more in agricultural than in non-agricultural jobs. Men wage earners are spread more evenly between agricultural and non-agricultural employment.

Village craftsmen/women are out of jobs on a large scale. The proportion of production workers has declined substantially in rural areas between the two surveys. This decline has been sharper for women. With very few alternative employment opportunities women are falling back to agriculture or forced to earn livings by unwanted activities such as commercial sex work.

Overall women earn about 4/5th of what men earn in agriculture but 3/4th outside of agriculture as daily wages. What annual payments are included in daily average earning these ratios go up slightly. Generally women have much less access to institutional credit, both at individual and household enterprise levels, irrespective of ecological regions, urban/rural areas are ethnicity/caste. However, Brahmin/Chhetri and Newar women have greater access to credit compared to women in other caste/ ethnicity. Women from low caste and disadvantaged ethnicity have no access to institutional credit at all. Women's access to credit is limited because both formal and informal credit institutions are geared to funding property owners.

All formal credit institutions seek tangible collateral for loan and women are effectively sidelined from institutional credit since women have little access to inherited property. The village moneylenders are also interested more in earning high interest or acquiring the debtor's property rather than financing.

Although using 1991 Agricultural Credit Survey data Sharma, found no significant difference in the poverty incidence between male headed (MHH) and female headed (FHH) households (50.7 percent vs. 47.2 percent), the employment and earnings scenario described above may have changed the situation in favor of men. Further, Agricultural Credit Survey data related only to rural areas, but gender inequality in employment and earnings opportunities may be reflected more in urban/rural differences and women's concentration in subsistence agriculture rather than in income differences in rural areas per se.

The process of dichotomization of production and reproduction must be stopped. This could happen in two ways. First women's access to better quality jobs in the organized production sectors could be facilitated by improving their access to education and improving their mobility by provision of easier transport facilities.

Secondly, assistance in their reproductive responsibilities by work sharing and introduction of simple technologies at home and provision of childcare facilities at the work place in the modernized sector would improve greatly their access to Jobs. In the context of mountain and hill areas road accessibility seems to be the most important factor for increasing women's mobility and access to education and health facilities.

Although some poor women may lose porter's work, transportation facilities are important to improve returns to women's enterprises. Otherwise benefits of productivity and income gains tend to be monopolized by the middlemen.

It is well recorded by now that introduction of cash crops or market oriented dairy in the already dichotomized communities tend to marginalize women, increase their work load and reduce their control over household resources. Proper attention needs to be paid to such side effects in project designs and appropriate measures incorporated in the projects themselves to take care of such unintended effects.

Policy packages must differ as per the cultural groups. In Indo-Aryan groups with already entrenched patriarchal value systems, the policy packages must address the systematic gender discriminations, while for the Tibeto-Burman groups the policy packages must be culture sensitive and designed with care not to introduce gender bias in employment or social behavior in general. Decentralization of decision making and people's participation in the real sense is a must in both cases.

A well designed program of enterprise development seems to have had a positive effect on women's status, both in the Indo-Aryan and the Tibeto-Burman groups in as indicated by the Dhampus case under the Annapurmna Conservation Area Project in Nepal. From the Dhampus study, three conclusions seem to be relevant:

a) Women's workload has declined in general and women's social status has improved both in the Gurung and Brahmin/Chhetri communities, both in the private and public arena.
b) Gurung women have benefited most.
c) Social differentiation is clearly visible; the low caste and the poor Brahmin/Chhetri women/men have benefited the least. The conclusion that the life-styles of the poor have remained more or less the same in-spite of the general prosperity of the area and expand job

opportunities is most telling. As such development programs must also be poverty-sensitive to reduce poverty.

Economic Opportunities

Women's economic opportunities can be increased on a large scale only through mainstreaming the gender perspective within sectoral programs. This is because development policies and programs impact on a large scale and cannot be reversed with small-scale individual project interventions. Individual projects should be promoted as catalysts, but they cannot solve the problem in a holistic manner. Acharya, analyzing Nepal's case summarizes the emerging gender issues at the sectoral level as follows:

a) ensuring adequate analysis of all programs and projects with a gender perspective;
b) gender sensitization of the implementation mechanism and machinery;
c) ensuring adequacy of measures initiated to ensure gender equity in project benefits; and
d) development of indicators and mechanisms, for a continuous monitoring and evaluation of policy, programs and project impact on women. This evaluation must be carried out in terms of not only their participation but their empowerment as well. In the current paper's perspective we may rewrite the points to incorporate ecology, ethnicity/caste and poverty sensitivity to sectoral programs. Land rights and other facilities in project resettlement of families should be given serious consideration in those areas where such rights do not exit.

Any assistance to resettled families and small businesses should include women on an equal basis.As far as measurement of women's contributions to GDP and economic welfare of the society goes Nepal is moving slowly to international standards. Efforts should be made to reflect the second part of the GDP scheme discussed above more fully.

Plans and Programs

At the National level, the government policies have tried to women's problems in various ways. The government had emphasized women's involvement in all programs and projects, recognized legal impediment to their economic empowerment and enunciated special programs for meeting their needs already in the Sixth Five year Plan (1981-1985). The Seventh Plan expanded on these themes.

The Eighth Five year Plan, declared, "the Government is committed to equal and meaningful participation of women in development." Nevertheless, at the program level there was no difference in the three plans. All three plans, with slight variations in emphasis, focused on smallscale income generation, education and training, and MCH and family planning programs for women. Required legal reforms were to be implemented to facilitate women's participation in development.

The Eighth Plan, in particular, mentioned about increasing women's representation at decision making levels in the government, non government and semi government sectors and a monitoring system for recording gender discrimination at work. A suitable organizational structure for coordination and monitoring of activities relating to women was also envisaged.

It has been a learning process as elsewhere with few achievements and numerous problems. In the Eighth Plan the focus was on mainstreaming. A number of positive developments have taken place during the last 25 years since 1980. Notable achievements include:

- Establishment of number of institutions, including a MWSW, a division in NPC, and WDD in MLD.
- Increase in women's participation in sectoral programs, such as farmer training's, forestry groups and skill training's to 16-20 percent.
- Initiation of specific programs for women which include ! Large, national level credit programs such as PCRW, WDP/SFDP, five regional banks and MCPW.
- Educational programs such as special provisions for female teachers, scholarships for girls, etc.
- Setting concrete targets for reduction of MMR.
- Extension of health facilities to increase the access of women and children to primary health care, expanding IEC programs for nutrition, health and sanitation

information and conducting immunization, nutrition supplement and vitamin "A" supplement programs.

– A comprehensive bill making women's right to property a little more secure and strengthening punitive measures against violence is pending in the Parliament.

The experience dealing with women's issues in the past two decades indicate that exclusive focus on women as an analytical category and efforts to cater to their practical needs for food, shelter, basic education and primary health are not sufficient for building an equal opportunity society for women and men. Moreover, in the absence of necessary structural and attitudinal changes, the prospects of her extensive involvement in programs and projects itself becomes constrained. This will effect the efficiency aspect as well.

From a review of developmental efforts in Nepal, Acharya writes, "Nepal has reached a stage on women's issues where the implementation aspects are most crucial. Right policy enunciation has been made at the macro level, but there are no mechanisms to implement them either at the macro, mesa or micro levels.

Women have gained somewhat in terms of educational and health status and political awareness, but gender difference in thermos of access to resources and positions of power have changes little, inspire of much rhetoric. Attitudinal changes required for effective implementation of policies and programs ion women have been rather slow to materialize . . .

The social attitude towards women has not changed much either. The family is still seen as the primary responsibility of women and good marriage and mother hood as the "ultimate goals" for them. This has effected various educational development and credit programs adversely.

Girls are withdrawn from schools and skill development programs, before they complete the courses because they have to be married off, credit can not be granted to the unmarried women because they shift their residence on marriage, they must start motherhood early because otherwise they will be stigmatized socially, they must start motherhood early because otherwise they will be stigmatized socially, they must bear constant domestic violence because that is the only shelter they have, etc."

Development Plans on Women

The Sixth Five Year Plan (1980/81-1984/85)

1. Attempt to involve women directly in agricultural training because overwhelming majority of women were involved in agriculture.
2. To encourage women in cottage and small industrial activities by providing them training, capital and marketing facilities because of extensive unemployment during agricultural off-seasons and carry out programs to raise women is income opportunities and status.
3. To involve women in population control activities so as to increase efficiency of population programs.
4. To increase the role of women in formal and informal education as also trainings on health and nutrition education.
5. To provide increased employment opportunities to educated women so as to make better use of their knowledge and skill.
6. To reform laws and regulations which inhibit women's participation in development.

The Seventh Five Year Plan (1985-1989/90)

1. To enable women to participate activity in the development process by providing appropriate opportunities, to foster self-reliance among women by increasing their productive capacity and to raise their social and economic status by this all round development.
2. There will be additional programs in agriculture for women in the field of agricultural extension. Quotas will be fixed in various training programs.
3. Training on basic health needs and maternal and child care programs will be conducted.
4. Literacy among women will be increased in the education sector quotas and special incentives will be used to increase female participation in education and various training programs
5. More emphasis will be given to development of cottage industries for providing work for women during the off-agricultural seasons. Special provision will be made for women in the provision of training facilities, credit and

other resources. Marketing facilities will also be developed.

6. Women will be encouraged to get involved in forest protection and preservation.
7. Facilities will be provided for participation in government and nongovernment organizations.
8. Nepal women's Organization will be facilitated to conduct development activities for women.
9. Legal reforms will be effected move provisions hindering women's participation in national development.

The Eighth Five (1992/93-1996/97)

1. The Government is committed to equal and meaningful participation of women in development process.
2. Programs designed to enhance women's participation will be included in economic and social sectors (agriculture, forestry, industry, health & education)
3. Policies will also be enunciated to raise employment opportunities for women in these areas.
4. Credit, technical knownhow entrepreneurship training & Market services will be extended.
5. Policies will be adopted to encourage the appointment of women the government, & nongovernment sectors and to provide them opportunities for career development.
6. Laws and by laws which hinder the development of women will be reformed.
7. Information on gender discrimination at work will be monitored and documented.
8. A suitable organizational structure will be formed for coordination and monitoring activities relating to women.

Such constraints have rather been universal. It clearly states that, in spite of much progress in many developing countries in the preceding five decades, everywhere the structure and quality of growth has not been satisfactory. It has been a "jobless, ruthless, rootless, voiceless and featureless growth." It has been very inequitable to women. In the same vein the Beijing Platform Action stated that " most of the goals set out in the Nairobi Forward Looking Strategies for the Advancement of Women have not been achieved.

Barriers to women's empowerment remain despite the efforts of government as well as NGOs and women and men everywhere." Particularly highlighted were: the persistent and increasing burden of poverty of women, inadequacies and inequality in access to education and training, health care and related services, violence against women, unequal access to power and decision making roles, inequalities in economic structures and policies and access to resources, biaseness in the mass media and the communication system and insufficient mechanism at all levels to promote women's interest and advancement.

Consequently, the task set by the United Nations for the fourth decade, is not only to increase women's participation in development par se. But to empower them in such a way that, they can bring about a fundamental change in those socioeconomic structures, institutions and attitudes that reinforce or/and introduce new forms of gender inequities. His Majesty's Government of Nepal has set it self a triple task of mainstreaming, eliminating gender inequality and empowering women and the Ministry of women and Social Welfare has prepared a detailed Action Plan for implementing the Beijing Platform for Action.

Specific Problems in Nepal among other things include:

- gender insensitivity of the sectoral and project implementing agencies in general;
- lack of capacity for planning and gender analysis in WID institution in general;
- general insensitivity of major training programs to gender issues;
- insufficient efforts to include women's representation decision making roles; and complete lack interest in women's programs at the district level and absence of a coordinating mechanism, complete lack of a monitoring and evaluation mechanism.

Conceptually, Nepal has taken note of these limitations and committed itself to the following plan of action in UN's Fourth World Conference on Women in Beijing.

- To revitalize women as integral rather than sectoral begins following a life cycle approach and redesign "mainstreaming" programs with this perceptive in sight.
- Reform of laws discriminatory to women, particularly relating to ancestral property and violence against

women, strengthen the law enforcement agencies for implementation of laws against violence and legal as well as rehabilitation assistance to victims of violence.

- To incorporate women's needs and concerns in poverty alleviation programs.
- To broaden the coverage of primary health care facilities, to reduce iodine deficiency, anemia and maternal mortality to half the current rates and to provide immunization coverage to 90 percent by the year 2000.
- To achieve universal literacy within the year 2000, and to increase women's access to technical schools and short term training through scholarship and quotas for female students.
- To institute within one-year regulations and mechanisms to screen and audit all programs and projects from women's perspective and to facility entry and career prospect for women at all levels of government institutions.
- To encourage and assist NGO's to work with community based organization for advocacy, institution building and delivery of services to women.

An Action Plan recommended recently by the MWSW for implementation of the Beijing Platform for Action expands upon the above themes relating them to the 12 objectives laid down in the Platform, pinning down the responsibilities for each action required.

The Ninth Plan Approach Paper sets triple objectives of mainstreaming, eliminating gender inequality and empowering women along the lines proposed by the Beijing Platform for Action. Mainstreaming section emphasizes the formulation of clearly defined policies, targets and programs are national and regional levels, improvement in information to reflect women's contributions to GDP, further institutional development and creation of a monitoring and evaluation mechanism.

Elimination of Gender Inequality includes reform of discriminatory laws, affirmative action in favor of women specific measures to eliminate violence against women, and information campaign for gender equality. Empowerment includes provisions for mandatory representation of women in policy formulation, ensuring their access to credit and land, meeting their health needs as women, education, training and technology, etc. Its details are still under preparation.

A Platform for Action

Nepal's development strategy in near future is expected to focus on broad based growth with emphasis on social and rural physical infrastructure. Given severe problems in implementation and general insensitivity of the HMG's implementing machinery to gender issues and lack of capability of WID institutions in general, the approach to gender should be multifaceted, including policies, capacity building and reorientation of sectoral programs and projects in gender perspective. The policies should focus on reform of the discriminatory laws and regulations, gender sensitization of the government and non-government implementing machinery, increasing the scope of sectoral objectives and programs related to women and funding gender sensitization institutional network, education and employment.

Policies

Legal Reform: Although legal reforms for equal rights in paternal property and increase in women's representation at higher political and administrative levels, are on the priority list of Nepalese women, given general resistance to this issue, policy dialogue with the government could focus on legal reforms for creating an equal opportunity society as targeted in the 9 th Plan Approach Paper. Particularly, equal land rights in the resettlement areas and equal access to public resources such as community forestry could be included in the current agenda.

Gender Sensitization: A policy decision on gender sensitization of the police and government machinery at all levels must be taken consciously and implemented vigorously. Gender sensitization is necessary at all political and administrate levels because no matter what manuals are provided, translation of programs into actions depends primary on human attitude to the issue at hand. Since gender bias is so ingrained in the social psyche and social behavior, it is necessary to sensitize the people on various and invisible indicators of gender biases. It has to be an on-going process because of the constant turnover of personnel at the district level and new recruits to the political leadership.

Women in Government Administration: Recruitment of more women in responsible positions must be a policy. The recent amendments to the Civil Service Act may be expected to facilities this process. Regularization of the WDD office and its staff into the government services needs immediate attention. Vacancy in district level positions of WDOs and moral of the PCRW staff is one of the constrains in micro-credit. Regularization of PCRW structure is a must for expansion of women's credits programs.

Overcoming Marginality: Marginality of women's components is a major issue in most sectoral programs. Real equal access to education, training and employment opportunities in all programs and projects should be ensured the gender both through policies and project intervention strategies.

Specific Projects: The government and the donors should continue to find specific projects for women to enable women to overcome the gender inequity entrenched in the social structure and social psyche.

Capacity Building: Capacity building may be facilitated by consciously provisioning for gender sensitization programs, in all projects for capacity building of relevant agencies. Capacity building efforts should encompass all levels off government administration and political institutions such as DDCs and VDCs. These should also include NGOs and the private sector.

Centrel Level

a) *The Women's Ministry and Women's Divisions or cells in sectoral Ministries/Departments*: These institutions lack staff and resources for fulfilling their mandates effectively as mentioned above. Sectoral Ministries also lack gender expertise to mainstream gender concerns. Resources should be allocated for building institutional capabilities for gender analysis within Women's Ministry or other relevant Ministries and institutions.

b) *Development of a regular Monitoring and Evaluation Mechanism and Procedures*: Monitoring is another big loophole in all programs. A monitoring mechanism needs to be developed as an integral part of the monitoring process in the Planning Commission. The Ministry of Women should be assisted in developing its own mechanisms to monitor and evaluate development programs from women's perspective. It should be helped to develop indicators for measuring the actual impact of various programs on women's social status and the process of empowerment. NPC should such as agriculture and forestry, education and health should be assisted specifically in capacity building for gender planning and monitoring.

c) *Development of a Training Infrastructure for Gender Sensitization*: Gender sensitization is a must for all staff (male and female) in the Women's Ministry and Women's Divisions and cells in various ministries as also the district and grass roots level workers. Various training institutions within and outside the government structures, e.g. Rural Training Academy, Staff College and Women's Training Centers (WTC), Universities and colleges and private sector/NGO training institutions, need resources and expert input in designing and integrating gender sensitization materials in their various courses and trainings as also developing new packages. Particularly WTCs, the Rural Training Academy and Staff College could be assisted in regularizing gender training in their own training calendars on a large scale. A review of all their training materials and integration of gender perspective in such training can help to gender sensitize the development programs on large scale.

d) *The problems of implementation of policies and management of facilities are especially severe in education and health.* Decentralization of decision making should be a priority area in both these sectors. This has been recommended by numerous reports and studies.But the process of decentralization has some how bypassed these sectors. For example, School Management Committees (SMCs) should be left free of political intervention, and given total power over school management including a role in pay scales, incentives, hiring and firing of the teachers. SMCs members should be parents who send their children to particular schools rather than partisan politicians. Certain proportion of SMC members should be constituted by mothers. Similarly, selected mothers or others or other's groups in the village should be represented overwhelmingly in Sub-Health Post

Management Boards. This Management Board should be given complete power over the SHP management including a role in pay scales, hiring and firing of staff

e) *The NGO movement in Nepal is nascent and much maligned.* But a few of them have emerged quite well at the national level as development NGOs delivering services to the population. A large number of NGOs especially at district and regional levels, however, lack expertise and have little capacity for delivery of services. These should be assisted selectively on the basis of their potentiality and not on the basis of political cronyism. The role of KMTNC in the development of ecotoursim and a few NGOs in social mobilization and credit delivery in Microcredit Project may be considered a success. But except for KMTNC, financial viability seems problems for most NGOs. According to MCPW's experience NGOS growing out of community based organizations (CBOs) or Cooperative Federations growing from below could be better alternative channels for service delivery and credit. Social Mobilization becomes more effective if initiated by rather than government agencies, as (CBO's) capacity in social mobilization is yet to be tested.

Women's NGOs have been more successful in advocacy and training rather than delivery of services per se. Their efforts for networking for advocacy and capacity building for gender sensitization and training could also be supported through donor funding.

District Level

DDCs, VDCs and the district level development administration. The district level political bodies and the line agencies have no gender expertise for mainstreaming the gender concerns. With the new Decentralization Act all development programs and projects are supposed to originate from the grass roots. As such gender expertise required from VDC to national levels. The government should initiate appropriate measures for setting and regularizing a mechanism for gender sensitization of the planning and implementation process from village to the national levels. A dialogue with donors will be useful in designing interventions for capacity building. Particularly, UNDP's Participatory District

Development Program (PDDP) needs redesigning for gender sensitive.

A second alternative, could be restructuring of the current Women Development Office operating under MLD at the district level to function as a coordination office at the district level. When PCRW was introduced in 1982, there were no large scale credit or community development programs directed to women in the country. Currently there are regional banks providing credit primarily to women. In addition thousands of NGO's and INGOs are operating their own small scale saving and credit programs. Nepal Rastra Bank funded Micro Credit Program has introduced a new model for providing credit to women directly through NGOs.

The PCRW model is also found to be very expensive model of credit delivery with 66 percent subsidy component. Some redesigning seems to be a must. The women Development Section at the districts therefore could be slowly divested of their direct group organization and credit preparation functions. These functions should be transfer to the banks themselves or to other financial intermediates such as NGOs or cooperatives, which are growing from below.

The Women Development Section should be assigned the functional responsibility of monitoring and supervising incorporation of women's concerns in all sectoral district and VDC level programs, organizing and facilitating gender training for politicians, administrations and field staff at VDC/ DDC levels, supervising and monitoring Micro Credit Program implemented through NGOs and reporting the progress on gender concerns to the Planning Commission and the Ministry of Women and Social Affairs required. This unit could be placed under Women's Ministry.

Project Interventions

a) The government along with policy initiative, capacity building, and mainstreaming, should also broaden the scope of standalone projects for women in fields where women and children predominate for example specific education and skill development or in the sector.

b) It is necessary to widen the scope and depth of mainstreaming by providing women, employment opportunities in nontraditional sectors such as paper manufacturing, software development, organized trading, etc. In Nepal even the so called traditional sectors such as garment making is monopolized by emigrant male labor. Sewing and knitting training have been widespread but not adequately linked to work in organize garment manufacturing industries.

Also targeting of training to particular groups will increase the efficiency of such training - for example sewing to the tailor cast and shoe making to cobblers. who are loosing jobs on a large scale due to availability of mass product garments and shoes, which are primarily imported. Minimum educational requirements and lack of information are a big hurdle to the respective service caste for getting into such trainings.

Designing industry has been largely male dominated. A study could be commissioned under assistance to CTEVE to explore possibilities of non-traditional sector employment for women.

Social Mobilization

Social mobilization, group formal education and credit are felt to be powerful intervention strategies for reaching women effectively and for their empowerment across all sectoral programs. Group mechanism does provide a basic commendation and scope for women's development and subsequent empowerment.

Women who are originally shy in public and imbued with little self-confidence to express their opinions in the public and may show considerable leadership capacities ultimately. Savings and credit as an initial inducement for group formation serves an useful purpose in bringing women together. It also could help women to raise household living standard to some extent and to meet emergency needs from group fund at reasonable interest rate. It empowers women to the extent that household menders and she herself feel that she is contributing to the maintenance of the household. This recognition by herself, her immediate family menders and the local community seems to be the most valued aspect of these small savings/credit and income generation programs.

Women who form groups are also able ultimately to influence some community action in favor of women, e.g., banning alcohol misuse in the villages. Ownership of a collective element for group sustainability.

However, group formation and its eventual sustainability is a long drawn out process. Further, for empowerment, improvement in gender relations must be an integral part of all social mobilization programs including credit.

Field observation reveals that often women are aware of the oppressive gender relationship in their own community but are helpless to do anything about it. When programs sidetrack such problems women become apathetic to the programs. Non-formal literacy classes must also form an integral part of group mobilization process both in the rural and urban areas. Education is a necessary element in empowerment of women.

Sectoral Issues

Mainstreaming should be the primary strategy for catering to the major needs of women at the sectoral levels. It needs to be direct to creating maximum access to sources of employment, credit technology educational and health facilities. At operational level, emerging gender issues may be summarized as

a) ensuring adequate analysis of all programs and projects with a gender perspective

b) gender sensitization of the implementation mechanism and machinery;

c) ensuring adequacy of measures initiated to ensure gender in project benefits; and

d) development of monitoring indicators and mechanisms to monitor and evaluate project impact on women in terms of not only her participation but her empowerment a well.

A few sectors are discussed below specifically as example.

Agriculture: The agricultural sector employs the largest proportion of women. Much of Nepal's agriculture, specially in the hills, depends on women. But women still form, less than 20 percent of trainees in agricultural training programs. Inspire of much rhetoric, little efforts and resources have been spent so far improving efficiency are concentrated precisely in these operations. Women's programs and administrative rules and regulations in agriculture. Very few women are represented at decision making levels. Finally, lack of access to and other resources severely limit women's choice in the agricultural decision making.

The Agricultural Perspective Plan (APP) explicitly seeks to ensure women's participation in agricultural program through staffing and attitudinal changes in the regular facilities rather than having separate facilities for them. APP expects to benefit women from high growth of dairy production, rapid growth in high-value crop and specific efforts to ensure women's participation in research, extension, credit and oversight, and access to fertilizer and irrigation. MOA should pay specific attention to the following recommendations in its sectoral programs and projects:

— all agricultural extension and farmer training programs involve both men and women on a 50:50 basis;
— special emphasis to involving the women in Tarai;
— initiatives for developing and disseminating women friendly indigenous technology for energy, food and fodder; particularly relevant are seed selection, post harvest cleaning and weeding operations;
- encouraging women's groups in natural resource protection and finally; and " ensuring women's equal access to land, natural resources and other assets (at least within Bank assisted projects).

Education and Training: The issues on education and training include social constraints on girl's schooling and rural/urban, regional and intergroup gaps in female education levels; heavy workload of girls, specifically for above primary age group and low quality of public school teaching, (it effects girls specially because more girls are likely to go to public schools) rigidity of formal schooling hours; high cost of girl's education; lack of innovation in all out of school training directed to women lack of need assessment and marketing research and lack of gender sensitivity in training materials, inappropriate methodology and pattern of training.

Programs and projects in the education sector pay specific attention to gender equity issues and ensure marketability of skills taught. Specific strategies for the education sector should include.

— continuation of revision of the books and the reading materials, female teacher and scholarship programs for on a broader scale;

- integration of gender as a specific subject on all primary/ secondary school teacher's trainings;
- provision for special schools in low caste localities because children from low castes are often mistreated by the teachers as well as students in mixed schools;
- provision for incentives not only for specifically disadvantage areas but also to educationally disadvantaged caste/ethnic groups, both in the hills and the Tarai areas; and " specific efforts to cater to 10-17 groups of girls, for example by splitting school hours in two - 4 hour shifts, allocating resources for girls' hostels on a larger scale, provisioning large scale and adequate scholarship to girls, recruiting and providing for training of female teachers on a large scale and provisioning for girl in selected areas, where strict purdha is practiced.

Particularly, with focus on human development, a series of projects are in the offing with special focus on teacher's training both at primary and secondary levels on a large scale, gender sensitization should be included in all training programs even if the subjects are science or mathematics. This will help to gender sensitize the future generation on a large scale. Otherwise it is felt that we are bringing generation of gender biased youngsters, and the task of debrain-washing them will never end.

Training's in skill development should match the nature of the industry feasible in the area, For example, training in computer skill can be useful only if concentrated in and around urban areas, while sewing, knitting and textile making have to be concentrated in batches to particular areas, where possibility of employment in such areas are high. Only then women can use them for income generation. An example in point is the knitting industry, which is generating good income for women in and around Kathamndu and Pokhara valleys, while in the Far-West it has been a total failure.

Tourism and Other Employment: Technological innovations are required to assist entrepreneurial women in reduction of production cost, product specialization and exploration of market niche. Specifically in the tourism sector which has large scale female participation, programs and projects should incorporate following strategy on gender. A separate program for women entrepreneurship development should be initiated.

A project for the promotion of women entrepreneurs could be considered in this context. The present skill development training provided by different organizations are traditional and lack management and networking components. To start with a national scale study is necessary to dig out the psychological, social and technical problems that the women face in business management and recommend solutions. Few organizations in the nongovernment sectors such as Women Entrepreneur's Association of Nepal (WEAN). Association for Craft Producers (ACP), Janakpur Women's Development Centre (JWDC) are working with women entrepreneurs. They operate on a very limited scale.

Major credit programs should devise mechanisms to facilitate access of organizations such as WEAN and ACP in Kathmandu. Association of Cottage and small Industries in Nepalgunj and JWDC in Janakpur to credit through NRB. Such associations could also be assisted in market niche exploration and cost redaction through technical assistance. Continuation of women's involvement in management of tourist facilities as planned under ecotourism component of the II Tourism Development Project.

Ensure 50-50 participation of women and men in all related training's because tourism sector employs women on a large scale, but they are concentrated mainly in traditional jobs such as, clerks and receptions. Few women have reached at the higher level of the organizational hierarchy. Establish a fund for rehabilitation of the commercial sex workers and public education packages to prevent trafficking, drug use, alcoholism and spread of STDS and AIDS in tourist areas. This should also ensure adequate credit access to women in the tourism sector expanding their business.

Rural Infrastructure: Rural infrastructure includes rural roads, irrigation facilities, rural energy sources and development of rural markets. Strategies in Nepal is likely to focus on rural infrastructure building for boosting a broad based agricultural development. But so far, specific attention to women's concerns in such projects has been minimal. Its future strategy needs.

— To ensure that women are provided with equal ownership and user rights in all transfers of public assets in these fields.

- To encourage and accord priority to women in forming water user's groups and in extension training, credit for establishment, operation and management of shallow tubewells and treadle pumps.
- To specify how the project specific gender policies are to be achieved.

6

National Policy

I. Nepalese Law

1. Forbidden Sexual Relations in the Ain of 1853

In contradistinction to the spareness of the Smrti, almost half of the contents of the Ain is devoted to detailed rules applying to forbidden sexual relations. These may be subsumed under three main topics : incestuous relations, inter caste relations and adultery. Incest, depending on the degree of kinship, inter caste relations either if contrary to the hierarchical order of the castes or between pure and impure castes belong to the category of crimes *(raja-khata)* and, as such, are punished by the State, according to the law. Adultery, in most Cases, is a private affair in which the decision rests upon the injured husband's will, though evidently in certain cases it may also involve incest (if the seducer is a close relative of the woman) or caste's disorder.

The possibility of kiiling his wifes' seducer given to the husband under certain circumstances is the private equivalent of capital punishment, but it is not a transfer from the State's power to execute criminals to a private individual; it is completely independent from criminal proceedings. In fact, the death penalty, according to the Ain, is mostly inflicted for crimes of blood, the rule ever and ever repeated being that life is taken in exchange for life, and suffering only very few exceptions. In matters related to sexual misdemeanor, capital punishment is only applied to incestuous relations with one's own mother, to the rape of a girl under eleven belonging to a pure caste by an untouchable and lastly to sexual relations of a slave with a woman of his master's family. If the seducer is to be killed, it is because of his relations with a married woman, but to be legal, such a killing requires complex personal and procedural conditions which we shall try to summarize.

2. Adultery Titles of Law and Terminology

2.1 Titles

The rules relating to adultery are gathered in a series of some eight chapters in the Ai.10. :

1. *Jari-ko* : "Of adultery";
2. *Pardesa janya-ko jari garnya-ko* : "Of the [man committing] adultery [with the wife of a man] travelling abroad";
3. *Phalana-sira bigrya bhamnya* "Of [the woman] declaring : I had sexual relations with such person";
4. *Tesro pari karni garnya* : "[Of the man] being the third to have sexual relations [with a woman]";
5. *Cautho-dekhi ubho pari rakhyaka swasni-ko jari garnya* : "Of adultery committed, being the fourth at least, with a kept woman [concubine]";
6. *Masinya jata-ko jari garnya* : "(Of adultery committed among the enslavable castes";
7. *Jari-ko phutakara* : "Additional rules concerning adultery";
8. *Swasni-ka mukha-le matra bhani jara katanya-ko* : "Of [the husband] killing the seducer on a mere declaration of his wife".

Some questions related to adultery are also treated in two more chapters (originally three) devoted to the customs existing among the Newar community : divorce on the woman's initiative *(pacuke)*, and punishment of sexual misbehaviour *(misakhata)*. But in these, rules and vocabulary differ deeply from the ones evidenced in the former set. The key words *jara, jari,* are never used in this context; and *sadhu* only once. The possibility of an injured Newar husband killing his wife's lover was not even imagined : the few paragraphs dealing with the sexual relations of a third person with a married woman merely mention the possibility of the husband having some marriage expenses, *(biha kharca)* refunded.

The space devoted to adultery, the presence of a chapter trying to draw a synthesis of the rules, their often realistic character, show that much concern was given by the legislator to a custom he did not wish to eliminate, but which was a potential threat to social peace in the kingdom.

2.2 Terminology, Jara and Sadhu

The cases of adultery which may lead to the killing of the seducer by the husband are described in the Ain under the title of *jari,* and generally the seducer is termed *jara* while the injured husband is called *sadhu.* We have already pointed to the fact that the Sk. *Jara is* rarely used in the Smrti, and as such was not borrowed as a technical term, but as a part of popular language. The word *sadhu* is also a Sanskrit loan word originally meaning "straight, right" which, in Nepali, apart from the well known meaning of ascetic, is also applied to "the injured husband who has the right to kill his wife's paramour". Its technical use in the Ain is not limited to this case, but the word is also applied to the man who is the victim of an aggressor or who kills a thief to defend his property, the opposition of *sadhu* with *cora* but also with "libertine" is also attested in the copper plate of Rana Bahadur.

The etymological connection of *sadhu* with its modern representative *sahu,* which, in modern languages, has only kept the meaning of "creditor" and is well evidenced as the complement of *asami* (debtor) in the Ain, was probably felt and influenced the technical use of *sadhu* as the "injured husband", implying a right of ownership of the husband on the wife. Such an implication seems for instance to be evidenced in §7 of *jari-ko* where the usual formula *sadhu-ko khusi* is replaced by *swasni-ka dhani-ko khusi* : "[punishment] is to be freely chosen by the owner *[dhani]* of the woman". Symmetrically, in §17 of *Jari-ko cora* is used for the, *jara* of *brahmana* "caste", who has been killed after having inflicted a wound (with a weapon, *hatiyara*) to the *sadhu.*

3. Rules and Customs

Adultery supposes the participation of three persons—a husband, a wife and a seducer. To each of them are related special personal conditions, which, when fulfilled allow the husband, if he decides to do so, to kill his wife's seducer and to punish her.

3.1 Conditions Related to the Husband

To have the possibility of avenging himself, the husband must belong to "caste killing the seducer" (*jara hamnya jata*). We have seen that the chapters devoted to their particular customs exclude the population of Newari origin from this possibility; among the other groups composing Nepalese society according to the Ain, some are explicitly enumerated as having the privilege, they include : the Rajaputa, Ksatri, Magara, Gurum-Ghale and the Sunuwara, *i.e.,* all the castes and ethnic groups belonging to the "cord-wearers" (*tagadhari*) and the "non-enslavable alcohol drinkers" (*namasinya matawali jata*). Though not included in this enumeration, brahmanas (Upadhya as well as Jaisi) are also expressly allowed to kill their wife's seducer.

Apart from these groups, the privilege of which needs not to be enquired upon, the Code admits that some castes, even with a very low status in social hierarchy, may proceed to such a revenge if they are entitled to do so by their ancestor's practices (*pita purkha-dekhi cali ayako)*; but there are certain limitations regarding this possibility for some of them. None of them is named and they remain mysterious. Most probably some of them are ethnic groups with strong patriarchal customs or castes having adopted this "Aryan" practice. The necessity of proving the ancestral nature of the custom may, as shown in a later edition, have had as consequence a subsequent inquiry by the legal authority. Such rules and restrictions imply that, though apparently independent of the caste's hierarchy, the privilege was mainly limited to martial tribes from the hills, which agrees with B. Hodgson's report of the custom.

3.2. Conditions Related to the Woman

Marriage is a notion quite difficult to apprehend in the Nepalese society of the nineteenth century. Christian monogamist societies establish a clear distinction between the married woman and concubines or mistresses. The first mentioned and her progeny are the only ones to have any legal status, while the others have no right at all. In contradistinction to this, the Nepalese system presented a continuum of levels, starting from the "lawfully wedded wife" and going down to mistresses, sometimes kept on a contractual basis. All of them have a legal existence, evidenced for instance by the right of their children to a share of their husband's property. The absence of specific words for husband and wife in Napali shows very well that marriage as an abstraction was never contemplated.

To the necessity for the husband to belong to a *jara hamnya jata*, is added the condition that the woman is a *aina-le jara hamna hunya-samma-ka swasni*, "a woman whose legal status is high enough for her seducer to be killed". From the formulation itself it is clear that while the husband's right depends on customary practice, the conditions imposed on the woman's status are determined by the law (*aina-le*) and, as such, may be modified by the legislator.

According to the Ai. 10, the husband belonging to a *jara hamnya jara* may kill the seducer of:

1. Women, he was the first to have sexual relations with, whether married with full rites or simply brought home when they were virgins.
2. Women, he was the second to have sexual relations with, who may be either widows or women he brought home when their former husband was alive. But in this case,
    (a) The women must originate from a caste having the privilege.
    (b) The husband must not have obtained her by paying a monetary compensation (*biha kharca*) to her former husband.
    (c) She must not be a widow belonging to a caste of a higher status than his own.

These complex and sometimes obscure rules have been drastically simplified in later editions of the Code. In the Ain of BS. 1992, women whose seducer may legally be killed must be of equal or immediately inferior status and belonging to the "cord-wearers", taken with full marriage rites (*bibaha gari lyaeki*), or virgins of equal caste whose rice is accepted (*bhata-ma sarobara gari rakheki*). No seducer of a woman who had a previous husband can be killed, excepting the case of an Upadhya widow brought publicly into his house by a Jaisi Brahmana.

3.3. *Seducers not to be Executed by the Husband*

Two kinds of prohibitions are mentioned in the Ain. The first is legal, which implies that if the husband transgresses it, he shall be punished as a murderer: if he belongs to a caste that can be executed (*katinya jata*), his life is exchanged for the life [he unjustly took] (*jyana-ko badala jyana jamcha*); otherwise his legal share in the family's patrimony is confiscated and he is condemned to life-prison (*damala*). The second is optional, of a moral character and devoid of legal sanction.

3.3.1. Legal Prohibitions

These legal prohibitions are grounded on religious considerations, the husband killing a *brahmana* would be guilty of *brahma-hatya;* the murder of a member of his *gotra* (i.e., an agnatic kinsman), would be a *gotra-hatya.*

A. Prohibition of *brahma-hatya* from the oldest sources of *dharma* onwards, the killing of a *brahmana* is essentially different from the killing of a member of another *varna,* as he who commits it, is not only guilty of murder but also of a "great sin" (mahapataka), called brahma-hatya, for which the only possible atonement is death. Whatever his offense, a *brahmana* is never to be executed. It seems however, that, before the promulgation of the code, injured husbands did not hesitate to commit such a horrible sin. This protection, originally a privilege of Upadhya and Jaisi, was extended, as in the case of exemptions from capital punishment to which it is homologous, to ascetics, mainly from brahmanic descent.

B. Prohibition of *gotra-hatya.* The idea that killing a member of one's *gotra* is a heinous sin, seems to be unknown to the Smrti. It results probably from the creation of a new *mahapataka* on the model of *brahma-hatya.* The fifteenth Tithi attributed to Rama Saha of Gorkha prescribes that king's collateral and members of his *gotra,* must not be executed even if they have committed a capital crime, but, instead must be shaven and banished from the kingdom; the same rule applies to *brahmana* and ascetics. This rule, one would have thought mainly inspired by political considerations, is followed by a gloss, probably written by a court pandita:

"If [someone] commits a criminal action for which his life is to be taken, it is written in the *sastra* that one must take the life of one who has taken a life, but if [the king] takes the life [of a member of his clan], he would be guilty of *gotra-hatya,* moreover, were he not to kill him, blame (*pratyavaya*) would attach [to the King]. This is why; saying [i.e., considering] that the expulsion from the country is strictly equivalent to an execution, it has been said one must expel [the culprit]".

The political chapters of the A.i. 10 seem unfortunately to have been lost , but such rules were probably applied to the King's and Prime Minister's families. It is instructing to remark the homology between the exemptions of capital punishment at State's level, and the prohibitions applied in the field of private revenge.

3.3.2 Optional Prohibitions

If the "religious" concept of *gotra-hatya* allowed the legislator to exclude the agents from the husband's wrath, no such way was opened for cognates. This is probably why, quite unexpectedly, recommendations of a moral character, devoid of any kind of legal sanction, are to be found in the text. They try to induce the injured husband not to use his right to kill his wife's seducer if he belongs to close cognates kinship, though he is entitled by the law to do so. The code's arguments are clues to the psychological background of the practice, as well as to the function of the courts in customary matters.

The killing of paramour not only originated in the husband's wrath, but also in social pressure. This is well evidenced at an earlier stage, in Rana Bahadur's copper plate which excludes from an official position the "Eunuch" unable to kill the seducer and to cut the nose of the guilty wife, but also in the very name of the fine (*namardi damda)* that the husband who, knowing she is unfaithful, still has sexual relations with his wife, has to pay according to the Ain. The cuckold suffered not only from jealousy but also, and maybe mostly, from *ridicule.* The legal obligation of having a document written under the control of the court, which at the same time verified if no prohibition of the killing was intended by the law, probably meant that the judge read aloud the chapter on the subject. So he had to mention that : "He who declares" "I do not kill the seducer"... is not considered as an impotent *(namarda),* but is said to be a wise man *(buddhiman),* the man who kills [his wife's] seducer when he is such a close relative is considered as stupid *(paji).* If the injured husband kills the seducer he commits no crime if such is the ancestral custom [of his clan], but if he releases him too, he commits no crime".

4. The Revenge of the Husband

4.1. Against the Paramour

Even if all the conditions for the killing were fulfilled, if the husband gave-up this possibility he could inflict other legal punishments on the paramour, these sanctions applying also in case the seducer belonged to a category he could not put to death.

4.1.1 Killing of the Seducer

The law which imposed drastic conditions on the status of the actors, did not care much about the circumstances of the killing as representatives of the state were not to be involved in it. Once the husband had taken the decision that was deemed to be legal, no one took much care to offer a chance of escaping to the culprit. Though the help of his kinsmen and of the authorities wits explicitly allowed for the capture of the seducer, with theoretically the husband should proceed the killing alone. But were he to kill him while he was escorted by the police on his way to the court, he was to pay a mere fine. The Ai. 10 remains silent about the killing procedure itself which is only described in later versions and was left to custom. The last edition of the Ain merely enjoins that a space of hundred foot must be left between the husband and the *jara,* but the rule only applies when the "cutting" is under the court's control, and in case of its transgression, a mere fine of fifty rupees is inflicted upon the judge and the husband.

4.1.2 Other Options

These may be classified under two heads, the first which consists in having the seducer humbled through some kind of mirroring private punishment, the second is a monetary compensation, either the confiscation of the seducer's share to the husband's profit or the payment of marriage expenses *(biha-kharca)* to compensate his loss. Lastly the husband may forgive the culprit and let him go.

A. *Humiliation of the jāra.* It has already been pointed to the fact that the cuckold not only suffered from jealousy, but also from social *ridicule.* The customary practices to avenge it try to inflict on the offender a corresponding public humiliation. This may consist in crawling under the husband's thigh (*taga-mani chiraunu*),a kind of symbolic copulation, to which may be added the licking of the sole of his foot (*taga-mani chirai paitalo-smeta cataunu*). These practices may be mere examples of a wider catalogue, mentioned here because they had different consequences on the status of the paramour.

This kind of popular entertainment was probably replaced in the case of *brahmana* by the forced ingestion of "uneatable" substances *(abhaks[y]a)* such as alcohol (*mada*), pork-meat (*sugura-ko masu)* etc., together with the tearing off of the sacred cord.

B. Monetary compensation. According to the Ain, this compensation could be of two kinds (a) confiscation of the legitimate share of the culprit to the profit of the husband *(aina-bamojima-ko amsa sarbaswa),* (b) payment of *biha-kharca.* It is quite difficult to distinguish between the cases in which one or the other was applied, though caste customs and maybe the legal status of the woman were involved.

While killing or public humiliation of the seducer are two possible outlets for the offended male pride of the warrior tribes, I would suggest that monetary compensations were first devised for *brahmanas* and then extended to other castes, in first instance to prevent *gotra-hatya* and, then as financial alternatives luring the possibly greedy *sadhu* into sparing the seducer.

4.2. Sanctions Against the Adulteress

4.2.1. Mutilations

In 1819 Hamilton remarked that, in Nepal, women, as in all Hindu governments, are never put to death; but the punishments inflicted on them are abundantly severe. The most 'common is the cutting off [of] their noses. Judicial mutilations are well attested in classical texts, and a special chapter is devoted to their redeeming through fines in the *Artha Sastra*. The cutting of various limbs, including the nose, in cases of theft is attested by the Nepalese Code of BS.1910, as a former practice, not to be applied anymore. Despite the similarity of the process, the ablation of the nose has a quite different meaning when applied to women. To cut off the nose of a thief is a way to inform people of his criminal record, to cut off the nose of a woman guilty of sexual misbehaviour is to deprive her of her beauty, her seduction, to prevent her from any further repetition.

Documents, prior to the Code, show that the mutilation of a woman could either be inflicted by the courts, as a punishment, or by the husband as a private revenge for adultery.

A. *Mutilation of women by judicial decision.* In the very important Lalmohars concerning the punishment of criminals in Tansen and Palpa published by the National Archives, the cutting off the nose is prescribed in association with degradation from caste for three women belonging to the Magar group. One in a case of infanticide of a child born from sexual relations with a slave, the second for abortion with the help of drugs of a foetus conceived through "incestuous" relations, the last for sexual relations with a Kami (untouchable). From the text of the documents it seems that these woman were not married, and that the punishment has no relation with adultery.

It has to be noticed that the comparative leniency shown towards brahmin males existed also in the case of females : in the same document an Upadhya widow who had committed infanticide after sexual relations with a Thapa Magar is not mutilated but banished after being excluded from water and paraded in the quarters with her face covered with black.

Such practices disappeared with the promulgation of the Code, where no allusion to the cutting off of the nose of a woman by judicial decision, whatever the sexual offense committed, can be traced.

B. *Private mutilations.* According to a copper-plate of Rana Bahadur Saha, dated from 1798 (BS. 1855), such a practice was a duty a State's officer could not evade without forfeiting his charge, a true test of virility :

"To the impotent who, knowing that someone else made [love] to his wife, could not kill the seducer, and after having killed the seducer could not cut off the nose [of his wife], no office should be given for his whole life".

Brahmani women were certainly excluded from the scope of this emphatic rule, their heads were shaved and they had probably to endure some kind of public humiliation whatever sexual offense they committed. Such shaving of the head, evidently aimed at the same purpose as the shaving of widows, that is depriving the woman of her sexual attractiveness, was admitted by the Code as a legal substitute for the ablation of the nose.

From this text presenting private revenge and the subsequent mutilation of the woman as almost compulsory, the Ain's compilers tried to depart, but their efforts were, at least in the beginning, hampered by the pressure of tradition. Forbidding the husband to cut off the nose of the adulteress and applying to him the general sanctions of criminal mutilations should have been a logical step following the proscription of judicial mutilations, but instead of confronting the standing custom, the legislator tried to find financial alternatives.

According to the law of blows and hurts, he who cuts off the nose of another man is sentenced to six years of imprisonment, to the double in the case of an aggression against a woman. This rule is repeated in the context of adultery but applies to the jealous husband of an innocent woman. If she is guilty of adultery, the husband who cuts her nose is merely compelled, if the seducer belonged to his Gotra, to pay a fine of Rs. 50, Rs. 25 otherwise. The first of these rules is probably the oldest and establishes a correlation between the sanctions applied to each cu1prit : the seducer belonging to the agnatic kinship must not be killed, consequently the woman must not be disfigured. The second, forbidding the mutilation, even if the seducer has been killed is, from a juridical point of view, an anomaly.

In spite of its almost pathological complacency for atrocities, Rana Bahadur's text, grounded in customary practices, showed a good deal of juridical common sense in presenting the woman's mutilation as a necessary, complement to the seducer's killing. The Ain's compilers, despite the subtlety they often displayed, do not seem to have considered the possible complicity between husband and wife and that by allowing the killing of the seducer while leaving the woman untouched they might open a way for legal murder. Wishing to eliminate unnecessarily cruel practices but unable to forbid the customary killing of the seducer introduced a legal incoherence which was, in practice, limited by the control of the woman's declaration by the State's representatives.

The legislator seems to have preferred financial incitation to criminal repression in order to protect the woman from mutilation : bargaining wrath for greed. Reform was achieved through manipulations of the right of the woman to keep her separate property. The husband who wished to avenge his wounded pride by disfiguring his wife, could do so, provided he paid a moderate fine, but he had in this case to forfeit any right on her separate property which he was allowed to seize if he abandoned violence.

No record exists to show how far this policy was successful. The cutting off of the nose of the guilty woman is alluded to as a common practice in the chapter devoted to [Women] declaring [falsely] "I had relations with such person". In the code of BS. 1992, the practice is merely prohibited, implying that no distinction shall be made between adulterous or innocent women : in every case the husband who mutilates his wife endures the same punishment.

4.2.2. Fines and Enslavement

The cutting off of the nose of the woman seems to have been distinctive of the cord-wearers and non-enslavable alcohol drinkers. If we come down to the enslavable castes, the situation is quite different. No allusion whatsoever is made in the chapter concerning adultery among the enslavable castes to a possible mutilation of the woman.

This may be accounted for by two reasons, the first being ethnic background, the other commercial interests.

Many of the ethnic groups considered as enslavable have a conception of marriage and family that differs widely from the patriarchal values that reign among the Indo-Nepalese, and do not feel adultery as a crime horrible enough to allow them to kill a fellow human and disfigure another.

As to the others, who seem to have had much more respectable practices, they seem to have been prevented from mutilating their wives by the general rule according to which the wife was enslaved if, and only if, her husband killed her seducer. Mutilation being customarily conceived as a counterpart to the killing of the seducer, it would have as consequence a loss of value of the female slave on the market.

5. Control by the State's Representatives

5.1. Power of Decision

The fundamental rule in matters of *jari* is that, as far as it is included in the scope of the legal sanctions allowed by the code, the husband himself, without any pressure from the authorities, must decide on a sanction which he shall himself apply to the *jara,* a principle encapsulated in the formula *sadhu-ko khusi humcha* : it shall be done according to the husband's desire. The "judge cannot oblige the owner of the woman" to choose a particular solution. The *jara* himself has more power than the judge as he may refuse to pay any monetary compensation to the husband and say : "If he is able to do it then let him cut me".

Correlatively, the one who takes the decision has to execute it. From the Ain's point of view, adultery by itself is not a crime, and the authorities stick to the principle that they are not to inflict capital punishment which must be an exchange for a life unjustly taken, and this extends to any kind of punishment. An exception according to which the *brahmana,* in case he was unable to punish his wife's seducer himself, could have the courts catch and sentence the *jara* to prison for life *(damala),* existed in the first edition of the Code, but was very soon cancelled.

When a conflict between private and public sanction exists, either because the woman relation with her lover is incestuous or because the hierarchical distance between them is such that it involves a crime, the husband's choice has to be respected by the courts unless he decides not to punish the culprits. In this case, the general sanctions of incest or of transgression of caste hierarchy are applied by the courts. The subordination of the courts to the husband's decision goes as far as allowing an untouchable guilty of sexual relations with a woman of a pure caste to escape any sanction if the husband, having decided to kill him was unable to cut him or only inflicted a wound on him.

5.2 From Customary to Written Procedure

The Nepalese conception according to which the woman's status is lowered every time she has sexual relations with a different man has a fundamental consequence on the husband's right to kill the seducer. Were he to execute a man who was not the first lover of his wife *(jetho),* he would, unless in some particular circumstances, commit a murder and be punished accordingly. This was not merely theoretical, the cases described in various chapters show that the possibility of having the husband accused of murder for killing a person in contravention with the law, was seized by the victim's kinsmen - who certainly dreamt of avenging the death of a member of their clan, and are shown as trying to corrupt the woman to have her proclaim their kinsman's innocence, as well as the woman's family to which the adulteress returned deprived of her reputation, her nose or her dowry.

Proof of adultery is not a problem when the culprits are caught in the act, or when the woman elopes with another man. In this case there is no doubt of the identity of the seducer, and the husband commits no fault in killing him, even if he is not the first lover of his wife. Furthermore the law considers that circumstantial evidence, such as the woman and the man "lying with touching knees", or a money transaction in a secret place are judicially equivalent to actual sexual relations.

The true problems arise when the husband suspects the wife's chastity or there is some evidence of the woman's misdemeanor, for instance pregnancy when the husband is abroad, but the culprit's identity is unknown, for in this case the seducer's identification rests on the woman's admission. The legislator's strategy which aimed at controlling the process of private revenge through representatives of the State got some support from the ideological background. The fickleness of women is a common remark in the Hindu Tradition from Manu-smrti onwards, completed by the blindness of the jealous husband it may lead to murder of innocents and endless blood feuds. To avoid fatal errors, the principle of a written admission of the woman was introduced in the customary practice. A written confession *(kayelan ama)* is the necessary formality for the State's authority to proceed to the punishment of any crime, on this very same model a "paper" *(kagaja)* became compulsory for the husband to punish the seducer. It is not certain that the presence of the local court was needed at first, but in a context of illiteracy, the writing of a document would automatically lead to its redaction through some kind of authority.

The substitution of public control to "private courts" afforded a better protection of the woman against the brutality of the husband and his family. Being specialized in enquiring about criminal cases, the courts should be more efficient in detecting the possible lies or half-lies of the woman and of the witnesses. To the protection of the woman was added a transfer of responsibilities: were the husband to kill a person later proved to be innocent, he could not, as far as the formalities had been observed, be prosecuted for murder. Written procedure meant better security as well as State's control.

5.3 Adultery When the Husband is Abroad

The husband's absence has traditionally been considered as a subject of a particular importance. The Tradition has devoted much space to the conduct to be followed by a *prosita-patikd* (a woman whose husband is abroad) and the only clear allusion to the husband's right to decide in matters of adultery in the *Artha-Sastra* appears in this context. It is evident that a woman who stays at home in the absence of her husband has more opportunities for misdemeanor than when both spouses stay in the same place. The woman might elope with another man, taking away property deemed to belong to her husband and her descendants. Such circumstances are a good test of how far the State is ready to involve itself in private affairs.

The kinsmen of the husband are entitled to act in his absence, but not to exercise private revenge in his name. They have to bring not only the guilty woman, but also the suspected paramour to the authorities. Here a document *(kagaja)* shall be written, then both culprits shall be given back to who brought them. The final decision must be taken by the husband when he returns home.

This theoretical neutrality of the authorities was, in fact, counteracted by an extension of the notion of theft : if the woman elopes with another man, he is reputed to have stolen everything she may bring along apart except for the "garments she wore on her body". Whichever part of her private or her husband's property she takes with her has to be restored to the husband's heir, and the thief seducer is to be jailed accordingly (i.e., on the basis of a month of jail for five rupees). Under the pretext of protecting private property, this was a way for the courts to sanction adultery, but this sanction had also a political background : it was meant to reinforce isolationism.

A distinction was made between three kinds of reasons for travelling: for the State's service, including war; for private or commercial reasons; for accepting an office in a foreign State.

Service to the State service afforded maximum protection of the husband's interests, the "thief" was to be kept in jail until the husband's return however small the amount he had stolen.

In case of travel for private or commercial reasons, the "thief " was kept in jail for the legal period and then released unless the husband had shown up in between.

If the husband was in the service of a foreign power, he forfeited all rights to kill his wife's paramour. With this last rule, the right to self revenge had become a political incentive, the true privilege of a true Nepalese.

From the preceding rules, it is clear that the legislator had no particular sympathy for mutilations or private revenge and did his best to limit them. To forbid them would have been contradictory to the golden rule of traditional Hindu policy since *Kautilya* : never oppose indigenous or traditional practices, but try to slowly integrate them and if possible get rid of them. To simply ignore them, as the classical texts did, would have been to neglect the dangers of such uncontrolled practices for a society on its way from segmentation to centralization and was impossible. The result, at the same time, was the establishment of an ever tighter control in which writing (written law, written documents) played an important part, and the transformation of a practice, never explicitly admitted by the Classical Tradition, into a symbolic Hindu privilege, belonging only to true Nepalese citizens, Nepalese who did not travel abroad except in the service of their government and did not serve foreign powers. International public opinion, to which the Ranas were more sensitive than was usually admitted, should, have induced the suppression of the private revenge for adultery, at least in the time of Candra Samser, as was the case for window-burning and slavery. However, it was not abolished until the promulgation of the first Muluki Ain in 1963 (2020 BS.).

Widow Burning in Nepal

Introduction[1]

Every suicide, even a religiously motivated one, causes dismay and often dumb amazement, especially when the person who used force against himself was known or identified with. The deed elicits horror and shock, and also grief and despair. Theories that propose to explain what cannot be grasped are of little help in such a situation. What good is it if Freud, in *Mourning and Melancholy,* says, "that perhaps no person finds the psychic energy to kill himself who does not first, in doing so, also kill a victim he has identified with, and who does not, secondly, thereby turn upon himself a death wish that has been directed against another person"? What good is it if Emile Durkheim, in his pioneering study *Le Suicide,* talks of social disintegration combined with a loss of orientation, as being one of the main causes of suicide?

Suicide as an existential problem and a social institution - that, to be sure, is something else. Given the fact that it is man alone, of all living creatures, who is able consciously to kill himself, suicide expresses much about a person's attitude towards life and death. And it is precisely here that grave differences exist between, cultures, differences that are among the most difficult to, gain a feeling for and so produce the most heated controversies.

Wherever "life is not of goods the highest" (Fr. Schiller in *Braut von Messina* - deriving from Zeno), wherever the image of the skeletal[2] Grim Reaper with the running hourglass, is unknown[3], wherever the fear of dying is perhaps different because connected reincarnation, wherever death does not occur in the storerooms of hospitals but almost publicly, wherever corpses do not disappear in coffins under the earth but are burned in thin cloths for all to see - there the motives for suicide are more relative in nature, whether it is committed by men or by women.

Widow burning, however, is not only in conflict with the Christian condemnation of suicide but also with the emancipated position of the woman, although even within Christianity the condemnation of suicide is rather late in coming. The Old Testament contains seven cases of suicide; the most famous in the New Testament is that of Judas. Women might become saints in the early Christian community defended their chastity by means of suicide. It was Thomas Aquinus who first declared suicide to be a mortal sin, and from that time on such victims were denied burial in cemeteries, and were interred as was done as late as 1821 in England - at crossroads, having previously been pierced through their hearts so that no evil spirit might arise.

However, suttee or - to use the Indian spelling - *sati* (which denotes both the custom and the person) is usually not regarded in the West as suicide. What is taken to be a heroic death, or at least one, springing from noble motives, in the Jain *sallekhand,* fasting to death among men, in Islamic or Christian martyrdom, and in Japanese *seppuku* or *harakiri* is not conceded to Hindu women. Nowadays they are usually held to be defence-less victims of a patriarchal society who have killed themselves or even been forced to do so out of a blind, antiquated and misplaced faithfulness to their husbands.

Given these cultural differences, the issue of suttee had to become one of the major reasons for clashes between British India and Brahmanical orthodoxy[4] which led to its final prohibition by Lord William Bentinck on 4 December 1829.[5]

I. Literary and Historical Sources

It was 24 years later that Prime Minister Janga Bahadur Rana set about promulgating the (Muluki) Ain, which contains the most detailed guidelines for the performance of *sati* found in South Asia (see below). There is numerous testimony in literary and historical sources to the fact that occasion enough existed to regulate the matter also in Nepal. Thus Francis B. Hamilton speaks in his *Account of the Kingdom of Nepal and of Territories Annexed to this Dominion by the House of Gorkha* (1819) of widow burning being "more prevalent" under the high castes of Nepal "than in any part of India... the vicinity of Calcutta excepted" (p. 23).

It is also the case that the earliest inscription pertaining to widow burning comes from Nepal.[6] It is dated Saka 386 (=464 A.D.), while the earliest Indian inscription is dated 510 A.D. In the Nepalese inscription it is written that the wife of the Licchavi king Dharmadeva, Rajyavati by name, wanted to perform *sati*. She was prevented from doing so, however, by her son Manadeva. On the western side of the long and tall pillar inscription one can read :

6 *prem[a]nā putram uvāca sāśvadanā yātah pitā, te divam*
7 *hā putrāstamite tavādya pitari prānair vrthā kim mama*
8 *rājyam putraka kārayāham anuyamy adyaiva bharttur ggatim 8*
9 *kim me bhogavidhānavistarakrtair āśāmayair bbandhanaih*
10 *māyā svapnanibhe samāgamavidhau bhartrā vinā jīvitum*
11 *yāmīty evam avasthitā khalu tadā dīnatmanā sūnunā*
12 *pādau bhaktivaśān nipīdya śirasā vijñāpitā yatnatah 9*
13 *kim bhogair mmama kim hi jivitasukhais tvadviprayoge sati*
14 *prānān pūrvam ahañ jahāmi paratas tvam yāsyasīto divam*
15 *ity evam mukhaparikajāntaragatair nnetrāmbumiśrair drham*
16 *vākpāśair vvihagīva pāśavaśagā baddhā tatas tasthusī 10*
17 *satputrena sahaurddhvadehikavidhinj bharttuh prākrty ātmanā*
18 *śīlatyāgadamopavāsaniyamair ekāntśuddhāsayā*
19 *[vi]prebhyopi ca sarvvadā pradadatī tatpunyavrddhayai dhanam*
20 *tasthau taddhrdayā satīvrqtavidhau sāksād ivārundhatī 11*

With affection (and) with a tearful face she addressed (her) son: "Your father went to heaven. O (my) son, as your father has gone today, what is the use of my breath [*i.e.*, life]. Take over, O son, the kingdom ! I (will) follow right now the path of my husband. What (use) is (it) for me to live without (my) husband by chains of hope made by the extension of (different) kinds of pleasures when the act of meeting is like an illusion and a dream. I will go !" Saying so, she (however) remained. Then she was addressed by her sorrowful son who had diligently pressed her feet against his head out of devotion: "What (to do) with pleasure, what with the joys of life when there is separation from you ? I will give up (my) life first, later I will go to heaven from here". With tears coming out from her lotus-like face, with a net made out of words she became like a trapped and tied bird, (and) therefore she remained. After she had, together with her noble son, performed her husband's obsequies she (lived) by the rules of good conduct, chastity, fasting (and) with a totally cleaned mind; (moreover) she always gave wealth to the brahmins to increase (her late husband's) merit, she remained, with him in her mind, according to the rule of the *sati* vow (so that) she really was like Arundhati.[7]

In this early poetic inscription it is clearly a matter of Rajyavati wanting to immolate herself out of grief and love for her husband. It is only because of her son's tears that she reverses her decision and henceforth practices the *sati* vow, by which is meant virtuous rules of widow-like conduct, such as chastity, poverty and humility.

For the more recent period repeated literary references to widow burning in Nepal can be found. Mention of it is made above all in the local chronicles, the *vamsavalis.* In historical sources, *sati* is mostly documented for the Rana and Saha rulers.[8] To give just a few instances : the wife of Rama Saha and the younger wife of Narabhupala Saha are said, for example, to have followed their husbands onto the pyre[9]. Of Bahadur Saha, one of the sons of Prthivi Narayana Saha, it is said that seven lawful and two common-law wives were burned together with him *(ibid.,* p. 149). The pregnant mother of Ser Bahadur Saha could be hindered at first, after her husband had died, but she performed *sati* immediately after her son was born (Hasrat, *loc. cit.).* It is also said that Prime Minister Bhimsen Thapa forced the main wife of Rana Bahadur Saha to perform *sati.*[10]

A popular Nevari song about this has been handed down.[11] In it there are lines to the effect that after the queen had heard in her exile about the violent death of her husband :

"I must commit sati." (4) [...] The people shed tears. (5) [...] There having looked at the face of his mother Queen Bijyalaksmi, the Heir Apparent [Girvana Yuddha Saha] shed tears from his, eyes. (19) 'Haya, King ! Haya, my son ! Do not cause trouble to your subjects! May you be able to strengthen your kingdom !' (20) Queen Bijyalaksmi mounted the wooden pyre. On her lips the Queen took the name of Rama. (21) Bhimasena Thapa was Kaji, Bhimasena Thapa was Prime Minister at that time. The Queen had to die a premature death. (22) The Queen died. Everyone present shed tears from his eyes. (23) (Lienhard's translation).

This particular case of widow burning can be confirmed from a document *(rukka)* from the year V.S. 1869 (1813 A.D.) filmed by the Nepal-German Manuscript Preservation Project (reel no. K 45/11 D) : six years after the suicide of his mother, Girvana Yuddha Saha fulfilled her wish and endowed *12 ½ ropani* of land to the Pasupati Temple.[12]

It is due to this forced immolation of queen Bijyalaksmi

that the popular belief arose that Nepal was cursed by her, so that altruism would never be rewarded in country[13]. However, in the middle of 19th cent., Bhanubhakta Acarya (1814-1868) still praised *sati* in his controversial poem *Badhusiksa* ("Teachings for the daughter-in-law") as one of the highest virtues for women.

(striko dharinapati jati ta aru thok dekhtaina manle rati /) yas lokma paralokma sukha dinya so heri janchan sari.[15]

(...) for giving luck to her husband in this world and the other world she should go for sati.

Moreover, there are cases of widow burning which do not conform to the normative prescriptions on *sati* in the Dharmasastra. Thus, both wife and mother commit sati after the death of Pratapa Malla,[16] or a servant of Narabhupala Saha kills himself after the death of his master together with the junior queen *(kanchi rani)* Samudravati in V.S. 1711.[17] Especially worth mentioning is the reason given for this incident in the Gorkhavamsavali (as quoted by Pant, *op. cit.,* [V.S. 2041], p. 1) :

euta kelo pani striko svani, savakko samid[18] *bhanyaka pranaka malik hun bhani pranatyaga garyo.* [For a wife (her) husband is the master of her life and for a servant his employer is the master of his life].

To be sure, there are also indications that Rana rulers objected to widow burning. Even Janga Bahadur Rana was basically against *sati,* although three of his wives had themselves immolated along with him.[19] In support of this, Oldfield reports that Rana Bahadur Saha successfully kept both the wife of his brother Barm Bahadur and the widow of his friend Barra Captain Singh from committing suicide.[20]

II. Widow Burning in the Ain of 1854

Even the (Muluki)[21] Ain of 1853/54 must be understood as a step towards the abolition of widow burning in Nepal. Section 94, with the title *Sati janya ko,* is - just as the text as a whole - composed in a syntactically complicated and somewhat contradictory language. The 19th of a total of 31 paragraphs may here suffice as a sample[22] :

sati jachu bhani pani khanyai solama cadhiago nadida sammamȧ solavata khasi ladi vagi valagari urhi bhagi va. malai napola darlagyo bhani vacyaka 'svasnilai bhatko' ra solama pugi agolai sakya pachi vacyaka svasnilai paniko patiya dida auval lai 'avala-0' 5 doyam lai 3 sim 1ai 2 caharalai I rupaiya godan dharmadhikaralai patiya dilai 'garai' dinu.

When a married woman says[23] : "I'll go to/as sati", when she pours water over her head[24] (and) mounts the pyre, (but when) she falls from the pyre before it is lit, (or) when she slips down (or) with her last energy stands up and runs away, and when she says : "Don't burn me; I'm afraid !" let a married woman who survives in this manner be accorded rehabilitation[25] for boiled rice (including water), (or), if the fire has already been started, rehabilitation (only) for water; furthermore, have her give *godan* to the *dhamadhikara as* (service rendered for) rehabilitation - (at the following rates :) for (a woman of) *avala*[26] rank 5 (rupees), for *doyama* 3, for *sima* 2 and for *cahara I* rupee".

Point for point, and placed within the normal scheme of legal dogmatics, the Ain's regulations affecting *sati* present the following picture.

Regulation for *Satī* According to the (Muluki) Ain[27]

Ain of 1853/54	*Differences in more recents Ains*
Satī is permitted for married women or women held to be married in the eyes of the law[28] § 1, 12) if :	
1. they are over 16 years old (§ 1- *3)*	MsA (§ 1) : 11 years
2. their sons are over 16 years old *(*§ 2, 31)	MsA : no least age is mentioned
3. their daughters are over 5 years old (§ 3, 31)	MsA 3 years, Ain 1927: likewise 5 years, Ain 1945 and Ain 1961 : both 12 years; Ain 1945 (§ 2) adds: "If the daughter is married, 10 years".
4. they have no other husband (§ 4)	
5. they are not pregnant (§ 6-7)	
6. their decision is freely taken and immediately carried out (§ 9-10, 12, 27), i.e. if a) no force (§ 16, 20, 22)	

b) no narcotization (§ 18, 20 22) or c) presuasion (§ 18, 20, 21, 30 was used	
7. but rather the attmpt was made to change her mind (§ 9-10, 14-15)	Ain 1945: (§ 1): If this not possible, the next government office should be informed.

Moreover, *sati* is expressly forbidden :

8. if "only" the son has died (§ 8),	MsA : § 4-5, Ain 1927 : § 8
9. in the case of female slaves and servents (§5; but cf. § 12 : a slave as a wife !)	
10. if the husband of a Brahmin woman has died in a remote area (§ 11).	not in MsA but in the Ains of 1927, 1945 and 1961 (in all cases § 4); Ain 1945 (§ 5): for rice-acceptable castes a second pyre is only possible, if the widow is over 45 old.

Two stages of immolation are legally pertinent in assigning punishment :

11. a ritual stage, namely the bath (*snāna*) by which *satī* is initiated, and for which an expiatory payment (*patiyā*) is necessary in cases of retraction; or the breaking of the bracelets (§ 25), by which the ritual decision to commit suicide is confirmed, and
12. a factual stage, namely the igniting of the fire (§ 11 and 13)

Thus in the case of an abandonment of intent it is amatter of importance when this has occurred, i.e.

13. after the bath and after the igniting of the fire (§ 14),
14. after the bath and after the igniting of the fire (§ 15) or
15. after the breaking of the bracelets (§ 25).

16. Further, the distinction is made between the main culprit,

instigator and accomplice : the main culprit is the person who lights the fire, the instigator the one who gives permission for *sati* to be performed, the accomplices are those who carry or merely accompany the widow to the pyre. The degree of punishment consequently depends upon the part played, and also upon nearness of kinship, age and caste status. Whether the son is punished, for example, when he allows an illicit *sati* to be performed on his mother depends upon whether he is over or under twelve years old, and whether or not he is a step-son (§ 25, 27).

---

17. The Ain also regulates questions of the wodow's hereditary rights when she lets herself be immolated, particularly with regard to land and personal property.

---

18. Interestingly, the text betrays no knowledge of the legal conceptof error that serves to mitigate or cancel punishment. If a woman mistakenly supposed that her husband had died and made preparations to have herself immolated, she would still, after the misunderstanding had been cleared up, be fined a penalty of 5 rupees a month or 4 months in prison.

---

19. The types of punishment include : capital punishment, incarceration for life or for a limited period, fines, confiscation of property (both real estate and personal property); moreover - as has been seen - expulsion from the caste. Whoever, for example, incites a mother to perform *sati* at the death of her son is given a life-term jail sentence or even the death penalty, if his status is that of a slave (§ 8). Particularly harsh punishments are meted out on those who narcotize a widow before her immolation, or use violence to force her (§ 16, 18, 21-22), or in cases where *sati* is performed for a man who is not her husband (§ 8 : Death of a Son). The Ain 1945 limits the punishments to 17 years imprisonment.

Basically, the first ten of these detailed regulations are in accordance with prescriptions one finds in the Dharmasastra, especially in the Nibandhas (Raghunandana's Sudditattva, Madhava, etc.). Its socio-political essence can easily be seen : the authorities wanted to insure by any means that *sati* would only occur voluntarily, and that small children or other husbands would not suffer from the widow's decision.

But there is one other thing that shows up clearly, namely the distinction between ritual and physical death. For, sections 13-15 stipulate whether *patiya* is given or not, and for what. If the widow, say, has taken the ritual bath and already mounted the pyre (cf. paragraph 19 mentioned above) but is then held back from burning herself as prescribed, she obtains *patiya* for rice and water, which is equivalent to being received back into the commensal community of family and caste. Similar is the case when she leaps or falls down from the pyre before it is lit; then, assuming she withdraws, she receives *patiya* only for water but not for rice, which signifies loss of her previous caste status.

The fact that, in spite of this regulation, widows who have announced their intention to perform *sati* but later changed their mind had difficulties returning to their family, or were even prohibited from doing so, can be seen from punishment being laid upon the members of the commensal community who refused water and/or rice in spite of the *patiya* (§ 23, 24).

Ritually, a widow is dead already at the point when she takes the decision, expresses it and confirms it by the ceremonial bath (water poured over head and shoulders) or breaks her bracelets. If she reverses her decision after that, she can be received back into society, i.e., her original commensal community, only by taking ritual countermeasures. We see here relatively unusual boundaries between life and death, a point I shall return to later.

Fire and water : both are, as is well-known, important for any kind of vow, in marriage, at oaths, etc. Fire burns, water washes away impurity. Given the performative unity of language and action in rituals, a solemnly declared decision, enforced by water and fire, can neither be repeated nor reversed. Therefore, it is ritually impossible to retract from *sati* as it is ritually impossible to re-marry under the condition that marriage is a life-long alliance. Once the pyre is kindled, there is no way back for the widow into the commensal community - and this is practically another term for society.

In Deopatan there is a gate, the so-called Satidvara, that sets this ritual threshold literally in front of your eyes :

formerly, when widows went through this gate, they too could no longer return. Today people still talk half-secretly about a couple of poor old beggar women who leapt from the fire and were no longer able to return to their families.

III The Abolition of Widow Burning

But of course, in Nepal too there are no legal suttes anymore. On 28 June 1920, almost one hundred years, in other words, after Bentinck's outlawing of suttee in British India, all forms of widow burning were also made subject to punishment in Nepal. This occurred in Prime Minister Candra Samser's amended version of the Muluki Ain, and the reason given for it is not only so obvious that it ought really to have occurred earlier, but also revealing in terms of the motives behind *sati*, for therein it says.

Sati is not a strict religious duty. Whoever does not perform *sati* does not automatically commit an offence.

Sati is performed in order to achieve certain goals, for example, heaven, fame or religious merit. But these a widow can also attain by other means, such as chastity.

As women are unable to understand the meaning of the sacred writings, they are often subject to being misguided and led with the sole object of insuring that relatives get her inheritance or possessions. This is to be done away with.

It is impossible to distinguish between genuine and ungenuine *sati*. While the institution of *sati* is basically praiseworthy, the harm arising from it is greater. Consequently *sati* is hereafter prohibited.

Although no cases of widow burning have been reported in Nepal in recent times, it nevertheless still stands in high esteem. This is seen clearly in a Nepali lexicon of law terminology from the year 1981. There *satitva* is first glossed simply as *suddhatva* "(purity)", before the presently illegal implications are cited.

IV. Differences between Nepal and India

There are altogether four basic differences in regards to widow burning between Nepal and India :

1. Nepal counts for the oldest inscription of widow burning.

2. The regulations of the (Muluki) Ain on *sati* are more

detailed than those of the Dharmasastra.

3. The documents of the Saha and Rana period suggest that in Nepal widow burning was mainly practiced among the ruling castes and hardly among Brahmins. However, the paragraph 11 of the Ain prohibits, in Accordance with the Dharmasastra, a second pyre for the Brahmin widow. Given the fact that a high number of Brahmins were included in the preparation of the Ain this could nevertheless be a more theoretical prescription. I have not come accross any indigenous or Western explanation for the well-known distinction between *sahagamana* and *anugamana;* to me it seems to be an expression of higher purity and honour of the Brahmin widow, and thus as a kind of status differentiation.

4. The fact that the regulations of the Ain on widow burning were formulated and finally promulgated only a few years after the prohibition of suttee in British India is well in accordance with Nepal's claim as the only Hindu Kingdom in the *kali(yuga)* who defends "old" Hindu ideals against the anti-traditional values from the West. The emphasis on *sati* has always been higher when power was in danger : in the decline of the Vijayanagar empire or the Rajput kingdoms, in Bengal through the somewhat more strict actions against widow burning by the British or even perhaps in the recent "fundamentalism, originated by the self-immolation of Roop Kunwar in Rajasthan which was declared by Ashish Nandy as "the desperate attempt to retain through *sati* something of the religious world view in an increasingly desacralised, secular world ".

V. Widow Burning and Asceticism

Here is not the place to deal with the fundamental changes in the status of Hindu women from the first centuries of the Christian era, which ultimately led to the institution of widow burning, such as the prohibition of divorce and widow remarriage, the conception of marriage as a ritual gift of the bride *(kanyadana)* and - connected with this - hypergamy, the impurity of women, etc.

I can also not go into detail on the pitiful fate of a Hindu widow and its implications for the origin of *sati* : the loss of respect among the commensal community, the loss of authority among members of her family, servants and slaves all the way down to outright molesting by male relatives, a deprivation of rights before the law, complete dependency upon her son, the more or less direct accusation of having been responsible for the death of her husband, no possibility to remarry... - with its many unfortunate consequences : a life full of deprivation, chastity, shorn hair, white clothes without ornamentation, a cold floor to sleep on - and with it all the constant danger of being cast out and ending up as a beggar or prostitute...

Suicide, of course, is not the only consequence of the widow's lot, for in that case it would have occurred much more frequently. But at times it has been an apparently legitimate escape route within Hinduism. India and Nepal have not defended simple suicide. The Jains, who have gone so far as actually to promote suicide, speak of simple suicide as being a childish death (*balamarana*), whereas they hold meeting death as a result of sacred acts like fasting, meditation, abnegation and prayer to be the wisest kind of death (*pandita-pandita-marana*). Among Buddhists, the desire to end one's life is one of the three desires that keep the fire of life burning.

In Hinduism, too, a widow who kills herself with pills or hangs herself for the death of her husband, is not a *sati*. On the contrary, India has gone so far as to condemn suicide for the most part, not because - as in Christendom - it contradicts God's will, but because it implies emotions (*raga*) and force (*himsa*) and thus acts counter to exalted Brahmanical principles of conduct. This is exactly one of the arguments Candra Samser used in the abolition of *sati* in Nepal and he proposed other means by which fame, religious merit or heaven could be achieved.

India and Nepal, however, have recognized religiously motivated or propagated suicide, particularly voluntary self-immolation, as being a means to enter Brahma's world. It was the ascetic, who in the final analysis provided the model for such means. Since olden times, or to be more precise, since the early Samnyasa-Upanisada, this class of persons was allowed to make the Great Journey *(mahaprasthana),* the trip to the northern region without return. For them the very act of initiation into a sect is itself social death signifying a complete expulsion from caste society - symbolized among some

Dasanamis by ritually amounting a pyre. For them life, when seen under perfect knowledge, is only a meaningless burden, and suicide, therefore, a religiously secure consequence, even if the pure desire for death is deemed an expression of the fact that perfect knowledge has not yet been attained.

The same applies to widows. And in fact, several Dharmasastrins place them on the same level, prescribing identical practices in eating and dressing for the ascetic *(yati),* for one who has vowed chastity *(brahmacarin)* and for the widow. The regulations of the Nepalese (Muluki) Ain also exhibit parallels between asceticism and *sati,* for example, the formal decision of the widow *(ma sati janchu)* and of the ascetic (*samyastam maya*) or in the cases of a withdrawal of the vow to commit *sati* or to enter upon an ascetic life : in both a ritual purificatory bath is necessary.

The introduction and above all the religious legitimation of *sati* in brahmanical circles is modelled after the ideal of the ascetic and not, as it is often stated, by a modification of an old, possibly chtonic warrior ethic of taking the wife/widow as personal property, booty and burial object. Seen from this brahmanically influenced world, in which men - as in the Jagannath Jannath festival in Puri - throw themselves in front of wheels of the processional chariot, leap from precipices and into holy rivers or starve themselves to death, it is no wonder that some enthusiastic women caught up in religious zealotry should also "seek heroism of death in order to attain heavenly bliss" (Winternitz, *op. cit.,* p. 82 - my transl.), and that such women should try, by way of the Hindu *ars moriendi,* to influence their life beyond the grave and their reincarnation. In a religion whose highest goal is not the freedom of the individual in the world but his liberation *from* the world, the, self-immolation of women can also be one of their few means to give their life, by a heroic death, a sacred meaning. Satis loose, after all, their personal names, are worshipped not as the faithful wife of their husband but as a generalized Sati goddess.

However, if *sati is* woven into brahmanical ideas and concepts, a wellknown dilemma immediately appears : through their desire for religious merit by self-immolation widows get caught up again in *karma,* "for her act is done out of desire, perhaps a desire for merit. But for those who seek *moksa,* the duties of the household life as a widow, in patient self-abnegation, are appropriate". In Indian folk religion, on the other hand, it is the concept of violent death including religiously motivated suicide that can lead to deification, while in the brahmanical traditions any unnatural death is more connected with ghost worship *(bhuta, preta* etc.).

Thus it turns out in the end that *sati* remains undecided under the well known and fundamental question of Hinduism: Is it deed or knowledge that leads to heaven and finally provides liberation? Is it the sacrifice, ascetic self-sacrifice and that of the widow, or the true and sacred knowledge of sacrifice ? No more and no less! The religious and historical achievement of India and Nepal consists perhaps in their having left this question open and not having followed a dogmatism by which women are, as in the European middle ages, hunted and burnt as witches.

AI warned against Criticizing Shariah

Islamabad, 25 May 1998 (NNI)—Threatening Amnesty International with grave consequences for criticism of the Taliban's human rights, its supreme leader Mullah Omar has said the student body is simply implementing and observing Islamic injunctions. In an interview with Voice of America, Mullah Omar said the Taliban would react sharply if AI continued the criticism. He rejected the AI report as mere allegations. "We are just implementing the divine injections", he maintained. He said the AI had criticized the Qisas and Diyat, which would cause losses to AI. Mullah Omar also refuted the AI allegation that the accused were not provided sufficient opportunity for defence. He said the judges were learned and aware of the judicial rules.

Amnesty International 1999 Annual Report

Tens of thousands of women effectively remained prisoners in their homes under Taliban edicts. Several thousand civilians, including possible prisoners of conscience, were taken prisoner. Almost all the detainees were reportedly tortured or ill-treated. Thousands of people were deliberately and systematically killed; thousands of others remained missing. Scores of civilians were killed in direct or indiscriminate attacks by all warring factions on the civilian population in residential areas. At least eight floggings, 14 amputations and 10 executions were announced, but the actual numbers were believed to be higher. [...]

Severe restrictions by the Taliban prevented UN agencies and NGOs from providing immediate humanitarian assistance to destitute families. [...] Fear of 'punishment' under Taliban edicts prevented tens of the Kings of Bajhang had more than one wife. The Brahmanas and the Ksatriyas of Western Nepal had their wives from almost every ethnic community. Hamilton has written that in the beginning the region of Parvat was ruled by a prince of the Jariya tribe. He gave his only daughter, who was the heiress of the throne also, to Dimba of the lunar pedigree. In this way the state of Parvat came into the hands of a Hindu king from a Jariya ruler.

Although all the prescribed forms of marriage were practiced in Western Nepal, *gandharva* and *raksasa* forms were very common among the Khasa Ksatriyas and the low tribes. The Brahmanas performed the *daiva* type of marriage and a king generally invited the bridegroom and offered his daughter as a gift *(kanyadana)* to him amidst different kinds of rejoicings. Rich dowry was given to the son-in-law by the parents of the daughter. When Prithvinarayan Shah got his daughter Vilasakumari Devi married to Prince Ranabhimasaha of Sallyan, he promised to give Korvang, Chhilli, Thapala and Phalavang as dowry to him. Ranabahadur Shah fulfilled the offer of the grandfather and when Girvan Yuddha Vikram Shah ascended the throne, he also affirmed his faith in the donation of his grand-father by giving a new copper-plate to Ranabhimasaha. In the same manner when Prince Gajarajasingha of Bajhang married Princess Sarasvatikumari Devi, he got Syudara, the governorship of Thalara and an annual salary of Rs. 4000 from King Girvan. These facts show that the Brahma and *Prajapatya* of marriages were quite popular in Western Nepal during the seventeenth and nineteenth centuries. After marriage till death no ceremony was observed in the life of an individual in the region.

On the death of the individual for 13 days his or her family and relatives had to observe *asaucha* (pollution). Shaving of the head and moustaches, *brahmabhoja* and *danas* of different kinds were three main specialties of the *antesthikraya*. After one year, the *varkhi sradhya* of the dead was also performed. Each year the progenies of the dead gave a feast to the Brahmans and offered some articles to the manes. This action was done by them on the *tithi* (day) of death of the individual in the dark fortnight (*pitrapaksa)* of the month of Aswin alone. When someone died in the family of the ruler, the subjects, who had no parents, used to shave their head and moustache on the eleventh day of mourning.

Position of Women

Women were highly respected in the beginning. If a king had no male progeny, but only a daughter, the latter used to inherit the throne of the father. This fact is nicely elucidated by the daughter of the Jariya ruler married to Dimba and Sakunamala, the daughter of Pratapanalla, married to Prince Punyamala of Gela. Women were not only respected but esteemed like goddesses. In an inscription of Prthvimalla, Dharmamala and Dipamala have been compared with Bhumi and Sri, the two consorts of Lord Vinsu. The copper-plates of the Mallas show that their wives provided active co-operation to their consorts in running the administration of the state. The contents *suputraparivaramsamasasti* (ruling well along with the son and the family) of a copper-plate of Karbarika Vivosasai make it clear that the wife of the king provided active administrative help to him. An examination of the history of Sallyan would reveal to the fact-finders that Vilasakumari Devi took the whole charge of administration of the state in her hands and her father-in-law and husband remained the silent spectators of administration till her death. She is continuously found writing letters to Ranabahadur Shah and receiving answers from him about the plans and tactics of letters' conquests of various states of Western Nepal. It was because of her active military support that the Gorkhalis were able to conquer Jumla. Doti and parvat without much trouble. Because of the statesmanship of Vilasakumari Devi, Sallyan became a big and most potential state of the Baisi group and preserved her entity till 1951. After some time another very important lady is seen in the royal palace of Sallyan. She was Toranakumari Devi, the wife of Narendrabahadurasaha who ruled Sallyan for about 15 years. The queen built a nice temple of Naravadesvara Mahadeva in the Dang Valley and donated enough land for the worship of the deity. She helped construct several broad routes in Sallyan and made laudable contributions to the development of agriculture and religion in the state. The temple of Siddha Ratananatha of the Dang Valley possesses several *lalamoharas* of the queen which contain the details of the provisions she made for the worship of the temple, maintenance of the ascetics who lived there and performance of various festivals connected with the deities of the shrine.

Surya Vikram Gyawali is of the opinion that Goddess Kalika of the Jumla Valley was a Brahmana lady in the beginning. Jalandhari Raja received the riches and ownership of the state because of his association with this woman. Owing to this fact, when Kalika died, he made a temple in her honour in Jumla. Finally, she came to be deified and worshipped by the people.

One paper document of Saturday, Jyestha-sudi- 12 of V. S. 1850 (1793) reveals that *sati* systems was widely practiced by the females on the death of their husband in Western Nepal during the medieval period. When Lalitasahi of Juvitha village died in the said year, his wife (*thakurani*) learnt herself on the funeral pyre of her consort. As the couple were childless, Narajitasahi of Gallagoan, Tibrikot, who lit the pyre, received the property of the couple. The document has been signed by six renowned Sahis of the region. Before this, in the fifteenth century, Queen *Chandravati* had self-immolated herself on the funeral pyre of Vaksaraja, the son and successor of Kalyala Baliraja. From a letter circulated in Bajhang after the death of Jang Bahadur Rana to deter the prevalence of the *sati* custom in the region, it is clear that for a fairly long time this system was widely practiced in Western Nepal. As the Ksatriyas of Western Nepal came from Rajasthan they preserved this custom in their families as a clan-tradition. However, evidences are not lacking when the mothers of small babies did not go *sati* but lived as widows and protected their progenies from varius kinds of odds and worries of the society.

Many women of Western Nepal were highly versed in different kinds of arts such as in dance and music. The palace of Semja remained perpetually echoed with the melodious songs of young maidens. The young people there always moved *matta* (intoxicated) on being pierced by the slanting eyes of the beautiful and amorous women (*ramaniya ramanis)* of the town.

The institution of the *devakis* is quite old in Western Nepal. It started during the medieval period when the Kastriyas began to offer their daughter to the service of the deities in the temples. Originally its purpose was pious but with the march of time they became public women and their progenies had to accept the hierarchy of the lowest castes of the society.

Dhanavajra Vajrachayra has written that females enjoyed more freedom during the Malla period in Western Nepal and queens were decorated with regal titles. The women of the noble families were often very religious. The mother of Krachalladeva was of the cow and the Brahmanas. The wife of Krachalladeva assiduously worked for the protection of the opinion that the woman should possess proper faith in religion and donate articles of different kinds from time to time for the happiness of the poor and the needy. According to her the most important religion of a woman was to serve her husband with complete dedication to him. Queen Mahalvasanta, the wife of King Malaibama of Parvat, literally followed this ideal of *bhakti.* Who was an exceptionally devoted wife of her husband.

During the fifteenth-sixteenth centuries position of women considerably declined in Western Nepal due to the influx of the Brahmans and the Ksatriyas from the south. Although the Brahmanas taught lofty ideals to the people of "vacant minds, ready to receive their doctrines", themselves they did not observe the Brahmanical traditions Hudgson has written that :

"They had sensual passions to gratify, as well as ambition. They found the native females-even the most distinguished nothing loath, but still of a temper, like that of the males, prompt to repel indignities. These females would indeed welcome the polished Brahmans to their embraces, but their offspring must not be stigmatized as the infamous progeny of a Brahmana and a Melchha - must, on the contrary, be raised to eminence in the new order to things proposed to be introduced by their fathers. To this progeny also, then the Brahmanas, in still greater defence of their creed, communicated the rank of sacred order of Hindustan; and from these two roots, mainly, sprung the now numerous, prominent, and extensively ramified, tribe of the Khasa- originally the name of a small clan of creedless barbarians, now the proud title of the Ksatriya, or military order of the Kingdom of Nepal. The offspring of original Khasa females and of Brahmans, with the honours and ranks of the second order of Hinduism, got the patronymic titles of the first order; and hence the key to nomenclature of so many stripes of the military tribes of Nepal is to be sought in the nomenclature of the scared order".

The sexual lust of the Brahmanas and the Khasas greatly contributed to the decline of moral standard among the females. To some extent the *devakis* of the region were also responsible for it. The *devakis* were promiscuous. The women of the low tribes of the mountains, called *Ketis*, were also promiscuous. Men of rank, even of the scared order, passed their nights in the company of these women, who often danced and pleased them, and by an excessive indulgence with them "soon they got exhausted" in their life. The sexual freedom of the males and females not only gave inactivity to the society but also brought innumerable *jharra* families into existence which had no respectable status in the society.

Inheritance of Property

Father was the head of the family. His sons had no right of partition during his life time. After the death of the father and mother, if necessary, in ordinary families the property of the house and land under their possession were equally divided among the brothers. As the eldest brother performed the *antesthikrya* of the father and *managed* the house for sometimes, he used to get a little more land and property from the brothers in the division, and it was known as *jethamsa*. The daughters had the right in the property of the father in case they had no brother. Two such cases are found in Western Nepal when daughters inherited the throne of their fathers after their marriage.

In case of the royal families there was no tradition of division of the principality of a king among his sons. There the eldest son of the king became the ruler and inherited the state. However, at times a lot of confusions are found in regard to succession in Western Nepal. In the Malla period once division of the state is seen in the last quarter of the thirteenth century due to the tug of war between Jitarimalla and Anandamalla for the throne. This trouble came to an end after the coronation of Pratapamalla only. In Bajhang when Saktisingha became the king, Jagatisingha revolted against him, came to Thalara and began to rule from there. The enmity of the two houses took such a deep root at the time of these two brothers that even today their descendants condemn each other's progenies. After the fourteenth century the kings of Bajhang and Thalara began to give share (*amsa*) to their younger brothers at the time of their coronation and this gave rise to the states of Bajura, Dugrakot, Channa, Khetada, Sunikot, Talkot, Pandrahavisakhada, Randi, Chaimpur, etc, in case of Bajhang and Talari, Gajada, Dogyala, etc, in case of Thalara. This system of giving *amsa* to the brothers first commened during the rule of Malaibama. Because of this mistake of the King Western Nepal came to be divided into twenty-two in the end.

On seeing the tradition of Bajhang. Kulapradipasaha and Samarabahadurasaha two brothers of King Narendrabahadurasaha of Sallyan, also demanded share (*amsa*) and created a very bitter family environment. When Narendrabahadurasaha got fed up with the trouble, he wrote a letter about it to Jang Bahadur Rana. The latter finally issued *rukka* from Kathmandu which contained that the state was a non-divisible entity and whatever Kulapradipasaha and Samaserabahadurasaha were getting earlier for their maintenance, that they should silently accept and serve the king faithfully. It was also said in the letter that if they did not serve their brother faithfully, they would lose that allowance also which they were getting so far from the state. After the instructions of Jang Bahadur Rana from Kathmandu, they began to do their work faithfully. The best evidence for the inheritance of property is a *lalamohara* which Raja Samaserabahadurasaha of Sallyan got from King Tribhuvan in 1936. It contains beautiful account of the rules which was followed in the division and inheritance of property by the people and the royal families in Western Nepal in the past.

Forced Labour and Slavery

Owing to low density of population and easy availability of immense land and forest-products, people of Western Nepal worked in their own homes and fulfilled the needs of their life without much use of money and dependence on the state. Because of the mountainous landscape, aristocracy of the region and needs of the military, labourers were in great demand in the region. Bulk of finest land was given as *virta* and *jagira* to the civil and military employees of the state. Therefore, governments were not in a position "to pay wages to a large number of porters and other labourers" engaged to meet the supply of the articles and foodgrains to the military and administrative staffs. Thus, forced and unpaid labour became necessary and compulsory.

One copper-plate of Jumla of Sake 1278 (1356) reveals that the females of the Brahmana caste also had to serve as slaves, if they did some heinous crime in their life. It shows that slavery was deep-rooted institution during the Malla period. The people of the low tribes and mountain tribes, and captured soliders of battles, had to serves as slaves. The entire adult male population, irrespective of its class and community, had to render compulsory unpaid labour service to the government. Only those houses were free from this obligation which supplied officials and military personnel to the governments and servants to the temples of the states. In Parvat even Brahmanas had to render compulsory unpaid labour service during the age of the Bama rules. They were remitted from this obligation in 1803 only. Herbs, drugs, articles for guests and mails were also supplied through such labourers. With the help of *Jhara* (unpaid) labour in 1796 a fort was also constructed at Jamla by the local administrator. Similarly, a bridge was built at Benighat, in the month of June 1805. The system of forced labour put the people of the region to a great hardship. As the labourers had to serve the state without any return, their life became miserable. After the conquest of the region by the Gorkhalis, even the pilgrims of the Mansarovar Lake began to force the villagers of the route to render "porterage services without any payment". In 1799 the government of Nepal "received report that the entire are a west of the Bheri had been ruined because of the indiscriminate use of unpaid labour services". Seventeen years after this, in 1816 the authorities of Doti were warned by an order from Kathmandu that they would be regarded as traitors if they expected unpaid labour "for the purposes other than the transportation of arms and ammunitions as well as of the sick persons...." Now the labourers got fifty per cent concessions also in their *walaka* levies.

References

1. Thanks for comments on an earlier draft of this paper are due to Andras Höfer, Julia Leslie and Mahes Raj Pant.
2. The representation of the *preta* as a skeleton stripped of flesh (cf. D. Schlingloff, *Die Religion des. Buddhismus,* Berlin 1963, Bd. 11, pp. 21ff. and pl. 1), a being which may be a burden upon, or even bring death to, those it has left behind, is not a picture of Death but of one "who has gone away", *i.e.,* a deceased person.
3. Even in Europe, Death was represented in such a fashion only from the 14th century on : cf. P. Westheim, *Der Tod in Mexiko,* Hanau [1989].
4. I will not discuss in this paper the history of widow burning in India. Among the more recent publications on this aspect I should perhaps mention : J.F. Sprockhoff, "Die Alten im alten Indien - Ein Versuch nach brahmanischen Quellen", *Saeculum* XXX (1979) : 374-433 (esp. pp. 421-28 and fn. 154 with further references); J.D.M. Derrett, "Anantarama's Defence of Suttee (c. 1818-1820)", *Our Heritage,* Calcutta Sanskrit College Research Series, no. CXIX, 150th Anniversary Vol., 1980; E.L. Stutchbury, "Blood, Fire and Mediation : Human Sacrifice and Widow Burning in Nineteenth Century India, *in* : M. Allen and S.N. Mukherjee (eds.), *Women in India and Nepal,* Australian National Univ. 1982, pp. 21-75; V.N. Datta, *Sati - A Historical, Social and Philosophical Enquiry into the Hindu Rite of Widow Burning,* New Delhi, 1988; Arvind Sharma (with Ajit Ray, Alaka Hejib and Katherine K. Young), *Sati - Historical and Phenomenological Essays,* Delhi 1988; Weinberger-Thomas, Catherine, "Cendres d'immortalite. La cremation des veuves en Inde," *Arch. Sc. soc. des Rel.,* Vol. 67/1 (1989): 9-51; J. Leslie, "A Problem of Choice : The Heroic Sa" or the Widow-Ascetic", in : J. Leslie (ed.) *Rules and Remedies in Classical Indian Law,* Leiden (1992). Cp. also fn. 5.
5. See for the history of the abolition of suttee in India : V.N. Datta, *op. cit.,* and V. Dalmia-Luderitz, "über die Verwendung der "Parliamentary Papers on Widow Immolation in India,

1821-1830", *in* : A. Jones (ed.), *Aubereuropaische Frauengeschichte-Probleme der Forschung,* Pfaffenweiler, 1990, pp. 41-66. Mulk Raj Anand, *Sati - A Writeup of Raja Ram Mohan Roy about Burning of Widows alive,* Delhi, 1989, presents not only the papers of the debate between Rammohan Roy and orthodox Hindus but also controversial articles, some of them very stimulating, from Indian journals on the death of Roop Kunwar, a young girl from Rajasthan who commited suicide after the untimely death of her husband in September 1987. For this, see also Julia Leslie, " Suttee or *Sati* : Victim or Victor", in J. Leslie (ed.), *Roles and Rituals for Hindu Women,* London, 199 1, pp. 8-11.

6. Dh. Vajracarya (ed.), *Licchavi Kala-ka Abhilekha,* Kathmandu V.S. 2030 : no. 2. For other editions cp. the overview in M. Slusser, Nepal Mandala, Princeton 1982, p. 404, to be supplemented by D.R. Regmi, *Inscriptions of Ancient Nepal.* 3 Vol., New Delhi 1983, Vol. I (text) and II (trans.), pp. 2-3 in both Vol.

7. Satis are often described as Arundhati, Vasistha's wife who is considered as perfectly chaste: cf. Winternitz, *Die Frau in den indischen Religionen, 1. Teil : Die, Frau im Brahmanismus,* Leipzig, 1920, p. 62.

8. It seems that the Mewars had a sceptical attitude towards *sati.* Among them girls are joined in marriage to Narayana in a special ceremony at a maidenly age, so that, *ritualiter,* they never become widows. As a result, remarriage occurs among Newars much more often than among Parbatiyas, but hardly any *sati.* However, there are cases of suttee among Malla aristocracy (see below).

9. Bikram Jit Hasrat (trans.), *History of Nepal as Told by Its Own and Contemporary Chroniclers,* Hoshiarpur, 1970, p. 120, 128.

10. Perceval Landon (1928), *Nepal,* 2 Vol., Kathmandu, 1976 (reprint)), Vol. 1, p. 75.

11. S. Lienhard, *Songs of Nepal : An Anthology of Nevar Folksongs and Hymns,* University of Hawaii, 1984, no. 95.

12. For more cases among the Ranas and Sahas see M.R. Pant, "Budhakaji Amarasimha Thapa paraloka bhaeko kura pareka, pacavata tatkalika aprakasita patra", *Purnima* 58.2 : 45-61 : letter of Bhimsen Thapa and Kaji Ranadvaja Thapa to Aniruddha Upadhyaya V.S. 1873 (Saun 30 gate), in which he mentions the *sahagamana* of his *kamcha mahatari,* and a letter of Cautara Bam Saha, dated V.S. 1873 (Saun 30 gate), in which mention of the *sahagamana* of his *kamcha mukhani is* also made, as well as a letter of Rajendra Vikrama Saha to Padmapani Pandita, dated V.S. 1873 (Magha 21 gate) which says : (*sri*

jethamumajyu)-le sahagamana garnubhayo.

13. See M. Hutt, *Himalayan Voices. An Introduction to Modern Nepali Literature,* Berkeley and Los Angeles 1991, p. 152.
14. See K. Pradhan, *A History of Nepali Literature,* New Delhi 1984, p. 41.
15. Quoted after P.M. Pradhan, *Adikavi Bhanubhakta Acharya,* Kalimpong 1979 (Makers of Nepali Literature Series).
16. See M.R. Pant, "Mahendra Mallako visayako kehi kura", *Purnima* 38.2 : 74-81.
17. See E. Thompson, *Suttee,* London, 1928, p. 38f. and 48f.
18. *s* for *kh* : *samid* from Persian *khavind (*= Skr. *svamin).*
19. Landon, *op. cit.,* Vol. I p. 154f., and Vol. II, p. 68. Cf. also Pramode Shamshere Rana, *Rana Nepal - An Insider's View.* Kathmandu, 1978, p. 46-47.
20. Henry Ambrose Oldfield, *Sketches from Nepal,* 2 Vols., London, 1880, Vol. 1, p. 251.
21. It is only from the edition of V.S. 2009-2012 onwards that the adjective *muluki,* "royal", was added to the title of the code : J. Fezas, "The Nepalese Juridical Tradition and its Sources - A List of the *ain* books kept in the National Archives . (Ms.), *in : Abhilekh,* Barsa 8, anka. 8, 2047 V.S., pp. 121-134.
22. I am preparing a critical edition and translation of this section along with a more detailed study on widow burning in Nepal.
23. "Sati", denotes in the Ain both the woman who is prepared to have herself immolated and the act of immolation.
24. A symbolic bath, such as is prescribed according to the Dharmasastra prior to *sati.*
25. Qnly the *dharmadhikara,* the "legal administrator" and house priest *(rajguru)* of the king, can confer *patiya,* which may be understood as the ritual preconditions for being taken back into the caste. In distinction thereto, a priest, *e.g.* of Pasupatinatha Temple, confers *prayascitta,* a type of purification of personal faults. Both concepts, however, are often used synonymously in the Ain. Concerning *dharmadhikara* see the long section 89 (Dharmadhikarako) in the Ain (ed. KNM); concerning *patiya* and *prayascitta* see A. Höfer, *The Caste Hierarchy and the State in Nepal - A Study of the Muluki Ain of 1854,* Innsbruck, 1979, pp. 185-188.
26. This and the following terms are tax classes and, indirectly, status categories, determined according to the quality of irrigable land : cf., for example, Topa Bahadur Simha, *Kanuni Sabda-Kosa,* Kathmandu, 1981, s.v., or U Muller, *Die eändliche Newar-Siedlungen im Kathmandu-Tal-Eine vergleichende Untersuchung sozialer und okonomischer Organisations-formen der Newar,* Giessen, 1984, p. 102.

27. Sources :
KNM *Sri 5 Surendra Bikram Sahadevaka Sasanakalama Baneko Muluki Ain.* Kathmandu : Sri 5-ko Sarkara (Kanuna tatha Nyaya Mantralaya), V.S. 2020 (hereafter called "Ain")
MsA The manuscript dated V.S. 1910,(1853) is kept in the National Archives, Kathmandu. It is a working copy with many additions of different scribes starting from p. 34[r] and ending on p. 856[r].
(Muluki) Ain of 1927 : *Muluki Ain,* 4 pts. and addenda, Kathmandu : Manoranjan Pres, V.S. 1927 (1870); of V.S. 1945 (1888) and 1961 (1905) : both ed..by Sri 5-ko Sarkara (Kanuna tatha Nyaya Mantralaya), Kathmandu. For further manuscripts and editions of the (Muluki) Ain see Jean Fezas, "The Nepalese Juridical Tradition...", *loc. cit.*

28. The Ain distinguishes between three categories of wives of the Cord-wearers *(tagadhari) : (a) viha gari lyayaka,,* "[virgins *(kanya)]* brought by performing a proper, i.e. "vedic" wedding ceremony" (= *vivahita);* (b) *diyo kalasa puji lyayaka, "[virgins]* brought by performing the [simplified] rites of the lamp and water pot" (= *lyaita); (c) manomanasa ga lyayaka,* "[virgins] brought by consent' (i.e. without any marriage ritual)" (also = lyaita). Cf. Ain (§ 317.2) and Hofer, *op. cit., p.* 74. The Ain (§ 94.5, cf., however, § 94.12) prohibits. *sati.*

7

Women's in Politics

The study of women's participation in politics raises the several issue of their systematic discrimination, and powerlessness, and under representation almost all over the world. Inspite of the enactment of important international legal instruments like Convention on Elimination of All Forms of Discrimination Against Women (1979) and Convention on Political Rights of Women's (1952) by the world body and holding of the Global Conferences on women like Nairobi Conference (1985) and Beijing Conference (1995), over the years, women's political situation all over the world has not improved very significantly. Except for few Scandinavian countries like Sweden (38.1%), Norway (34.4%), Finland (31.5%) and Denmark (30.7%), women's representation in the Parliaments is none too impressive even in the advanced democracies like the U.K, the U.S.A., France, and others.

In fact on an average women constitute only 10 percent of all elected parliamentarians worldwide. While searching for an independent identity and 'space' for themselves, women have seriously questioned and challenged the existing structures, and value systems that perpetuate inequity and discrimination in society and politics. Such efforts by women to reverse the situation have brought them into a situation of direct confrontation with forces of conservatism and reaction. Access to the political power and decision making process is considered as an index of the overall status of women in society. In a patriarchal and male dominated society like Nepal where women are systematically discriminated by according them a low status, the inadequate and unfair representation in politics has been a historical reality. Even compared to some countries in the South Asian region Nepal's situation is not very encouraging.

Women in Parliament

At the present, the Parliament in Nepal is represented by 12 women, 7 (3.4% of the total) in Pratindidhi Sabha-the lower house and 5 (8.3% of the total) in Rastriya Sabha-the upper house. The composition of women legislators in the present Parliament is not very different from the first elected Parliament in 1991 in which Pratinidhi Sabha and Rastriya Sabha were represented by 8 and 3 women legislators respectively. The under representation of women in the national legislature violates the spirit of the Constitution of Kingdom of Nepal, 1990 which makes it mandatory for the reservation of minimum of 5% seats for women besides instructing everybody to promote gender justice.

In a background of the tremendous contribution and sacrifices made by women to the success of the Jan Andolan-1990 (Peoples' Movement for the Restoration of Democracty-1990) such a gender gap in women's representation is, indeed, a unbearabale response to women's aspirations the political parties in Nepal. The inflexible and conservative attitude of almost all political parties is evident from the fact that none of them could display the spirit of magnanimity towards women in distribution of parliamentary tickets limit set by the constitution. Even the veteran women politicians and seasoned political stalwarts were lumped in the reservation basket. The political background of the women candidates shows that most of them also do not possess an independent political identity of their own. Many of them have been initially projected by the parties on account of their very close family relationship that of widow, daughter-in-law etc, with some senior male leaders.

It is evident that most of Nepalese women politicians, like their male counterparts, belong to the small upper strata of urban, middle class, upper caste (primarily, Bahun, Chhetri and Newars) and educated elite background. None of them come from the rural, grass-root and under class or low caste background. Grossly inadequate representation of women in the national legislature has negatively affected the enactment of gender sensitive legislations like the Women's Property Right Bill. Because of the numerical weakness and lack of confidence among the women Member of Parliaments, they appear to be incapable of influencing the rigid attitude of their male colleagues so far. Women's representation in the local level politics has undergone a dramatic expansion following the enactment of the legislation requiring the election of at least one women representative from each and every ward committee of Village Development Committees (VDC). Municipalities and Metropolitan cities.

Few of the discussed causes that greatly marginalize women in politics are as follows:

- Patriarchal and male dominated society which treats women as the second class citizens and compels women to accept the low and subordinate status in society.
- Low level of literacy and political awareness among women.
- Economic dependency of women on male members of the family as a result of denial of the property right
- Lack of family and support for active participation in politics which compels many women to choose between home and public life.
- Lack of confident, competent and credible women who can act as the role models for other women at all levels of society
- Growing criminalization, corruption and lumpenization of polities, thereby, making it increasingly difficult for the women to participate actively in the polities.
- Weak civil society and isolationist as well as divisive tendencies among the women groups and other alternate groups have provided a carte blanche freedom to the unprincipled and amoral people to misuse the political power.

Tendency to distance from the political process and obsession with the NGO type project oriented activities have resulted in loss of credibility for the most of women groups, who, otherwise, could have made very useful intervention in the political challenge ahead.

Problems

Since the dawn of democracy in 1990 Nepalese women are trying to confront multitude of problems and challenges simultaneously. It is the presence of both opportunities and challenges that spurs Nepalese women into action. They have already succeeded in a great deal in sensitizing a large section of society, both male and female, towards the gender sensitive issues like women's property right legislation need for increased reservation for women in different levels of polity to enhance their political participation. However there is a need for the consolidation of gains already made by women in politics. There is also need for promoting the upward political mobility of the women who have been elected in the different levels of the political system. Equally important is the need for conducting the effective advocacy and lobbing for greatly expanding the level of political reservation for women in order to bridge the gender gap in politics.

Herein lies the greatest challenge for all women leaders, politicians, activists, researchers and gender sensitive individuals to develop an overarching vision and concrete strategy for action and building up a broad countervailing unity and solidarity, cutting across all the conventional barriers, in order to attain their cherished goal of full equal participation in politics. Women's participation in the various levels of decision making is an essential prerequisite for the establishment of equality, development and peace. Women constitute about 50% of the total population of Nepal but yet their participation in the various levels of decision making is negligible. The political space all over the world is monopolized by men. In many countries women have played a very important role in the independence movements for democracy, but their participation in the various spheres of public life has continued to remain minimal in comparison to their male counterparts. The political participation of women in the South Asia region is not very encouraging.

In many countries of South Asia special provisions; have been made to increase women's political participation, yet the percentage of women in the higher levels of the political power structure has not risen. There are various factors that have discouraged women from taking an active part in politics.

The main reasons are due to the amount of violence, corruption and manipulations, which are present there. Many women who have excellent leadership qualities are unwilling to participate in politics because of these factors. It is therefore essential to make politics clean and green so that the flow of women into the political arena in enlarged.

Rule of Ranas

For about a century of isolation, roughly between 1850-1950, Nepal was ruled by a feudal family-the Ranas, who called themselves kings. The Ranas ruled in Nepal for 104 years, during which time the people were deprived of fundamental rights. In 1950, the rule of the Ranas was overthrown by a movement jointly involving the people of Nepal and the king. During this historical mass movement the women of Nepal played significant roles. They not only participated in demonstrations but also raised the awareness of the people through radio programmes and establishing women's organizations to motivate women. Many female leaders worked underground and some of them were arrested for distributing pamphlets. Even at the time of autocratic rule female leaders worked hard establishing schools, demanding voting rights for women and mobilizing a lot of women through organizations with an objective of fighting against the Rana rule.

After the political change of 1951, when democracy was established women's organizations were influenced by party politics. Women were represented in the National Level election of 1958. One woman was elected into parliament and several were nominated into the National Assembly. But in 1960 the parliamentary system of government was banned by His Majesty the king and the partyless Panchayat System was established. Women activists protested hard against this Royal proclamation which was undemocratic. A few women activists were jailed for a long time or more than two years due to their political views and actions.

For more than thirty years there was no organised party system but women worked underground mobilizing other women. Though there were women' s organizations established by the government under the Panchayat system, they were not able to mobilize large numbers of women. Constitutional provisions to involve women at the grassroots level were made but the number of women in Parliament was very limited during this period. In 1989 there was mass movement for the restoration of democracy.

At this point of time, many female leaders were jailed. The

participation of Nepalese women for the restoration of democracy is a milestone in the history of popular mass movement women from various political parties, social workers, NGO activists and students leaders all contributed greatly to the success of this movement.

New Constitution Favoured Women

After the restoration of democracy a new Constitution of Nepal was promulgated which provided women with equal political rights. The provision formulated states that women can vote, compete in local and national elections, involve themselves in political parties and support and adapt any political ideology. The constitution also states that all political parties must have at least 5% candidates for house of representative. Three seats must also be reserved for women in the upper house of Parliament. The new ordinance Act of 1997 made another provision to increase the participation of women at a local level. This act states that one seat must be reserved for women in each ward of the Village Development Committee.

Due to this compulsory provision about 40,000 female candidates were elected in the local level election of 1997. This provision really forced all parties to support a female candidate and encouraged women to become involved. Women's political participation at a grass roots level has clearly increased but it is too early to say whether any positive change in the lives of women will come about or whether female politicians will be able to raise women's issues strongly. The number of women involved with politics on a National level is negligible. The political participation of women has not increased very significantly in the recent election.

Assembly, the Upper House of Parliament three out of sixty members were females. Therefor 4.9% of the total numbers of Parliament were female in 1991. When this figure is compared with the percentage of females in Parliament in 1986 (5.7%) it is clear to see that a decreasing trend in female participation is present. This trend is further confirmed by the mid-term poll of 1994 where the number of women elected was only seven. Participation in Village Development Committees (VDC) and Municipalities is also very low. According to the Election Commission's report of 1992 the number of candidates in the VDCs were 102,502 out of which the number of women candidates were 956 which is 0.9%. The number elected were 241 which 241 which 0.55% out of 44,662 members. Even the constitutional provision for integrating women into the various levels of the political power structure has failed to increase women's participation.

Thus the women's movements have been able to generate awareness and encourage women to fight for their rights but still few women are taking up active roles in the political scene. Many countries of South Asia; except Nepal, Bhutan and the Maldives, have produced female Prime Ministers and President yet even these successful examples have failed to encourage women to participate in politics.

Reason for Low Political Participation

1. *Patriarchal Values and Norms*: The main reason for low political participation of women in politics is the patriarchal structure of society. According to our traditions and culture the participation of women in politics and the public eye is against the generally accepted role of women. The patriarchal values have subjugated and distempered women.
2. *Lack of Institutional Support*: Though there are many institutions established for the over all development of women there is a lack of institutional mechanism, which can encourage and support women to take part in elections. There are many women's organizations related to different political parties but they have not been able to provide moral and financial support to women who are interested in becoming involved in politics.
3. *Criminalization*: Criminalization in politics has increased rapidly in recent years. Mafia, money, manipulation and muscle power, i.e. 4-M, have played dominant roles in South Asian politics. Because of this scenario it is very difficult to motivate and encourage women to come forward and take part in this "dirty game". Women feel that it is not their territory, that men are better players than themselves. This view is simply not true. Women can be just as good, if not better when it comes to these dealings.
4. *Lack of Family Support*: Family support can either prevent

or promote women from participating in politics. Women who come from families with a strong political history will often be encouraged to continue the work of past relatives. Women generally need to receive permission from their husbands or fathers in order to embark on a political career. Without this permission and support it would very difficult for women to become successful politicians. This is not only because of the financial help, which is so often required, but also for moral encouragement.

The role which women have in the home gives additional ties to female politicians, which reduce their mobility. Women who are married and trying to bring up children while keeping a home will find it almost impossible to work full time as well. This problem is enhanced in a country like Nepal because of the large family sizes that put additional burdens on women.

5. *Wrong social and cultural views*: It is generally expected by a majority of people, both male and female, that the women's role is in the home. Women are considered stupid and ignorant when it comes to matters of any real importance. When they are constantly being told that they are not intelligent enough to participate in politics it is no wonder that they do not believe in themselves. Women are encouraged to believe that politics is much too complicated for them to understand and so it is best left to men. They should stay at home, cooking and cleaning and having children. Women who do have a slight inclination to achieve something in life might be encouraged to be a nurse, midwife or school teacher as these are jobs in their league.

6. *Lack of Education and Awareness*: We have already seen that the literacy rate of women is considerably lower than that of men. Boys are encouraged to attend school whereas girls are of more use in the home. This denial of a basic education means that the majority of women do not realize that they are not receiving their full rights. It is difficult to teach them when they cannot read and difficult for them to stand up for themselves when they can not write.

7. *Economic Dependency:* Funds are required in order to embark upon a political career, the majority of women are

financially dependent upon their husbands or fathers. Women without money do not have the freedom to make their own decisions and do as they want. A women who wants to become involved in politics but has no funds must have funds must have the support of her family. This can be difficult to obtain because of the cultural way of thinking.

In order to encourage more women to participate the following activities should be formulated:

1. *Awareness raising programs*: There is a definite need to raise awareness throughout the country to the ability and potential of female politicians and also to encourage women to come forward as political candidates. People must be encouraged to vote for female politicians. The programs must try to change the concept that politics is a "dirty game" that is not suitable for women.
2. *Leadership development*: Leadership development programs for women would promote their confidence and teach them that they are capable of occupying political positions. The public relations and management skills of women could also be developed in these programs. Training would encourage them to take part in politics as well as raising the political consciousness among women. There is a great need for political reform. Clean elections need to be brought about along with an election system that is favorable for women's political empowerment.
3. *Support from women's pressure groups*: Pressure groups and support groups should be formed throughout the country to work as lobbying groups in conjunction with political parties. Their aims should be to increase the political participation of women at various levels of the power structure and to support women eager to take part in politics.
4. *Increase the number of seats reserved for women*: The existing constitutional provision related to women's politics is very limited. More seats should be reserved for women at all levels of the political power structure, not only at the higher level.
5. *Economic empowerment*: Women must be given the opportunity to become economically independent so that they are able to make their own decisions without needing

the permission of their husbands of fathers. There is a great need to change all the discriminatory laws related to women.

6 *Change in the negative role the media*: In many countries of South Asia the media have been playing a negative role by projecting stereotype roles for women. There is a great to change the attitude of the media through various gender sensitive-training programs.

7. *Change in traditional beliefs and the values system*: The belief that women are weak, sexual objects must be changed. These types of beliefs are deeply rooted in our society. The main task is to change the traditional believes of people through positive promotion of the values of women.

8. *Awareness about women's rights*: Women's rights are human rights. This message should reach all segments of society. Various awareness programs should be organized to create awareness about these issues.

9. *Encouragement from political parties*: The role of the political parties is very important for increasing women's political participation. It has been observed that women are not encouraged by the political parties to participate in political sphere. All the political parties should reserve at least 30-40% of their positions for women in all parts of the party hierarchy, especially at the decision making level.

It will be impossible to create any change in policies without increasing the representation of women in the various levels of the political power structure. Women need to learn about politics, its impacts and its positive consequences. They must understand the importance of their vote. Everyone must realize that women are essential parts of a political system that is free from corruption and exploitation. The voices of women strengthen democracy and will lead to a peaceful, developed and equal society. Political parties should encourage more women to enter into politics. They should not be used only as vote banks. Instead, they should help bring about change to the present political structure that is biased against women. This reform should be designed to place measures on expenditure, control violence, ensure voter registration and fair canvassing of votes. There is a great need to reserve seats for women to help curb the vast difference between the number of males and females holding political power.

A review of the experience of Nepalese women's struggle to achieve human rights and political rights during the decade since the dawn of democracy also shows that it is not very different from that of their global counterparts, particularly the South Asian sisters. Instead, in Nepal's context, the situation of women is even more pathetic and grave as they are still treated as the second class citizens. Extremely low social status and disproportionately low representation of women in all walks of public life mirrors the marginalization, subordination and dehumanization of Nepalese women. Since 1990, the Government of Nepal has been making continuous efforts to enhance the women's status and empower them by guaranteeing the "right to equality" under the Constitution of the Kingdom of Nepal, 1990 and implementing various gender sensitive development programs and ratifying 16 important international human rights instruments, including the CEDAW. The constitutional provisions related to the "Directive Principles and Policies of the State" have set guidelines for the state to pursue a policy of encouraging the women to participate in national development by making special provisions for their education, health, employment and welfare.

Moreover, the Constitution also makes the mandatory reservation of 5% seats for women in both houses of the parliament. "The local Representatives Act, 1996" makes the reservation of 20% seats for women in the grassroots political units-the Village Development Committees (VDC) and Municipalities. As part of the post-Beijing Conference initiative, a separate Ministry of Women and Social Welfare has been established. The newly established Ministry has formulated the Gender Equality and Empowerment National Work Plan, 1997. The ongoing Ninth Five-year Plan Document has specially targeted the women in its overall poverty alleviation strategy. Moreover, in accordance with its commitment in the Beijing Conference, 1995, HMG's Ministry of Law and Justice has submitted a gender sensitive amendment Bill to the Parliament with a view to amend various discriminatory and derogatory provisions in the Civil Code (Muluki Ain). This proposed amendment provides women an increased leverage in the inheritance rights, marriage, divorce, adoption, abortion, violence, rape etc. Nepal has also been actively involved in the preparation of the draft of the "SAARC Convention on Preventing and Combating Trafficking of Women and Children for Prostitution." Which is expected to be ratified in the forthcoming overdue SAARC Summit.

Thus it could be regarded as an important step in promoting the rights of girls child and women in the region as well as in fighting against the most abominable trade and trafficking of innocent girls and women for immoral purposes.

No less noteworthy is the emergence and growth of the NGOs and human rights organizations committed to the cause of women. Not only have these organizations contributed a great deal through advocacy and action to the sensitization of the society to the issues related to women's empowerment and welfare, they have also succeeded in forcing the otherwise reluctant and indifferent government, political parties, legislature and judiciary to respond to women's issues on many occasions. The under representation of Nepalese women in polities is a social and historical reality. Women are silent and disproportionately represented in Nepalese politics. Women have been treated as the 'Vote Banks' only by the political parties and politicians alike. Looking at the functioning of political parties in Nepal it appears that women are treated only as the ornamental showpieces or the auxiliary force. This is also evident in the only nominal representation in the party central committees as well as in the low priority or position accorded to the party sister organizations compared to other party related fraternal organizations like the students and youth groups.

The inflexible and conservative attitude of almost all political parties, irrespective of their high sounding promises and radical rhetoric, is evident from the fact that none of them could display the spirit of magnanimity towards women candidates in distribution of the parliamentary tickets exceeding the mandatory limit of 5% set by the constitution in all the general elections held so far the pervasive gender discrimination in politics makes even the veteran woman politicians feel bypassed, ignored and insecure. Very few of the women politicians or members of the parliament projected by political parties possess an independent identity of their own. Their political background has been usually characterized the ascriptive dynastic patronage by a powerful leader and non-merit factors etc. It has been experienced that in a country with patriarchal society like Nepal powerful socio-economic, cultural and institutional barriers have blocked all but the most tenacious women from politics. This could be the main reason for fitful, sporadic and episodic participation of woman in politics. Hence, because of the dependence of women politicians upon the patronage and support of the senior male politicians in the party and because of their political vulnerability a decade long experience of women in the legislature shows that they have not been able to develop sufficient confidence or capacity to push through the woman friendly legislation's like the "Women's Inheritance Bill" or "Reproduction Rights Bill" etc.

Neither have they been able to espouse the agenda different from male counterparts, aimed at restoring the health of our dysfunctional political system. In the last general elections held on May 1999, out of 2,238 candidates for 205 seats only 135 were women and as many as 113 constituencies did not have any women candidate at all. Looking at such political exclusion and marginalization of women, it could be conjectured that at this rate woman will take many more centuries to enjoy equality with men.

In spite of the dismal scenario at the national level, women's representation in the local level politics has undergone a dramatic expansion following the enactment of the Local Bodies Act, 1996 which required the election of at least one woman from each ward committee of the VDC and municipalities. As a result, the elections to the local bodies held on 1,007 and 1998, returned more than 40,000 women representatives. It constitutes almost 20% of all the elected office bearers. Without doubt, the representation of such a large number of women belonging to the heterogeneous socio-economic and political backgrounds in the grassroots units of the political system can be expected to have a long-term catalytic impact in the society and politics.

Issues affecting realisation of women's rights are:

— Patriarchal and male dominated society, which, on one

hand, oppresses and marginalizes women by compelling them to accept the low subordinate status in the society and on the other hand, discourages women's political participation by making it matrilineal dynastic, ascriptive and patronage oriented;

- Lack of political will and appropriate implementation machinery has made mockery of a number of progressive legislation with good intentions;
- Low priority given to women's programs by the government always results in 'tokenisms' and resource shortages;
- Growing criminalization, violence, corruption, derailment of democratic norms, values and rising cost of electioneering acts as deterrent against women's participation;
- Lack of strong, confident, competent and credible women leaders who can act as the 'role models' in motivating increasing number of women to participate in politics and human rights activities;
- Weak civil society, political indifference and apathy of women activists, upper caste elitist social background of civil society activists;
- Low level of female literacy and political awareness among women; and
- Economic dependency of women and lack of family support for active political participation.

Socio-cultural Aspect of Gender Equity/ Equality and

Democracy in Nepal

In Nepal, women had experienced unfairness and injustice in the autocratic political systems of the past and continue experiencing it in the democratic, multi-party political system of the present in legal, political, economic and socio-cultural fronts. Legal, political and economic aspects of gender discrimination and democracy are the subject matters of other three articles. I, therefore, will focus on discussion and analysis of socio-cultural aspects only. This article is divided in five sections: (1) meaning of democracy, (2) meaning of gender equity/equality, (3) socio-cultural fields of gender inequality, (4) socio-cultural factors of gender inequality, and (5) means to reduce/eliminate socio-culture-based gender inequality.

Meaning of Democracy

Democracy means different things to different people. Its meaning differs among individuals, ideologies, paradigms, cultures, and contexts (Diamond, Linz and Lipset, 1989:xvi). Max Weber defined "democracy" as the universal access to public positions and increasing sphere of influence of public opinion. Diamond, Linz and Lipset (1989:xvi) write, ".. democracy-or what Robert Dahl terms "polyarchy"-denotes a system of government that meets three essential conditions: meaningful and extensive competition among individuals and organized groups (especially political parties) for all effective positions or government power, at regular intervals and excluding the use of force; a highly inclusive level of political participation in the selection of leaders and policies, at least through regular and fair elections, such that no major (adult) social group is excluded; and a level of civil and political liberties-freedom of expression, freedom of the press, freedom to form and join organizations-sufficient to ensure the integrity of political competition and participation."

Jayal writes, "On the societal front, the limits on effective democracy stem from a combination of (i) inequalities in social relations, and (ii) the logic of democracy itself. Inequitous social relations may derive not only from economic inequalities, but also inequalities based in, for instance, gender or caste. The concentration of social power is not reducible to, and can be undesirable as the concentration of economic power, and indeed we know that the institutions of society are frequently undemocratic, as they actively neglect or subordinate weaker social groups. Social relations of domination and subordination tend to distort democracy, such that the voice of the powerful gets expressed (through interest groups, for example) while the powerless go largely unrepresented, except in the formal and ineffectual sense of periodically participating in elections."

Political scientists have identified various types of democracy. Lipsitz mentions majoritarian; liberal and egalitarian democracy and Held mentions liberal, protective, developmental, competitive elitist, radical development, legal, classical, direct and participatory democracy. Barber has identified three essentials of democracy: national government elected by the people, constitution and human rights. He further mentions four requirements of democracy: democracy must control violence; democracy must provide freedom and equality; democracy must require real law; and democracy needs reason. In the history of two and a half century of territorial unification of Nepal, Nepalese people experienced 18 month-long democracy in 1959-1960 and 10 years of democracy after the people's movement of 1990. Till now, unfortunately all disadvantaged groups, including Dalits, women, indigenous peoples, Muslims and Madhesis, have not yet experienced the taste of democracy other than freedom to be organized and make demands of political nature.

Gender Equity

UNDP, in its Gender Reference Guide about Mainstreaming Gender Equity defines gender equality and gender equity to mean subjective and objective situations. Gender equality "refers to norms and values, attitudes and perceptions, required to attain equal status between women and men, without neutralizing the biological differences between being women and men." Gender equity refers to "fairness in women's and men's access to socio-economic resources" and also it is a "condition in which women and men participate as equals, and have equal access to socio-economic resources."

Equity means fairness or right judgment; and equality does not necessarily mean equity. The taken-for-granted meaning of equity and equality is very problematic in Nepal as elsewhere in the world. "'Equity,' in law, is a set of rules that was originally developed to overcome inflexibility in government decisions. 'Equity' is based on broad principles of reason and justice. It allows the law to adjust to special circumstances of case." "In the early days, the laws were often applied so strictly that they created injustice." According to the MIT economist Lester Thurow, "Equity is the more philosophically and economically complex concept because it is highly normative and focuses on the just distribution of economic resources." "Equality does not necessarily imply equity." Equality is a more straightforward mathematical concept that reflects the extent of differences with respect to the possession of any desired goods, resources, or services.

According to C. Douglas Lummis 'equality' has "taken on

certain toxic meanings" in development discourse. According to him:

> "In the various notions of equality, it is possible to distinguish two families of meaning. In the first, equality indicates a kind of justice or fair treatment. In the second, equality indicates sameness or homogeneity. In some contexts the two meanings may overlap or converge, but they are different. To treat people justly may require treating them differently; on the other hand, to treat them as if they were the same is not necessarily to treat them justly. Moreover, the two meanings are different in kind. Equality as justice is a value statement concerning how people ought to be treated; it refers to relations between persons. Equality as sameness, however, is an allegation of fact; it postulates common characteristics in people. A value statement may be derived from it. However, if equality as sameness is asserted as a value, it may turn out to allege not a fact that is, but a fact that ought to be created. When this notion becomes attached to power, the consequences can be frightening."

Sometimes equality may not be effective, for example, many men practice polygyny and very few women practice polyandry. Equality does not mean that if men practice polygyny, women should demand for polyandry to be equal. Similarly, in polyandry society, it does not mean that men should demand for polygyny. Instead, in both types of polygamous society it is desirable to demand for monogamy with equal respect for husband and wife. Similarly, sometimes equality produces inequality. For example, in equality of opportunity, "What is equal is not the people, but the rules of the game." The main object of this competitive game is to produce inequality. It is a device for legitimizing it. "To accept equality of opportunity is to accept the game, and to accept the game is to accept the identity of player."

In Jurisprudence, "formal equality" accepts sameness but in "substantive model of equality" equality in result is desired, not just equal opportunity, and de facto equality, not just de jure equality, and special measure (unequal), as the corrective measures against socially constructed and historically determined discrimination.

Inequality is a political problem, not of poverty as some people believe. Till now, Minister for Justice and the Ministry of Justice, Justices or Judiciary, Executive, Legislative, Media, Civil Society Organizations, including Human Rights Organizations, have failed to give due justice to women. For example, implementation of CEDAW (Initial Report v Shadow Report), equal property rights Bill, pro-abortion Bill, elimination of women trafficking, etc. have not been implemented seriously yet. Also, it is difficult to imagine fairness and justice under the Muluki Ain (National Code) based on Dayabhag and Mitakshyara Sampradaya of Banaras and Bengal Gharana and also under the Hindu State and Hindu-biased Constitution.

Socio-cultural Fields of Gender Inequality

In Nepalese society there are many socio-cultural fields of gender inequality and some may be common to all culture but many vary from one culture to another. Some socio-cultural inequality occurs at the household level and some occurs at the community level. Many researchers and gender experts have noted that the status of women of indigenous ethnic groups is relatively better than those of the Hindu women. This true to the extent that the former society is characterized by egalitarian or flat or horizontal social structure whereas the latter is characterized by a vertical or hierarchical social structure with purity and pollution of caste, women and foods. It, however, should be noted here that many indigenous ethnic groups have been influenced greatly by the process of Hinduization and Sanskritization initiated by the Hindu rulers under the state patronage. Therefore, status of women in such Hinduized families is similar to those of their Hindu counterparts.

Household Level

Gender inequality at the household level is very conspicuous. Gender discrimination is widely prevalent from birth to death. Family members learn it through the processes of socialization such as conditioning, imitation, indoctrination, anticipatory socialization and active gender roles. It is a bitter fact that most of the families in Nepal are authoritarian, not democratic for women and girl child of the family because of persistence of the following types of gender discrimination:

Daughter as a liability: In Hindu society daughters are taken as liabilities. Very often parents want sons, not daughters. If son is born, parent celebrates by throwing out a big party for all relatives, friends and community members but if daughter is born they become sad. Sons and daughters are further discriminated in child care, foods, clothing, education, play, work and social mobility. Most of the parents do not want to invest money for daughter because they believe that she is some one's property, not theirs.

In non-Hindu society and culture, particularly those of the indigenous peoples such as Gurung, Magar, Rai, Limbu and Tamang traditionally there has been no discrimination between son and daughter. They generally do not take daughters as liability. However, in the last 230 years, the process of internal colonization or Hinduization or Sanskritization has forced some indigenous people to emulate Hindu social and cultural values. In such families, like in Hindu families, daughters are taken as liability.

Daijoo/Tilak related Torture: In Hindu society and culture daughters do not get parental property but during daughter's marriage, the groom's family demand cash and kind which many bride's parents cannot afford. Daijoo/Tilak is widely prevalent in the Madhesi communities of the Terai. The problem is indeed very acute in these communities. If the bride brings less amount of Daijoo/Tilak, she is often harassed and nowadays, there is increasing cases of bride-burning by the groom's family members. Also, many brides commit suicide due to depression resulting from such harassment.

Untouchability: All Hindu women are treated as untouchables for four to five days during menstruation and for few days after child delivery.

Untouchability is not practiced by indigenous peoples but it is practiced half-heartedly by those who are Hinduized or Sanskritized. In far-western and mid-western Nepal, Hindu women must live in a small hut called Chhaupadi or in cowshed during menstruation and child delivery.

Dalit women (and men) have been traditionally treated as "untouchables." Though the Muluki Ain (New National Code) of 1963 abolished untouchability, its practices continue unabated. Dalit women are not allowed to fetch water from public water sources, enter the temple and other public places. Many Dalit women are sexually exploited but if they should become pregnant boy friends abandon them or if their boy friends marry them, they are not accepted by their (husbands') families. Their children become citizenshipless as they are not entitled to get citizenship certificate without known fathers.

Child-marriage, polygamy, mismatch marriage and lesbianism: Child marriage is still prevalent in some Hilly areas and in most parts of the Terai. Although the Census data of 1991 show that mean age at marriage has increased from 15.4 in 1961 to 18.1 in 1991, 7.6 percent girls are married at the age of 10 to 14. Married girl child are deprived of education, increase workload, and suffer from health, including reproductive, problems. Polygyny is widely practiced, whereas Polyandry is practiced by some mountain-communities, such as: Dolpali, Lhopa, Baragaunle and Manange. Polyandry has been a customary practice but polygyny exists though the laws have made it illegal.

Mismatch marriage is also common in the Hills and Terai. Often the husband is aged and girl-wife is either a teenager or very young. Most of them become widow when they are still young and widows have low social status in the Hindu society and culture.

It is thuse evident that there are few but gradually increasing cases of lesbian marriages. Such practices are not allowed in the Nepalese society, they, therefore, are facing hard times in living normal conjugal life. Domestic violence: Domestic violence, both physical and mental, appears to be one of the very widely prevalent problems in Nepal. Almost all women victims do not speak out against the violence done by their male family members.

Community/Societal Level

There are many socio-culture-based gender inequalities at the community/ societal level. These are:.

Prostitution and Trafficking of women and girl child: This is a common problem of poor women and girl child of many castes and ethnic groups. Every year thousands of innocent women and girl child are sold by their fake husbands, relatives, friends and brokers in brothels in India. Many women and girl child resort to prostitution in the country as a last resort for their livelihood. It is indeed a shame to have a prevalence of trafficking of women and girl child in democracy.

Bonded labor: In the western, mid-western and far-western Terai, bonded labor (Kamaiya) was prevalent until it was abolished recently by His Majesty's Government. All the family members of such laborers were exploited by their landlords throughout their life by engaging them in agricultural and domestic works. After freedom from bonded labor, these bonded laborers are having a hard time to make a living due to government's failure to rehabilitate them properly.

Deuki, Jhuma, and Kumari: Due to some traditional religious practices, some women lose their freedom to live the life of their own choice. In Baitadi, adistrict in far-western region, some girls, from the poor families are purchased by rich "high caste" people and offer to the gods as Deuki. Later, these girls practice prostitution.

In the mountain region, Buddhist families offer their second daughter to the monasteries where they live a life of Jhuma. They must practice celibacy for life. The Newars of Kathmandu Valley have a tradition of living goddess called Kumari. These Kumaris must live in the temples until they menstruate. After menstruation they are no more eligible to be the goddess Kumari and later many of them remain single because of the belief that whoever marry them should die.

Badi: Women of one of the Dalit caste groups called Badi located in Nepalgunj and some villages in Banke district in mid-western region and in some villages in Dhangari district in far-western region have been forced by the society to engage in commercial sex works as their only profession. No rights on women's own body: Nepalese women do not have right on one's own body. They have no right on their reproductive health. They have no right to decide when to become pregnant, how many times to become pregnant, and whether or not to do abortion.

Patriliental/Patrilocal: It is tradition that married women change their family names to adopt the family names of their husbands and live in their husband's home. As women have to leave their maiden family name and natal home, obviously, they are psychologically dominated by their husbands and their family members, who are more like strangers than family members. Husband and wife relationship would change substantially if both husband and wife should live in a new home. Son(s) and daughter(s) inherit father's family name. Therefore, it is not surprising to hear common beliefs that sons open the door to heaven and that parent make efforts for having a son even if they already have many daughters only.

Illiteracy: According to the Census of 1991, the overall female literacy rate (6+ years) of both male and female combined is 39.6 and that of women is 25. The literacy rate of both Dalit and indigenous women is negligible. The literacy rate of Dalit women is low because of social discrimination, particularly untouchability and that of the Indigenous women, who speak their own mother tongues, is low because of imposition of Khas Nepali language in the class rooms and the offices. As long as literacy rate remains low, women will not be able to become public and subsequently, they will be deprived from meaningful participation in the public sphere, including politics.

Social values: Hindu social values have a direct bearing on gender discrimination. FWLD have listed some of the popular beliefs, including dhilo paye, chhora paye ("let it be late, but let it be a son"), chhora paye swarga jaane ("the birth of a son paves the way to heaven"), chhori ko janma hare ko karma ("a daughter is born with doomed fate"), chhora paye khasi, chhori paye pharsi (if a son is born, it is celebrated by sacrificing a goat, if it's daughter, a pumpkin is enough"), mare paap, pale punya ("it's a sin if the groom kills the bride, charity if nurtured"), and swasni macheko buddhi pachhadi ("women are always shortsighted").

Socio-cultural Factors

Even in democracy, if certain dominant socio-cultural factors are not addressed properly, gender inequality would continue to reproduce and democracy may be challenged by these factors.

Patriarchy

In Nepal we have mostly patriarchal societies. Patriarchy, following Sylvia Walby, is "a system of social structures and practices in which men dominate, oppress and exploit women". In such system men control women's labor power, reproduction, sexuality, mobility, and economic resources, including property. In Nepal and other South Asian societies, patriarchal institutions include family, religion, legal system, political institutions, media, and educational institutions

It is recognized by all that the position of women belonging to indigenous peoples is better compared to the Indo-Aryans or Hindus. Girl child and women of Indigenous peoples have better social status at home and in the community but they are totally absent in public offices. Many indigenous peoples were coerced to go through the process of Hinduization or Sanskritization or Nepalization resulting the loss of their traditional language, religion and culture. In such cases, the males of indigenous communities may be even more stricter than their Hindu counterpart in exploiting, subjugating and oppressing women as the saying goes, naya jogile kharani dherai ghascha ("new hermits rub their bodies with more ashes").

Hegemony

Historical unfairness and injustice were and are created by Bahunbad or Brahmanbad (Brahamanism) or Hindu cultural values. Women in general have become its victim and women belonging to so-called "low caste" or Dalits and indigenous ethnic groups have become double victims: one as women in general and the other as Dalit/indigenous women.

One of the emerging patterns of Nepal's democracy is a tendency of the ruling political party or parties to maintain, sustain, and reinforce the process of hegemony or domination, on the one hand, and homogenization of culture and ideology, on the other; both have been continuing since the project of territorial unification in 1768. Such a coercive practice goes against the very social structure of Nepal and the spirit of democracy.

It is a fact that Nepali social structure has been characterized by diversity in ecology, caste and ethnicity, language, religion, region, and culture. It is also a fact that democracy implies pluralism, and therefore, it is only in democracy various groups, including those of the minorities, interests and demands can be articulated, fulfilled, safeguarded, and preserved. Equally true is a fact that democracy would no more remain as democracy if diversity or pluralism is destroyed. Contrary to democratic spirit, there has been a domination or hegemony of specific caste (Bahun-Chhetris), regional (pahadiyas), gender (men), linguistic (Nepali), religious (Hindu) groups in all public sphere, including politics, bureaucracy, police, military, education, medicine, engi-neering and culture for the last two and a half centuries. It should be noted that although Nepal is a small country in terms of geography, but both biological and cultural diversities are great.

If democracy has to function in its true sense of the term, people belonging to all these different groups should have equal opportunity to contribute for the national development of Nepal. Religious, cultural and social dominance of Hinduism, Hindu values, and caste and ethnic fairness and justice have negatively affected to non-Hindu women. Women of so-called "high castes" are victims by their so-called "high caste" men.

Due to the Hindu values of purity and pollution of castes and foods and hierarchy Dalit women have become triple victims by "high caste" men and women, by their own and other men. Similarly women of so-called "Matawali" ("liquor drinking caste") or indigenous ethnic groups, who are more than 61, and other religious/linguistic groups are double victims Once they are victimized by men as a women. Additionally, they, as a group with their own distinct culture, religion, language, are victimized by the dominant groups who follow Hindu culture and religion, and speak Khas Nepali language. Similarly, Hindu men and women dominate non-Hindus, particularly animists, Bon, Buddhist. Lamaist, Islam and Christians.

Khas Nepali language speaking men and women dominate women who speak their own mother tongues-there are more than 125 languages and dialects in Nepal. Also, Pahadi or Hill men and women dominate Madhesi men and women. These differences have come to surface because of socio-cultural diversity. Principle of equality is based on a criterion of inclusion and subsequently "cultural differences between communities, their ways of life, systems or moral values, modes of dress and address" are now accepted positively.

The theorists of cultural differences have made two arguments about the inadequacies of the principle of formal equality: one, "equality assumes that equals should be treated equally and unequals unequally" and hence, 'by ignoring cultural differences, however, the idea of formal equality treats unequals equally"; and two, "equality requires that equal treatment be given to all culturally distinct communities." It is unfortunate that women activists and leaders of so-called "high castes" are for gender equity and gender equality. Also, they are not sensitive enough about domination, suppression, oppression and subjugation of the later groups by default of being the women belonging to "high castes". Continuing exclusion, marginalization and alienation of Dalit, indigenous nationalities, Madhesi, and Muslim women do not help to achieve gender equity and gender equality in Nepal.

Nepalese society is characterized by socio-cultural diversity and it has implications in differential gender inequality. The diversity is reflected in caste and ethnicity, language, religion and region.

In terms of race, Caucasians and Mongolians together comprise most of the population of the country and Dravidians and Proto-Australoids comprise minority population. Among the Caucasians, Brahman/Bahun, Kshatriya/ Chhetri, Vaisya and Sudra are further divided into numerous caste and sub-castes. The remaining three racial groups comprise 61 indigenous peoples or nationalities. There are Muslims, Sikhs, Bengalis among other groups. Compared to so-called Hindu "high caste" women, other women, together with their male counterparts, are discriminated in language, religion and culture. In the case of Dalit women (and men), they have been treated as "untouchables" though the New National Code of Nepal abolished untocuhability in 1963.

Women belonging to various nationalities, Madhesis, and Muslims who speak their own mother tongues are discriminated by the state in the use of their language in the local bodies, government owned media and schools. Subsequently many girl children and women remain illiterate and uneducated. Girl child and women belonging to Khas Nepali language speakers are in more advantageous positions because of the Constitutional provision of Nepali as the only official language.

In fact religion affects women differentially. Hindu women are more privileged than non-Hindus such as Animists,

Bon, Buddhists, Lamaists, Islam and Christians. The democratic constitution of Nepal has declared Nepal as the Hindu country.

The most important means to reduce, if possible to eliminate, socio-culture-based gender inequalities are gender struggle for decentralized household, selective cooperation and partnership and selective antagonism and confrontation, positive discrimination (equality of opportunity and equality of outcomes), reform or movement or revolution. One of the main gender struggles that should be waged is at the household level. Such struggle should be directed in two fronts, one within the household and another between households and larger institutions. The struggle within the household, following Hartmann should focus on both fronts, production and redistribution. At the production front, women should struggle to achieve equity in housework and in redistribution of family income. I believe that women, as indicated by Hartmann, should "resist doing housework and rearing children, at least many children" and perceive their economic security in self-reliance. Similarly, struggle between households and larger institutions, following Hartmann, should focus on household production versus production organized by capital and the state and in redistribution in terms of taxes.

Even in democracy, many men tend to believe that women's equal right movement is directed against men and that women can actually gain nothing with such confrontational approach. They interpret equal property rights and right to one's own body as women's ploy against men. Also, gender sensitization programs have been blamed for increasing family conflicts. On the other hand, some gender activists believe that the whole movement is not really against men-therefore confrontation or antagonism is not required.They say that what is required and desired is partnership between women and men and girls and boys. Some other gender activists believe that selective confrontation is required if women's plight should be heard by men and also if women should really achieve gender equality and equity.

One of the most debatable social issues in Nepal is positive discrimination or affirmative action for women and other disadvantaged groups. In Nepal although policy makers are yet to be convinced but all gender activists and activists of other disadvantaged groups very strongly believe that it is one of the very effective means to bridge the gender gap that has been manufactured in centuries.

Although advocates of democracy believed that a colour-blind policy would ensure equality in all spheres of social and political life, the ideologues of cultural differences has shown that the obliteration of differences cannot ensure equality and by treating unequals equally, it actually violates the principle of equality. The task of democracy was still unfinished. While legal barriers to equality had been removed and public places and institutions were now open to all, people of different races and gender could neither participate on equal terms, nor use the available opportunities to an equal degree. Year of subordination had seriously handicapped the members of the discriminated communities and placed them at a disadvantage in at least three ways,

(a) it had diminished their motivations and aspirations.
(b) although jobs were formally open to all, the marginalized groups were unable to compete successfully with the members of the better-off social groups
(c) children of the dominant social groups performed better in standard examination.

In Nepal gender activists are demanding for substantive equality because the Constitution of the Kingdom of Nepal, 1990 has already granted formal equality. The Constitution has made it mandatory to all political parties to reserve five percent of candidacy during the general election, gender activists are demanding for 20 to 33 percent of such reservation, not just for candidacy to loose but to win.

So far women's equal right movement has been more reformist than a real movement or a revolution. In the past women's movement was welfare oriented, which was essentially a reformist approach. After the re-establishment of multi-party political system or democracy in 1990, women's right activists have gradually moving towards generating a movement but critics often charge that domination of educated, urban and upper and upper middle class women of certain caste, religion, language and culture and their orientation to projects have distorted the nature of the movement. It is true that until now instead of being a grass roots level movement women's movement has become a policy targeted movement with little success.

Trafficking of Women: Human Rights Violations

The coalition of about 60 non-governmental organisations (NGOs) had just joined hands as a unified front to combat the trafficking of Nepalese women and girls when a gang of seven traffickers was arrested immediately in Kathmandu by the local police. In fact, news about the arrest of people for trafficking, their release and their rearrest have become an everyday phenomenon in Nepal. Another news story during the same week also noted that 21 girls were recently rescued from Indian brothels with the help of the Indian police and sent back to Nepal. While fresh incidents of the trafficking of women and girls persist, those who are already worn out, HIV-infected and have lost their material value in the sex market continue to return home to Nepal. Traffickers do not fear the police or the legal regime that is put in place to prevent, counter or combat them. Corruption is pervasive everywhere, and the criminal justice system, as far as it relates to the police and local administration, is also not an exception. As such, the problem of trafficking in women and girls, an insidious form of violence, continues to flourish in Nepal. There is no data, but a rough estimation indicates that thousands of Nepalese women and girls are trafficked to India annually. They are generally trafficked for the purpose of domestic servitude, sexual exploitation or forced labour, including prostitution. Many people think that such factors as a lack of viable economic opportunities at home, the continued lower status of women in society, a lack of preventive information, etc., are the contributing factors, but this assumption is not true. No one wants to be trafficked simply because there is a good reason for it. In fact, if these were the true factors, all Nepalese women or girls would have been in the brothels of India or abroad by now.

All Nepalese should fight such negative propaganda that is instigated by traffickers and their accomplices. In fact, trafficking in women and girls has become one of the fastest growing enterprises in Nepal. The extent of the criminality of the people in this trade has become stronger than the social capacity of public institutions to confront it. Traffickers in women, much like narcotic traffickers, operate boldly across international borders using the local means of communication and trade. The low risk of prosecution, the enormous profit potential, official corruption and the open international boarder, etc., are the major factors that make Nepal a haven for traffickers.

Most of these enterprises are led by Indian dons who have their offices on the other side of the international border and whose illegal enterprises are directed toward Nepal. Those who are arrested only happen to be the intermediaries working in the actual context. These intermediaries lure victims with personal counselling, false promises of jobs as nannies, cooks, waitresses, sales clerks, etc.

Once they cross the international border, they notice though that the people who gave them company until then have left them and that the language, style and attitude of the new caretakers who replaced them are different. By this time, however, the motherland is too far, and the clutches of the criminals are too strong. The women and girls confront their abductors, cry and try to run away, but they find that they are virtual prisoners with no resources, little recourse and no protection against the violations of their person and human rights.

Well-established criminal agents traffic in these women and girls, often capitalising on the simplicity of rural women, rising unemployment and the disintegrating social networks in the countryside of Nepal. This increasingly serious problem is going to have a notorious impact on the country's social fabric very soon. The hope that the newly established Human Rights Commission would mean a radical new start in instilling respect for human rights has not yet been fulfilled. As in many other social sectors, the government of Nepal does not have a well-formulated plan to address the areas of prevention, victim assistance and protection and enforcement. There is not even governmental machinery that is consulting closely with NGOs, like the present 60-member coalition, which are working in the area and which have programmes to warn potential victims of methods used by traffickers. Some of these NGO representatives can be helpful in addressing the issue by watching source, transit and destination countries, by calling popular attention to the problem and by developing strategies for combating this egregious human rights violation. There is not even a public awareness campaign at the present time. At the minimum, such a coalition and its continued activities can ensure that young women and girls are educated about this problem so that they will not fall prey to traffickers' tactics of coercion, violence, fraud and deceit. It can also create the pressure of public opinion on law enforcement agencies to prevent women and girls from being trafficked and to ensure that traffickers are punished. There is also a need to review existing criminal laws and their current use to determine if they are adequate to prevent and deter trafficking in women and girls, to recommend any appropriate legal changes to ensure that trafficking is criminalised and that the consequences of trafficking are significant and, lastly, to review current prosecution efforts against traffickers in order to identify additional intelligence sources, evidentiary needs and resource capabilities. The only mechanism is the police force, which deals with the problem without trained immigration and law enforcement personnel to enhance their ability to effectively implement border security and to identify traffickers and the victims of trafficking.

Frequently the police also complain about the narrow legal bases of judges and public attorneys that prevent enhanced enforcement of laws against trafficking. Some studies have been done by NGOs, and many important issues have already been highlighted by the media, but they need to be analysed again with all parties cooperating and working together. There are, moreover, some other issues that have hardly been raised by any quarter. There is, for example, a need to examine the current treatment of trafficking, including an effort to determine ways to insure the provision of services for victims and witnesses in settings that secure their safety, precautions for the safe return of victims and witnesses to their places of origin, witness cooperation in criminal trials against traffickers and the consideration of temporary and/or permanent legal status for victims and witnesses of trafficking who lack any legal status. Fortunately, as yet, Nepal does not have an organised flesh trade within its political frontiers, but prostitution has existed in one form or another in some segments of Nepalese society for a long time. It is only in recent years though that prostitution has spread in places where large projects are being implemented, roadside markets are being developed or wage labourers continue to live in huge numbers for a long time, including prostitution that flourishes in hotels in partnership with the police or local administration in urban areas. Thamel, for example, has always been known as a place for paedophiles or sex with minors, so much so that pimps around Bir Hospital and the Gongabu bus terminal constantly appear to be busy all afternoon. The law, however, has never focussed on women and children in order to protect them from incidental or commercial sexual abuse. No attempt has been made until today to focus on trafficking and prostitution, analysing the existing laws, penalties, sentencing patterns, reporting requirements, law enforcement capabilities and victim assistance programs.

In fact, the real problems begin, not with the law, but with the capacity and bona fides of politicians and law enforcement agencies. If the political will is there, Nepal can virtually eradicate prostitution and put a stop to trafficking that originates from this country. No matter how much progress the country makes in combating violence against women, reforms unfair inheritance and property rights and strengthens women's access to fair employment and economic opportunities, the existing open border arrangements that were introduced in 1950 must end in order to save the country from the vices that originate on the other side of the border but for which the Nepalese people are made to pay incessantly. The appropriate response to all allegations of violations of human rights and humanitarian law-wherever in the world they are reported-is that they must be rigorously and independently investigated. Where proven to be well-founded, those responsible have to be brought to justice.

8

Assessment

Many women in Third World Countries like Nepal are mainly involved in domestic work which is not recognised as productive work. All unpaid help by women in family farms and businesses also goes unrecorded. This shows that although women generate a substantial amount of goods and services in the economy, they are not considered 'econo-mically active' by data collectors.

Indeed Women's involvement in income generating activities enables them to be liberated from economic dependency on men. Their active partici-pation in the financial system also broadens their horizon of, development in terms of, education, and family as well as social welfare. The crucial importance of access to the credit system becomes clearer when one realises how, in the face of grinding poverty, many of the poor women take the initiative to become mini-entrepreneurs. They acquire goods and services with a resourcefulness and determination born within themselves and aspire to a better life. Credit assists rural women to establish an enterprise and accelerates capital formation, employment generation, social responsibility, and partnership of rural women in socio-economic development of the country. In order to achieve socio-economic development of poor rural women, who are in the majority, basic facilities like credit extension services, drinking water, health care and skill development are essential.

PCRW Programme

The major programme developed for women's development is the Production Credit for Rural Women

(PCRW), imple-mented under the aegis of the Ministry of Local Development.

The PCRW programme is aimed at:

- Establishing linkages between rural women and support services/facilities to be provided by government and NGOs.
- Facilitating the life of rural women by engendering self-confidence and feelings of equality among them, by taking steps to eradicate the existing backwardness, illiteracy, superstitions and by transforming backward traditional thinking through the implementation of various social and community activities.
- Providing support and assistance to rural women to adopt appropriate technologies which save time and reduce workload so as to utilise their time and labour in gainful activities.
- Enhancing the involvement of NGOs in women's development programmes.
- Creating awareness extensively among women to organise themselves collectively for creating demand for their skills and products at local levels and increase their absorptive capacity.
- Coordinating the development activities carried out by government and NGOs.

PCRW is implemented in a systematic manner. The steps involved include the following:

- Rapport building among staff, involved in programme management, the target groups and the community in order to establish mutual trust and understanding among each other.
- Identification of existing skills, needs and potential of rural women by conducting a household survey and studying their socio-economic situation.
- Motivation of rural women to prioritise their needs and that of their community, based on the findings of the household survey and focused group discussions.
- Development of management capability of rural women to lead, organise and manage the activities for themselves and for their communities.
- Linking women with banking services to enable them to

avail loans on group guarantees to carry out self-employment and income generating activities;

– Assisting women to form Self-Help Groups and to assume the responsibility for group activities to strengthen and develop these SHGs.

Production credit is given to the rural women for various income generating activities without collateral security. The Women Development Division (WDD) conducts household surveys and organises women into groups.

Sectoral classification of the PCRW loan indicates that there is a diversity of loan disbursement to rural women. Livestock seemed to be the most important sector for rural women.

A large number of training activities were conducted under the PCRW programme in order to enhance women's participation in the financial system. These training activities were conducted mainly in the rural areas with the objective of imparting it sense of equality and confidence to rural women so that they could improve their lot by participating in developmental work through access to credit facilities.

Rural women, men and children benefited through different kinds of community development activities conducted under the PCRW programme. Such activities were child care, vegetable production, parasite control, adult literacy, health care, drinking water facilities, rural tool preparation, afforestation and environmental conservation, and family welfare.

Two Rural Development Banks (RDB's) were established in the eastern region – Biratnagar and far-western region-Dhanagadhi. These RDBs were the prototype of the Grameen Bank of Bangladesh. They were established to fulfil the following basic objectives:

– Provide banking services to the rural poor.
– Provide credit for increasing income and employment opportunities of the poor and help reduce the level of poverty among the rural population in general and women in particular.
– Create awareness and raise the level of, income in the rural poor.
– Develop an institutional mechanism for linking savings

with credit and thereby initiate self-reliant economic development activities for strengthening rural economy.

Better performance of RDB Biratnagar might be attributed to the managerial efficiency and geographical and infrastructural accessibility in the eastern part of the country. By April, 1994, it had organised 5,993 rural women into 1,200 groups. 4,602 women, out of above group members, borrowed Rs. 19.8 million for conducting micro-enterprises related to agriculture, cottage industry, services sector and retail trade. The rural women were able to make a saving of Rs. 9.69 million with 100 per cent repayment of matured loans.

Hundreds of NGO's have been functioning in different parts of the country. NGO activities were further enhanced after the restoration of the democratic government in 1990. The Social Services National Coordination Council (SSNCC) is the supreme body of NGOs at the policy level. However, each NGO functions independently. There is a special wing, Women Service Coordination Committee (WSCC) under SSNCC to coordinate women development. NGOs specialising in women development are present in all the five development regions. In addition, there are some other NGOs and SHGs which are dealing with saving and credit functions in rural areas. The Self-Help Fund (Swalamban Kosh) and the Pauper (Nirdhan) are two recognised NGOs functioning respectively in the eastern and western parts of the country. They have adopted the Grameen Bank Model for poverty alleviation in rural areas. This model has also been followed by most of the NGOs working with credit for women development.

NGO's and Women Development

The NGO's working on women development focus on providing women with sustainable development oppor-tunities so that they can become self sufficient and are able to undertake income generating activities. Training becomes an invaluable and effective means of imparting skills and initiating women into the mainstream of socioeconomic development. Most of the these training programmes are confined to the rural areas, where poverty dominates the household and where its impact is the greatest on women.

The interest rate was comparatively low (14 per cent) based on the current rate of interest taken by commercial banks and the Agricultural Development Bank. Informal sources naturally charged a higher interest rate compared to formal sources. The annual interest from the informal sources ranged from 30 per cent to 60 per cent depending on the situation and place. Generally, it is easier to access credit through informal sources rather than formal resources. However, loan conditions were made easier in special credit programmes designed for women beneficiaries, and credit was advanced mainly against group guarantees.

There are many constraints that hinder, women's participation in the credit system. Women in all of the four geographical locations and varying ethnic combinations had faced the many problems. Illiteracy and low level of education was the main constraint that hindered women from access to credit.

The Caste system and ethnic factors were also a major social constraint. Geographical constraints played an important role. Inaccessible localities made development efforts difficult. Ignorance of credit facilities was another problem. Women beneficiaries lacked knowledge about the credit system and profitable business due to illiteracy and poor communication.

Low level household income limited women's participation in the credit system because of the additional excess burden of household chores, high frequency of child bearing, family responsibilities and services as well as male domination in external dealings. Women beneficiaries were asked to make suggestions for increasing women's participation in the credit system. Their suggestions included increase in the level of education: providing massive training; identification of more profitable enterprises; reduction of child bearing rate through birth control, inculcating all attitude of respect for women; sharing of household responsibility by men and women; giving the opportunity for income generation; and providing credit to the women/beneficiaries at their doorsteps on flexible terms.

Since Nepalese society is comprised of various castes and ethnic groups, their sociocultural values must be taken into account before launching women development activities. The focus of the credit system should be the middle age and married group because they tend to be reliable borrowers.

Therefore married women of middle age should be given preference when providing credit. A vast majority of women beneficiaries were illiterate, only a few women had achieved literacy through the adult literacy programmes. It was obvious that this factor was a major hindrance in dealing with the credit system. The findings indicated that an extensive functional literacy and schooling programme was required to redress this major shortcoming.

Since the gross annual family income of the respondents was small, falling well below the defined low income group, extensive rural credit programmes should be launched in support of rural women. The respondents average household farm size was 0.83 hac in totality of all the surveyed areas. This reflected that the small borrowers were small farm families, so micro-rural credit programmes must be made accessible to the small farm rural women..

Empowering the Women of Nepal

Against the backdrop of the Himalayan mountains lies Nepal, one of the world's poorest countries. With a population of 22 million, less than the State of California, Nepal has an annual per capita income below that of Haiti. Fifty-three percent of the population subsists on less than $1 a day, and the percentage of income-poor is not expected to improve dramatically since demographers anticipate that Nepal's population will double in twenty-seven years. Meeting these challenges is central to the U. S. Agency for International Development's (USAID) Mission in Nepal.

Nepal is one of only three countries in the world where female life expectancy is lower than that of males (52.6 years compared with 55.4 years). Its maternal mortality rate is estimated to be 515 per 100,000 births, second only to Bhutan in the Asia region. For children under the age of five, the death rate for girls is considerably higher than that of boys.

In the agricultural sector, women are key participants. They are responsible for 60 to 70 percent of output, working more than three hours longer each day than men (an average of 11 hours a day, compared with 7.5 for men). According to USAID/Nepal, the greater work burden of women, their generally poor health and limited access to health care, and a persistent gender gap in education are severe constraints to the country's economic growth.

Strategy of USAID

To help Nepal obtain greater economic growth, USAID recently revised its strategy for reducing rural poverty. Its focus is now on three strategic objectives: sustaining increases in the sale of forest and high-value agricultural products, reducing fertility and improving maternal and child health, and empowering women. USAID/ Nepal is the only USAID mission to identify increased women's empowerment as a strategic objective, although India has a special objective to expand women's role and participation in decision-making. The USAID mission in Nepal has defined empowerment as women making choices that enhance their well-being, as well as that of their families and communities. The mission expects that its new, integrated empowerment program will result in measurable behavioral changes in women. These include women becoming more active participants in their households and communities and contributing more to the growth of Nepal's economy and their own prosperity.

The mission faces obstacles in this effort. In the Nepali context, empowering women and bringing them into the development process is inextricably bound to the dominant Hindu social structure, which influences all aspects of social, cultural, and economic life. This structure assigns women to restricted roles within the inside world of household and family responsibilities.

To reach its goal of empowering women, USAID/ Nepal is carrying out three critical interventions. The first aims to increase women's literacy, the second supports women's economic participation through access to credit, and the third offers advocacy training and education on women's legal rights. Literacy is the foundation on which the other development interventions build, the starting point for empowerment. Economic participation is the anchor in the empowerment program. It helps women put cash in their own hands, giving them a greater voice in household decision making, especially on spending for the family. Legal rights education and advocacy training build on the other interventions to transform women's perceptions about themselves as actors in their communities. Individually, these interventions have a significant impact on Nepali women. Although Nepali women play a vital role in the economy through unpaid work in the home, their contributions to household incomes remain largely unrecognized. The intervention to strengthen women's economic participation is based on the assumption that bolstering their contributions to household income will increase their influence over decisions related to household spending. Research has shown that women are more likely than men to spend income on nutrition, health care, and education, so putting money in their hands through microenterprise development should result in the household spending a larger share of its income on the family's well-being. USAID/ Nepal also anticipates that women who come together in economic empowerment groups will remain active participants long after completing a literacy program, for example.

During 1997, nearly 24,000 women became active members of savings and credit groups, making monthly deposits into savings accounts. More than 20,000 of these women took out loans and either started or expanded 6,000 microenterprises. Even in the less accessible areas of the country where formal banking services are often unavailable, more than 2,000 women received USAID loans for microenterprise activities.

In 1991, Nepal had one of the lowest literacy rates in the world for women, with only about 22 percent of woman (15 to 44 years of age) able to read or write. Lack of reading and math skills have placed these women at a disadvantage in the labor market and the political arena.

With the aid of local non-governmental organizations (NGOs), USAID/Nepal initiated literacy programs in 1995 to help Nepal respond to the problem. The NGOs established thousands of literacy groups around the country, and by 1997, more than 400,000 women had been made literate. USAID estimated that by 1997, the literacy rate for adult females had risen to 32 percent.

USAID's literacy training has had a broad effect. A 1997 survey showed that literate women put a higher value on keeping their daughters in school. In those areas where women had received basic literacy training, only 4 percent of girls never attended school, compared to almost 20 percent in areas where the USAID/ Nepal programs were not available. Literacy skills have also increased women's ability to use credit effectively. In 1996, nearly half of the graduates of USAID-supported literacy classes became new borrowers. A 1997 study showed that course graduates articulated an increased awareness of the advantages of borrowing money to start a small enterprise and a better understanding of loan repayment requirements.

Lack of a full participatory role in the life of the family has often prevented Nepali women from having a voice in community affairs. USAID/ Nepal's strategic response was to integrate the development and use of advocacy skills into a revised practical curriculum on legal rights and responsibilities. Over the past three years, more than 85,000 women across the country have completed legal rights and advocacy training programs funded by USAID/Nepal. Nearly 1,000 advocacy groups have been formed. These groups have undertaken a wide variety of actions on both individual and public issues. A 1997 sample survey showed the groups have confronted a number of social problems including domestic violence, alcoholism, and gambling. They have also campaigned for better and more accessible primary education, and they have called for the increased availability of oral rehydration therapy and polio vaccines. Finally, they have carried out community development projects such as repairing school buildings, installing water pipes, and planting community forests. The advocacy groups have spoken out on national issues such as women's right to own property, caste discrimination, and trafficking of girls. Recognizing that access to income increases their decision- making role in the family and community, they have demanded greater access to economic interventions.

The initial research from a 1996 case study of six rural communities and a 1997 survey of rural Nepali women lends credence to the mission's hypothesis that women who participate in an integrated empowerment program of economic participation, basic literacy, and legal rights and advocacy interventions are more likely to increase their influence over decision making within the household and to participate in initiating collective actions for social change. Women who participated in the earlier USAID/ Nepal empowerment program showed higher levels of shared decision-making than women who had not participated. Sixty-eight percent of participating women increased their decision-making about spending household income at least slightly. This household income was spent mainly on household well-being, such as the purchase of additional food, to pay for medical treatment or children's education. Empowered women also invested in productive assets, they repaid loans, and they increased their level of savings. At the same time, according to the research, women's groups initiated an average of 23 collective actions annually, demonstrating a link between women's increased confidence and their active participation in the life of the community.

Bibliography

Acharya, Meena, *Women and the Subsistence Sector: Economic Participation and Household Decision-making in Nepal,* Washington, D.C.: World Bank, 1983.

Allen, Michael, *The Cult of Kumari: Virgin Worship in Nepal, Kirtipur*: Institute of Nepal and Asian Studies, Tribhuvan Univ.,1975.

Bajracharya, Deepak, et al., "Women and the Management of Energy, Forests, and Other Resources", *MPE series* No.3. ICIMOD, Kathmandu, 1990.

Basnet, Mira, *The Role of Women in the Movement for Democracy in Nepal,* Variety Printers, Kathmandu, 1997.

Bennett, Lynn, "Tradition and Change in the Legal Status of Nepalese Women", in Status of Women in Nepal. Vol. 1, Part 2, 1979.

Bhatt, N., L. Shrestha, B.T. Slayter, and I. Koirala, "Managing Resources in a Nepalese Village: Changing Dynamics of Gender, Caste and Ethnicity", *IIDS*, Kathmandu, 1994.

Boserup, Easter, *Women's Role in Economic Development,* George Allen and Unwin, London, 1970.

CEDA, *Statistics of Women in Nepal,* Vol. 2, Parts 1-9, 1981.

Centre for Women and Development, *Production Credit for Rural Women: An Impact Evaluation Study*. Kathmandu, 1989.

CERID, *Education of Girls and Women in Nepal,* Tribhuvan University, Kathmandu, 1986.

Goonting, D., *Preliminary Research Findings,* "An Impact Study of Micro-Credit Intervention for Disadvantaged Groups: The case of PCRW in Nepal", USRPD, University of Guelph, Canada, 1994.

GWPIG, Beyond Beijing; *Women in Nepal Towards the Year 2005*, Kathmandu, 1996.

Inserra, Anne E., "Women's Participation in Community Forestry in Nepal: An Analysis for the Forestry Development Project". USAID, Kathmandu, 1987.

Majupuria, Indira, *Nepalese Women: A Vivid Account of the Status and Role of Nepalese Women in the Total Spectrumof Life - Religious, Social, Eenomie, Political and Legal: Focus on Equality, Degelopment and Peace*, Lashkar, India: M. Devi, 1989.

Ministry for Local Development/ HMGN, *Women Development Program: Progress Report*, 1995/96. Kathmandu.

Ministry of Education/ HMGN, *Education for Girls and Women in Nepal*, Kathmandu, 1986.

Ministry of Women and Social Welfare/HMGN, *Program for Encountering Violence Against Women* (draft prepared for the Ninth Five-Year Plan), Kathmandu, 1996.

Rana, M. S. J. B./Shah A. J., "Role of Women in Nepal's Industrial Development: Status, Constraints, Opportunities and Prospects", *Vol. I & II., prepared for HMGN and UNIDO*, Vienna, 1987.

Shrestha, Kapil, *Women's Political Participation in Nepal: Perspectives and Challenges*, Kathmandu, 1998.

Index

A

Abolition of widow burning/Sati, 200
Abortion
  laws, 105-107
  unsafe, 108
  reforms, 109-110
  legalising, 109
Action Plan (Women's Ministry) problems, 162
Access to land and property, 125
Adultery, 175
  when husband is abroad, 189-190
  rules relating to (8 chapters), 176
  cases in Ain, 177
  conditions related to woman/husband, 177-78
Agricultural perspective plan (APP), 80, 171
Agriculture Sector, 79
  and women, 3, 80, 130, 146, 154
  and women participation in training programme, 170
  and women's issues, 80
AIDS
  awareness, 40
  cases Nepal, 39-40
Ain (Muluki)
  Nepalese law, 175, 195-96
  widow burning, 195
  Regulation on Sati, 196
Alcohol movement against, 16
Amnesty International warning by Taliban, 204
Amsa System, 210
  and division of Nepal, 210
Ancestral Kinship, 31, 34
Asceticism and widow burning, 203
Aungsabanda (coparceners in property), 30, 103-104
Awareness of women's rights, 226

B

Badi caste and traditional prostitution, 46-51
Badi marriage system, 49
Badi women, 237
Bajang and Thalara kings and *amsa* tradition, 210
Baseline surveys sex workers, 42
Bombay brothels, 41
Bonded labour, 237
Brahmanical ideas and Sati, 203
Brahmana hatya prohibition, 180

C

Capacity Building, 165
Carpet industry women in, 133
Centres for Higher Learning, 9
CERID (Research Centre for Educational Innovation and Development)
  -study, 54)
Changes in women's lives study, 1

Child labour, 84, 136
 working conditions, 136
 girl/boy participation, 136
Christians condemnation of suicide, 191
Chandra Shamsher Rana, 28
Citizenship laws
 discrimination in, 3, 84, 101
Civil Service Act (age of entry women), 23, 86
Commercial Sex workers (CSW's)
 age group, 75
 STDs, 42-43
 categories, 45
Commercialization indicators, 140
Compelling Factors women's education, 72
Community Based Organization, (CBO), 167
Contractual Rights, 36
Concerned center for child workers in Nepal (CCWIN)-
 Studies, 55-56
Control over sexuality
 legal instruments of, 38
Constitution
 of 1990, 66
 of Nepal, 4, 23, 65, 84, 137
Constitutional guarantees, 137
Convention on the Elimination of all kinds of Discrimination Against Women
 (CEDAW), 3, 65, 227
 provisions, 98
Cross Cousin marriage
 Badis, 49

D

Daijoo/Tilak, 235
 socio-cultural factors, 238
Dalit community, 88
Dalit women, 235, 240
 conditions, 89
 oppression, 87-88
  economic, 89
  education, 90
  health, 90
  political, 90
  social, 89
 sexual exploitation, 91
 programme
  recommendations, 92
Daughters/girl child rights, 120, 235
 discrimination, 65
 inheritance, 30-31, 33
 disadvantages, 32
 as liability, 235
 circumstances, 32
Death rituals, 205-206
Death penalty (Ain), 175
Decade for women, 22
Decision making powers
 causes, 67
Decision making participation in, 4
Defective Value system, 32, 35
 characteristics, 26, 39, 238
Deficiencies in literacy programmes, 57-58
Delegation to the government, (Women's issues), 14
Democracy
 establishment, 221, 230, 239
 meaning, 231
Deuki (Devadasis), 46
Deuki, Jhuma, Kumari, 237
Development strategy Nepal, 164
Developmental
 efforts (Nepal), 154
 plans on women, 160
  and Five Year Plans 6-8th, 160
Devakis (W. Nepal), 208

Dhampus study on woman's status
change, 156
Dhampu categories of women
present, 49
Discriminating
in law, 3
in education, 33
Discriminatory laws, 116
Discrimination against women, 97
Discriminatory Provisions in the
code of country-writ, 66
Division of Labour, 7
in household, 138
District Development Committees
(DDCs), 85
women in, 167
Donors (women's movement), 17
Dowry
deaths, 74
prevalence, 74

E

Economic activity rates (women),
3, 79, 128
and ethnic factors, 147
Economic contribution of women,
24, 63-64
issues preventing, 76, 125
Economic Dependancy impact, 119
Economic opportunity increasing
of, 157
Education Sector strategies, 171
Education Programmes in Nepal,
54, 72
Educating girls/boys
attitude, 55
Educating
social/religious values, 56
Education/Training issues, 171
Elections 1999
performance of women, 229
Elimination of gender inequality,
163
Empower Dalit women of Nepal,
93-95
American Faction, 94
Employment opportunities
women changes in, 142
Employment status changes, 145
Empowerment, 163
Epistemological issues, 6
Equal access to opportunities, 165
Equal Inheritance Rights
Barrier, 117
Lack of, 119
political parties on, 121
New Legislation
recommendation, 123-24
Equal pay, 82, 138
Ethnicity and caste factor in
economic activities, 147
Evaluation/monitoring of
empowerment process, 157

F

Feminisation of
agriculture, 154
poverty, 83
Female/male headed
enterprises earning rates
comparison, 150
houses, 83
Female literacy rate, 72, 238, 256
Female labour force
in agriculture, 130
and institutional credit, 149
Feminist theories/ feminism, 9
Flesh trade
causative factors, 48
Fines and enslavement
(adultery), 186
and ethnic groups views, 186

Forbidden Sexual Relations
topics, 175
Forced labour (slavery West
Nepal (Jumla copper plate)
evidence of females, 211

G

Gender and public/private
spheres (GAPS), 7, 20
Gender and Development (GAD),
7
Gender Based violence, 74
Gender Equality
definition, 232-33
socio-cultural fields, 234
in households, 234
Gender discrimination legal
provisions, 103
Gender Empowerment measure
(GEM), 2
Gender inequalities
community level, 236
Gender Equality and
Empowerment
National work plan, 227
Gender issues, 6, 11
sectoral level, 157
operational level, 170
Gender Sensitive Development
Index, 2
Gender Sensitive Index, 21
Gender Sensitization, 164
Girl/Boy child
Comparison on education, 55
Girls Education
parental values, 57
social/religious values, 55-56
programme, 54
Girls attitude education/
marriage, 159
Girls status/values, 55
Goddess Kalika (Jumla) legend,
207
Gross Domestic Product (GDP)
growth rate, 140
women's contribution, 150
formal/informal sector, 151
estimates, 151
Govt plans and programmes, 158
Govt Administration
women in, 165
Training, 166
Gotra Hatya
prohibition (legal), 180
Govt policy on gender
trafficking, 75-76
Grassroots level organisations,
21
Group formation
services, 169
sustainability, 170
Gurkha imperialism, 5

H

Hegemony of ruling party, 239
Health Sector implementation of
policies problems, 166
Hindu religion and women, 11
Hinduization (Nepal), 25
Hindu law, 99
Hindu Varna system, 25
History-Nepal, 5
HIV
status, 39-40
education, 41
infections and trafficting, 244
Household Maintenace Activities
Value Added study, 152
examples, 153
Househods and gender equality,
234
Human Development Report, 1997,

2
Human Rights Violations and Trafficking, 244
Hypersexualization and Badi caste, 47

I

Illicit relations and gender relations, 25
Immunisation
gender gaps in, 71
coverage, 163
Indo-Aryan community and marriage, 69
Incest, 175
Infant and child mortality rates and status, 71
Informal sector women in, 134
Infertility and remarriage, 37
INGOs
funding of projects on sex workers, 47
Income generating activities literacy programmes, 61
Inheritance of property
West Nepal, 209
rights, 29, 77, 99
Institutional Credit access to (women), 24, 78-79, 126, 149, 253
constraints, 253
International Instruments Prohibiting slavery, 98
Intervention strategy, 168
short/long term, 20-21
Intercaste marriage, 25
Islam
gender discrimination, 11
Issues marginalizing women's rights, 229-30

J

Janakpur Women's Development Centre (JWDC), 173
Jara and *Sadhu*
terms in adultery,177
fundamental rule on decision, 187
Jayasthiti Malla (King), 25
Judiciary women in, 86
Junga Bahadur Rana, 28
guidelines for Sati, 192

K

KAP (Knowledge Attitude and Practice) studies, 43
Knowledge (manufacturing) in women, 8

L

Labour Act, 82
Labour Force Participation Rates, 127, 129
Labour Regulations favouring women, 137-38
Landholding size, 79-80
Language
issue (text books), 59
that dominates 240
Law classification of women, 37
Laws on trafficking, 76
Legal Reforms, 164
Legal prohibition of killing a seducer in adultery, 180
Legal instruments on control over sexuality, 38
Legal Relations, 29
Leftist Women's Organisation, 10
Liberalization impact, 140
Literacy programmes, 20, 58
training packages, 60
logistics, 58-59
text books, 59
monitoring of, 60
Literacy
Programme deficiencies, 57-58

rates, 54 , 238, 256
Local level issues
means used, 14
Local Representatives Act, 227

M

Malla period
division of state (W. Nepal), 210
fight for the throne, 210
Maintenance Rights unmarried woman, 103
Managerial class women in, 82-83
Managerial/Supervisory functions and women, 132
Manufacturing sector
women in, 3, 131
Manab Nyaya Sastra, 25
Marriage hype (West Nepal), 205
Marriage
and property rights, 30-33
mean age at, 56, 69
and schooling, 56
importance of, 68
system, 4
Market Production definition, 150
Maternal Mortality Rates, 70
Media
negative
campaign by, 117-18
role, 226
Micro Credit Programme, 168
Ministry of Women and Social Welfare (MWSW)
Action plan for implementation
of Beijing Platform for Action, 162
Mitakshara Dayabhaga school, 99
Modernization process positive/negative aspects, 139
Monitoring/evaluation, 157, 165
Mother's Groups, 21
Mother's nationality, 3
Mother and Child Health Workers (MCHW), 70
Muluki Ain (National Code), 5, 26, 28, 77, 99, 103, 175, 195-96, 234
Mutilation of adultress, 184

N

National Code of Nepal (Ain), 99
legal rules, 5, 26, 28
inheritance, 77, 99
National Issues, 13
Rights/Violations, 13
National School curriculum redesigning, 20
Nepalese law, 175
Nepalese egal system, 99
Nepalese Universities, 9
Nepalese politics women in, 3
Nepal National Education Commission, 53
Nepal Education System Plan (NESP), 53
Nepal Rural Credit Review Study (NRCRS), 79
Nepalese Women Voter's League, (NWVL), 21
New constitution and women, 222
Newari song on Sati, 194
New Muluki Ain, 100
Ninth Plan Approach paper and development, issues, 163
NGOs
in AIDS campaign, 41
in sex workers study, 44
in Nepal, 167
role, 18
and womens development, 252
Non-traditional sector
employment scope, 169
Non agriculture sector, 81, 140
work in, 144, 154
and ethnic groups, 148

O

Occupational distribution and ethnic/caste group-wise, 147
Occupational Structure Changes, 141-42
Old Testament on suicide, 191
Optional prohibitions of killing of seducer by husband in adultery, 180

P

Paedophiles, 247
Panchayat regime and women, 10
Parliament representation of women—in worldwide, 217
Parliamentary members women as , 24
Partition Rights, 114
Participatory District Development Programme, 167-68
Patriarchy features, 2, 238
Patriarchal
  values/norms, 223
  society, 1, 23, 26, 139
Patrilineal/Patrilocal society, 237
Patrilineal descent, 177
PCRW (Production Credit for Rural Women), 17, 24, 86
  programmes, 249-51
  model (introduction), 168
Penal system, 25
Pesaa (trade) girls-status, 49
Plan (Five Year) Focus on Women, 158
Political parties
  and gender issues, 20
  on equal inheritance rights, 121
Politics
  women in, 217
  cause of marginalization, 219, 223-24
  problem, 220
Polygyng, 78
Poor health, 70
Poverty incidents male/female headed household, 155
Positive
  discrimination. and women, 103, 242
Positive development women empowerment, 158
Population composition
  majority/minority groups, 241
Proof of adultery, 188
Project interventions, 168
Property law, 33, 78
Property Rights, 102, 112
Prostitutes, 29, 41-42
Prostitution seminar on, 44
Pro-women legislations, 66
Punishment on trafficking/rape, 76
Public resources/ decision making access and control, 139

R

Racial Groups (Nepal), 4
Racial/ Religious categories women, 19
Ranas Rule (1850-1990), 221
  discrimination in, 5
Rana Bahadur Saha
  copper plate on mutilation of adultress, 184
Rape punishment, 76, 105
Recruitment policies women, 19

Religious
clusters, 4
diversity, 4
values, 56
Reservation of seats in parliament, 227
Revenge of the husband in adultery, 182
Rights/programmes, 13
Right to
identity, 27, 36
equality, 101
freedom, 102
against exploitation, 102
property, 27, 102-103
Royal Palace women
contribution, position, 206-207
wedding dowry, 205
Rules (suggested by law) to be practiced by women, 38
Rural Development Banks (RDBS), 251
Rural infrastructural strategies, 173
Rural Society, 68

S

SAARC Role, 1-2
SAARC convention on the prevention and combating of trafficking in women and children for prostitution, 228
Sanctions against adultress, 183
mutilation prohibition Brahmin woman, 184
Sati, 28, 192
guidelines for, 192
cases, 194
regulation in Ain, 196
Savings and credit in group forming, 164
Seducers
in adultery rules for Ain, 179
identification, 188
Self employed women, 81, 134, 145, 154
Seminars on women issues, 14
Sex industry (Nepal), 43
Sex Ratio women, 72
Sex Workers
categories, 45
research, 43
Single women discrimination against, 138
Social attitude towards women's status, 159
Social cast hierarchy, 11
Social mobilization, 169
Social Services National Coordination Council (SSNCC), 252
Social taboos, 39
Son preference, 12, 64
South Asian Society, 2
STD and migrant labour, 41
STD and sex workers research, 43
Status (Nepali women) indicators, 71
Suicide, 191
and widow burning / sati, 191
Succession law on death of husband/wife, 37
Supreme Court's verdict on discrimination
provisions, 66
in property laws, 114
System of National Accounts (SNA)
production boundary, 150
items missed in GDP, 152

T

Taliban edicts impact on women, 204

Tenancy Rights daughters, 104
Text books literacy material, 59
Tibeto-Nepalese women status, 63
Tourism Sector
programme/projects, 172
women in, 133
Traditional Prostitution, 46
Trade Union Act, 82
Trafficking in women as HR violation, 244
Trafficking prevention camps, 44
Trafficking of children, 75
Training in skill development, 172

U

Unemployment rates and women, 134
Unmarried women
maintenance rights, 103-104
property rights, 114, 120
Unpaid work women in, 24, 128, 134
UN Conference on Women
Beijing, 162
Plan of Action, 162
USAID Mission to Nepal, 254
strategy, 255
literacy programme, 256
loans to women enterprises, 251
empowerment programmes, 256-58

V

VDC's (Village Development Committees), 48, 85, 219, 227
Village Health Workers (VHWs), 70
Vilas Kumari Devi (Princess)
marriage,
military participation, 205
Violence against women, 73
causes, 74
forms, 74

W

Wage employment
role, 145
agriculture/non-agriculture sectors, 146
earnings rate
men/women, 146
rural/urban, 147
trend, 154
Westernization, 5, 16
Western world knowledge
learning of, 8
Western Nepal
Sati, 207
Devakis
prevalence of, 208-209
position of women (15-16 centuries), 208
inheritance of property, 209
Widow burning, 191
earliest poetic inscription on, 193
differences Nepal/India, 200
abolition, 200
Widowhood, 69
Widow's
rights to property, 31, 34, 103
remarriage and property rights, 104, 120
Wife's share in property, 120
Women's Bills, 229
Women's consent in marriage, 37
Women in development, 7
Women's causus in Parliament, 21
Women's Education Programme, (WEP), 59
Women's Equal Rights Movement, 243
Women Enterpreneurs Association Nepal (WEAN), 173

Women enterpreneurs, 135, 149
    programmes projects, 173
    problems, 83
Women's Rights
    Movements, 15
    Commission, 25
Women's Ministry and staff with gender expertise, 165
Women's/Men's
    earning, 155
    comparison, 155
Women's production increasing ways of, 155-56
Women's Organisation 1947-52, 9
Women in
    local level politics, 219
    Parliament, 218, 222
    politics
        causes of marginalization, 219
        measures to promrote, 225
Women's production dichotomy, 156
Women's political Participation issues, 86
Working conditions industries, 132
Women enterpreneurship programme/project, 173

Y

Year of subordination
    way of being handicap to discriminated, 243